Hiking through History
Alabama

Hiking through History Alabama

Exploring the Heart of Dixie's Past by Trail from the Selma Historic Walk to the Confederate Memorial Park

Joe Cuhaj

FALCON GUIDES

GUILFORD, CONNECTICUT
HELENA, MONTANA

To my historian daughter Kellie. This proves the apple doesn't fall far from the tree.

FALCONGUIDES®

An imprint of Rowman & Littlefield
Falcon and FalconGuides are registered trademarks and Make Adventure Your Story is a trademark of Rowman & Littlefield.

Distributed by NATIONAL BOOK NETWORK

Copyright © 2016 by Rowman & Littlefield

Photos by Joe Cuhaj

Maps: Melissa Baker © Rowman & Littlefield

British Library Cataloguing-in-Publication Information available

Library of Congress Cataloging-in-Publication Data available

ISBN 978-1-4930-1938-0 (paperback)
ISBN 978-1-4930-1939-7 (e-book)

∞™ The paper used in this publication meets the minimum requirements of American National Standard for Information Sciences—Permanence of Paper for Printed Library Materials, ANSI/NISO Z39.48-1992.

Contents

The Hikes

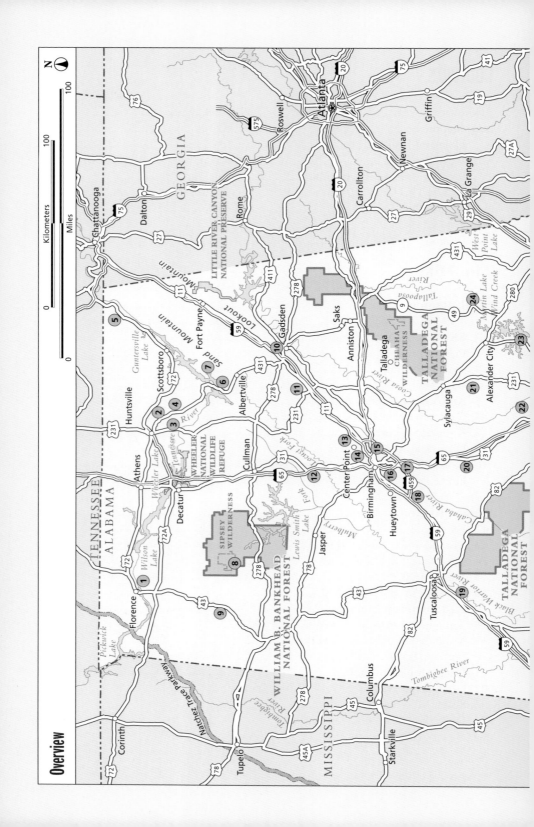

Overview

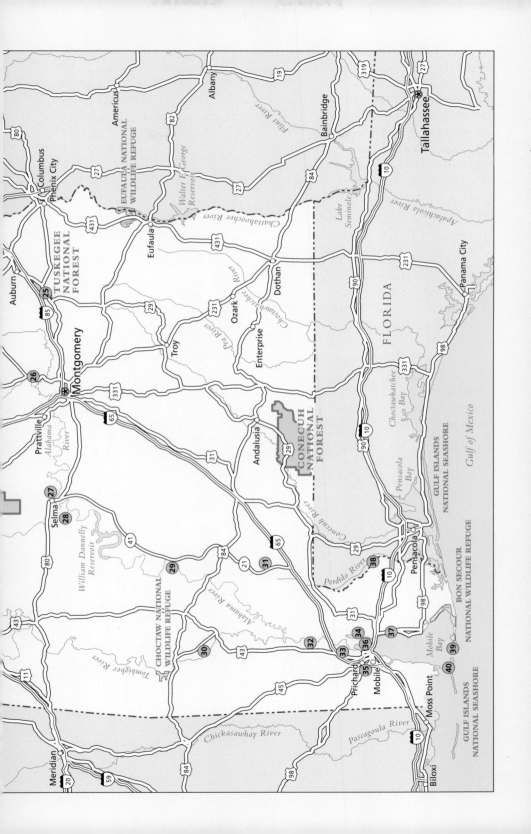

Acknowledgments

There are several people and organizations I need to thank for helping me put this book together, including Ike Lyon with the US Army Corps of Engineers, Janice Barret with Wild South, Cathie Mayne with the Huntsville Land Trust, and the Alabama Trail of Tears Association. And, of course, I once again have to thank my wife, Maggie, for joining me on this little adventure, and Archer the Wonder Dog (it's a wonder he put up with this).

Introduction

I can't tell you how excited I was when I was asked to write this book. Besides hiking and writing, I am a history geek. I love stumbling onto little-known facts about historic events, and my DVR always has several shows recorded from the History Channel, Discovery Channel, or Smithsonian Channel, so writing this book was a true joy.

My goal was not only to present the more famous aspects of Alabama history but also try to burrow down and present some little-known aspect to each hike and hopefully bring it to you not in a stodgy seventh grade history teacher voice but with the excitement that I experienced as I learned about Alabama's rich history.

Of course our travels will take us to the "Big Three" when it comes to Alabama history—Native American, Civil War, and Civil Rights history. Native Americans and Paleo-Americans have inhabited the forests, rock shelters, and rivers of Alabama for over 10,000 years. Sadly their story culminates in their removal in the 1800s during what is known as the "Trail of Tears" (TOT). Several hikes will take us to TOT significant areas, such as the Smokerise Trail in Huntsville, an actual route used during the removal, and the Dismals Canyon where Chickasaw Indians were interned before their removal with 90 percent dying en route.

Just about every hike has a bit of Civil War history attached to it—none more so than the Confederate Breastworks Trail at Historic Blakeley State Park. The park was the site of the last major battle of the war, concluding just hours after Grant surrendered to Lee in Virginia. And we'll take a hike with a twist at the Confederate Memorial Park near Verbena, the site of a retirement home and grounds established by a Confederate veteran (later funded by the state) to help wounded veterans who were broke, homeless, or severely injured following the war.

And no history book about Alabama would be complete without walking the streets of Selma, where in March 1965 brave marchers met billy clubs and tear gas as they crossed the Edmund Pettus Bridge on their 80-mile walk to Montgomery, which ended with the signing of the Voting Rights Act that guaranteed the right to vote for all races, sex, and religions.

And that is only the tip of the iceberg. There is much more included, like hikes to active archaeological sites and giant rock shelters.

Now I know a lot of you will ask why your favorite rail-trail or city historic walk wasn't included. I shied away from these as much as possible. This is a book about traditional hiking trails, after all, with three notable exceptions: the Port City Historic Walk through downtown Mobile with 300 years of history, the Selma Historic Walk where "Bloody Sunday" occurred in 1965, and the Vulcan Trail, which played an important part in the mining history of the Birmingham area.

So there you go. Time to go hiking. Enjoy!

Flora and Fauna

Alabama is truly blessed with natural resources, particularly when it comes to the plants and wildlife found here. In fact, scientists recognize the state as being one of the most ecologically diverse areas in the country. Take aquatic wildlife, for example. The state has more species of mussels, snails, turtles, and crawfish than any place in the country. The state's rivers, streams, and lakes boast 350 species of freshwater fish—that's one-third of the total species in the entire nation. The Cahaba River alone, in Birmingham, has more species of fish per mile than the entire state of California.

Yes, Alabama is blessed.

As you walk down the state's trails, spend some time taking in the trail "amenities"—our abundant wildflowers. In marshes and streams there are the bright yellow to scarlet colors of trumpet honeysuckle. In late spring the fences and trees are hugged by the vines of Carolina jasmine with its yellow blooms. Bright yellow balls of honeycomb head bloom in late summer in the bogs and savannahs across the state, while a tremendous variety of lily find refuge here, including merry bells with their thin, delicate stems; hay-yellow bells; and the Cahaba lily, which grows in the swift currents of rivers and has a wide, white bloom and long, narrow, fingerlike petals.

Two-thirds of Alabama remains covered in forest, with southern yellow, loblolly, longleaf, and slash pines dominating in the pine forests. Several varieties of oak thrive here, most notably the water and live oak. You will also most likely see sweet gum

and hickory along your journeys. And springtime brings bursts of color with white flowering dogwoods and magnolias filling the forests with their fragrant aroma. On these hikes you will encounter trails littered with leaves from the aptly named bigleaf magnolia, with leathery leaves that are bigger than the size of your hand.

In springtime mountain laurel and a wide variety of azaleas line many of the trails, giving life to the forest after a drab gray winter. The fragrance is wonderful as you stroll across a ridgeline.

Needless to say you will run into the more common species of wildlife as you hike in Alabama, such as white-tailed deer, gray squirrels, and chipmunks. Wild turkeys dart out in front of you from the brush. Black bears have made a huge comeback and can now be found in most regions, though are not readily seen. The Mobile-Tensaw River Delta has the largest concentration of black bears in the state.

On the wild side the American alligator, one of only two species of alligator in the world, can be found in the South and Gulf Coast regions. Gators are naturally afraid of humans and would rather dart away than confront you. Normally they feed on fish, frogs, snakes, turtles, birds, and small mammals. Having said that, don't tempt fate. Despite their short, stubby legs and apparent slowness on the ground, they can move very fast out of water for a short distance, and dogs and children frolicking in a lake could be in danger. Just keep your distance.

From north to south you will have a chance to see a wide variety of birds, the more common being blue herons, egrets, turkey vultures (which many confuse with hawks when soaring above), and red-tailed hawks. You may also spy ospreys, bald eagles, red-cockaded and pileated woodpeckers, and a book full of smaller birds like finches, starlings, wrens, and thrushes.

Weather

Alabama has a little bit of everything when it comes to weather, from cold, snowy winters in the north to hot, humid, subtropical weather along the Gulf, and everything in between.

Many say that the weather in Alabama is perfect for hiking year-round. Well, that's not quite true. There are a couple of notable exceptions, and they all revolve around the summer months.

Alabama is in the Deep South, and the heat and humidity of summer can sometimes be brutal, with heat indexes well above 100° F. Along the Gulf the subtropical climate makes things worse with frequent, sudden, and severe pop-up thunderstorms. In fact, the city of Mobile, lucky them, has earned the distinction of being the wettest city in America on numerous occasions.

The Gulf also has the added disadvantage of the possibility of hurricanes. While Alabama's footprint on the Gulf is relatively small compared to other states, some devastating hurricanes have made landfall here and did considerable damage, not only on the immediate coast but far inland as well, from flooding and tornadoes.

In the north average temperatures range from 46° F in January to 80° F in July. Colder temperatures are more frequent in the north, and yes, you may experience significant accumulations of snow.

Down on the Gulf average temperatures range from 52° F in January to 85° F in July. Cold snaps of below 30° F, even near zero, do occur, but they are few and far between and short lived.

Restrictions and Regulations

It should go without saying but still needs to be said: The historical hikes I'll be taking you to over the next few chapters are fragile, not only their environment but also the artifacts and relics found there. While the managing agencies and cities do an excellent job of protecting them, they can't do it on their own.

As you walk these trails, do not touch any artifacts you find, and most certainly do not bring them home with you. In many of the parks, artifacts are federally protected with heavy fines and possible imprisonment for breaking the law. If you find an artifact during one of your hikes, look but don't touch, note the location, then when you get back to the trailhead, report it to the managing agency as soon as possible for them to investigate.

Camping is allowed in most of the parks and forests we will visit. Please refer to the "Trail contacts" section of each hike for information on who to contact for reservations, fees, and regulations. As of this writing things were changing, especially in the state parks and state forests where budget restrictions were keeping this information in flux.

For camping in national forests, there is usually a small fee for campground sites for both primitive and improved (with water and electricity). Backcountry camping is allowed along the trails at no additional cost. Follow the policy of dispersed camping, where campsites are spread far apart and at least 100 feet from the trail. In some areas others have already established campsites close to the trail. If this is the case, rangers suggest using these sites to minimize any further camping impact. And again, contact the "Trail contact" for more information, including restrictions on building campfires or transporting firewood to an area, which can bring disease to a forest.

Dogs are usually welcomed on the trails, but a leash is required unless otherwise noted. And hunting is allowed in national forests and Forever Wild properties. Contact the national forest, district forest ranger, or the Alabama Department of Conservation and Natural Resources (DCNR) for hunting seasons, which can restrict camping locations and hiking trails. This is noted under "Special considerations" and "Trail contact" for each hike as needed.

How to Use This Guide

This guide contains everything you will need to know about each hike and arm you with information to determine if it is a trail that you want to experience or not.

The guide has been broken down into the four regions identified by the Alabama Department of Tourism: North (Huntsville), Central (Birmingham), South (Montgomery), and Gulf Coast (Mobile and Baldwin County).

Each hike is broken down for easy reference as follows:

Summary: Each hike begins with a short summary to give you a taste of the hiking adventure to follow. You'll learn about the trail terrain and what surprises the route has to offer. If your interest is piqued, read on; if it isn't, skip to the next.

Start is a brief, single line describing exactly where to begin your hike. For example, the north end of a parking lot or the kiosk next to the bathhouse.

Distance: The total distance for and type of hike—loop, out and back, etc.

Hiking time: This is the time it should take for an average person to hike the trails. I have noted in this section where you might want to add time to your hike, such as if there is a museum of interest along the trail.

Difficulty: A subjective description because we all have different skill levels, but it will give you a good general idea of how difficult a hike is: Easy (relatively flat trail, shorter distance), Moderate (slight elevation gains, longer distance), or Difficult (steep climbs, long distance, or technical challenges).

Trail surface: What the path will be like underfoot—dirt, rock, sand, asphalt, etc.

Best seasons: The time of year when you will get the most enjoyment from the trail described.

Other trail users: Who you will encounter on the trail, such as joggers, cyclists, etc.

Canine compatibility: Whether or not dogs are allowed on the trail. Sometimes they are allowed but not recommended. It will be noted here.

Land status: Who owns or manages the property; for example, state park, national forest, or privately owned.

Nearest town: The town nearest to the trailhead.

Fees and permits: Lets you know if admission is charged or if you need a permit.

Schedule: What days of the week the trails are open and what the hours are, and what the hours are for any ancillary attractions such as museums.

Maps: Additional maps to refer to that will help you understand the trail route, such as USGS topographic maps, *DeLorme Gazetteer* pages and grid coordinates, or brochures available at kiosks or park offices.

Trail contact: Who and how to contact people with additional information about a trail.

Finding the trailhead: Mile-by-mile descriptions of how to get to a trailhead, including GPS coordinates.

The Hike: After the lead-in we get to the real nitty gritty: a full description of the hike and the history that will unfold before you.

Miles and Directions: A full mile-by-mile description of the twists and turns of a trail and where you should see certain features.

Sidebar: Expanded historical articles of interest that relates in some way to the trail you are reading about.

Tidbit: Shorter, more concise bits of historical information or trivia that relates in some way to the trail you are reading about.

How to Use the Maps

Overview Map

This map shows the location of all hikes described in this book, so you can choose a hike based on geography or the type of history it follows, or see which hikes are nearby. You can find your way to the start of the hike from the nearest sizable town or city. Coupled with the detailed directions provided in the "Finding the trailhead" entries, this map should visually lead you to where you need to be for each hike.

Route Maps

This is your primary guide to each hike. It shows all the accessible roads and trails, points of interest, water and geographical features, towns, and landmarks. It also distinguishes trails from roads. The selected route is highlighted, and directional arrows point the way.

Trail Finder

Best Civil War Hikes

7 Cave Mountain Loop
22 Confederate Memorial Park Nature Trail
34 Confederate Breastworks Trail
39 Fort Morgan Loop
40 Fort Gaines Loop

Best Civil Rights Hikes

27 Selma Historic Walk

Best Native American Hikes

5 Cave Trail
8 Kinlock Shelter
19 Moundville Archaeological Park

Best Hikes for Nature Lovers

2 Monte Sano Nature Preserve Loop
25 Bartram Trail
32 Mound Island
40 Fort Gaines Loop

Best Hikes for Children

3 Plateau Loop
12 Fossil Trail
37 Village Point Park Preserve Loop

Best Geology Hikes

8 Kinlock Shelter
9 Dismals Historic Gorge
12 Fossil Trail

Best Industrial Hikes

13 Mine Ruins/Crusher Trail
17 Red Mountain Mine Trail
18 Tannehill Historical State Park Loop

Best Hikes for Dogs

25 Bartram Trail
29 Nancy's Mountain
38 Perdido River

Map Legend

Municipal

≡(65)≡ Interstate Highway

≡(331)≡ US Highway

≡(700)≡ State Road

≡(569)≡ Local/Forest Road

= = = : Gravel Road

= = = = Unpaved Road

+—+—+ Railroad

—··—··— State Boundary

—•—•—•— Power Line

Trails

- - - - - - Featured Trail

- - - - - - Trail

Water Features

⬭ Body of Water

≈ Marsh

〰 River/Creek

≋ Waterfall

⚲ Spring

Land Management

▱ National Park/Forest/Monument

▱ National Wilderness/Recreation Area

▱ State Park/Forest, County Park

▱ Preserve

Symbols

▲ Backcountry Campsite

▭ Bench

⏝ Bridge

▥ Boardwalk/Steps

◣ Boat Launch

■ Building/Point of Interest

▲ Campground

∩ Cave

† Cemetery

⌶ Gate

▲ Mountain Peak

🅿 Parking

⊞ Picnic Area

🏠 Ranger Station/Park Office

🚻 Restroom

⬔ Scenic View

🮲 Tower

○ Town

① Trailhead

❓ Visitor/Information Center

NORTH REGION

This walk through Alabama's past begins in what is called the North Region, an area ranging roughly from just north of Birmingham to Huntsville and the Alabama/Tennessee state line. Much of the history you will explore in this region comes from Native American folklore, ceremony, and tragedy.

The folklore is found in sites like Noccalula Falls Historic Gorge. Now a beautiful park operated by the city of Gadsden, the park and the towering waterfall were named for a beautiful Indian princess, Noccalula, who met her demise from the top of the dizzying heights of the gorge that was carved centuries before by the magnificent waterfall.

Explore Native American ceremony in places like Kinlock Shelter, an amazing tall, deep rock shelter with petroglyphs dating back centuries. Walk in quiet solitude as you retrace the steps of Native Americans who were forced from their homes by the US government in one of the most tragic episodes of American history, the "Trail of Tears."

You will also visit plenty of local history, including a walk to a local cemetery that was established deep in the woods along the banks of Lake Guntersville during the late 1800s, and a loop around the top of Monte Sano State Park, where in the 1800s thousands would flock to a swanky hotel to cleanse themselves of yellow fever in the fresh mountain air. This is also where famed rocket scientist Wernher Von Braun established an observatory for local students and scientists to do some star gazing. The observatory is now open to the public so that you, too, can explore the stars.

1 TVA Nature Walk

History abounds along the trails at the Tennessee Valley Authority's Muscle Shoals Reservation. Along this 2.7-mile-long loop you will experience the handiwork of the Civilian Conservation Corps (CCC) from the mid-1930s, pass the site of a town that was once a major Southern shipping hub, and walk a half mile over the Tennessee River on a lovingly repurposed 1840 railroad trestle.

Start: East side of the TVA Nature Trail parking lot

Distance: 2.7-mile multi-loop

Hiking time: About 1.5 hours

Difficulty: Easy to moderate with some stair climbing

Trail surface: Dirt footpath, some asphalt, some stone stairs

Best seasons: Fall–spring

Other trail users: Joggers and cyclists

Canine compatibility: Leashed dogs permitted

Land status: Tennessee Valley Authority small wild area

Nearest town: Florence

Fees and permits: None

Schedule: Year-round, daily sunrise to sunset

Maps: USGS Florence, AL; *DeLorme: Alabama Atlas & Gazetteer*, page 17, C7

Trail contact: Tennessee Valley Authority, SB1H, PO Box 1010, Muscle Shoals 35661; (256) 386-2543; tva.gov/river/recreation

Finding the trailhead: From the intersection of US 72/US 43 and AL 133 in Florence, take AL 133 south 5 miles (you will cross Wilson Dam along the way). Turn right at the TVA Nature Trail sign onto Thunder Road. The parking lot is ahead in 500 feet. The trailhead is on the east side of the parking lot. GPS: N34 46.806' / W87 39.392'

The Hike

At first glance the 25-acre Tennessee Valley Authority's Muscle Shoals Reservation doesn't look like it would be a great hiking destination with its extensive paved jogging trail system and roads that loop around the property, but take a closer look and you will find an amazing place to hike and one that is crammed with history.

Located high above Pickwick Lake, which was formed by Wilson Dam, the reservation has a total of 11 miles of trails that wind through a beautiful landscape and take you back in time to 1813.

The dam and surrounding infrastructure was a monumental undertaking by the US War Department's Army Corps of Engineers. The project was started in 1918 under orders of President Woodrow Wilson. It included the building of a dam to power two new plants that would process nitrates for munitions during the First World War. Your trek begins on a trail called the Old First Quarters Trail, the name this area was given during the construction project and where housing for the crew was located. Along the route you will see a retaining wall and a bridge built during this time period.

Jutting out 1,500 feet over the Tennessee River, this old railroad bridge has seen its share of history and is now a key element of this hike.

You will also be treated to some of the handiwork of the Civilian Conservation Corps. As you make your way west on the Rockpile Trail, which was built by the CCC, you will climb sandstone steps that were constructed by the Corps and will give you a good cardio workout. Your reward is a good view of the river from the stone overlook built by these young men in the mid–1930s. Near the overlook you will also see stone foundations, the remnants of the living quarters used by the Corps of Engineers.

As you make your way around the bluff and head down toward the river, you will be walking in the footsteps of those who used to call this place home back in 1813 in the town of Southport. The Tennessee River was once a major waterway for shipping in the 1800s, and the town of Southport capitalized on this by becoming a major hub for shipping cotton. In fact, the town was recognized as the "greatest cotton town east of Memphis." The only indication today that the town once stood here is a historical marker.

Next you come to the highlight of the trip, the old railroad bridge. The state of Alabama authorized the construction of the bridge to span the river and awarded the contract to the Florence Bridge Company. Construction began in 1832, with the grand opening of the new toll bridge held in 1840. The bridge saw many severe storms in its day, two of which severely damaged the structure. The Memphis and Charleston Railroad made repairs to the bridge, which then reopened in 1858 as a double-decker affair with trains using the upper deck.

The new structure didn't last long, however; in 1862 Confederate soldiers burned the bridge to deter the advance of Union troops during the Civil War. Five years after the war, the bridge was reborn, with both decks rebuilt and put back into service, but in 1892 a coal train with five cars crashed through the span to the riverbank below. Miraculously no one died in the accident. The bridge was once again rebuilt, with the lower deck used as a toll bridge while trains continued to use the upper deck. The toll bridge closed in 1933; the upper deck shut down in 1988.

Finally, in 1993 the latest owner of the bridge, Norfolk-Southern Railroad, donated it to the Old Railroad Bridge Company, which in turn restored a half mile of the lower deck, converting it into a walking trail. Today you can walk that span to the middle of the Tennessee River for a wonderful view with the upper deck providing shade.

▶ Many believe that the old Alabama motto, the "Heart of Dixie," came directly from the Civil War, since Montgomery was the first capital of the Confederacy. In fact, it was part of a promotional campaign for the state in the late 1940s/ early 1950s to change the previous motto—the "Cotton State."

The trail is not blazed but is well-worn and easy to follow. There are directional signs at intersections to help navigate the paths. This is a wonderful hike to do in the fall, through the mixed hardwood forest that lights up the trail with fiery orange, yellow, and red colors.

Miles and Directions

0.0 Start on the east side of the parking lot where you can see the entrance to the paved Reservation Road Trail. Walk only a few feet to the east on the road; just before coming to a metal gate, turn left (north) onto the dirt Old First Quarters Trail (a sign shows the way).

0.1 Cross an impressive bridge built by the CCC and come to a Y intersection. The right fork leads to the CCC Pavilion Trail. Take the left fork to the northeast to continue on the Old First Quarters Trail. A deep runoff or seasonal stream bed parallels the trail on the left. (**Option:** Take the CCC Pavilion Trail to add 0.6 mile to the hike where it loops back onto the Rockpile Trail.)

0.3 A retaining wall built by the CCC can be seen on the opposite side of the trail to the left. In 250 feet come to a T intersection with the Rockpile Trail. Turn left (northwest) onto the Rockpile Trail. In a few yards cross a 50-foot bridge over the runoff to the west and come to a Y. The Loop Trail is to the left and leads back to the parking lot. Take the right fork to the north and continue on the Rockpile Trail. In 50 feet Pickwick Lake and the Tennessee River are in front of you. The trail makes a left turn and heads up stairs.

0.4 Come to the top of the stairs and the overlook. Walk around the left side of the building and pass another short stone structure. In 150 feet come to another Y. Take the right fork to the southwest and continue on the Rockpile Trail, walking along a tall bluff.

TVA Nature Walk

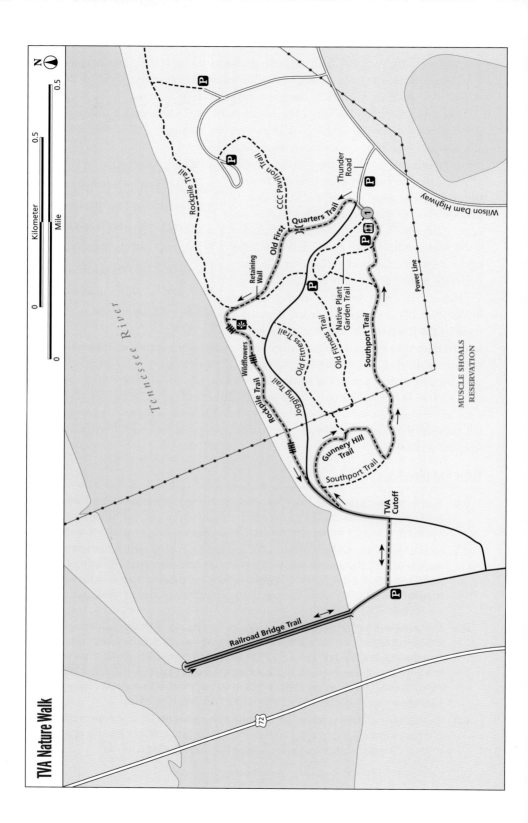

The telltale stonework of the CCC demarcates a wooden bridge along a section of the TVA Nature Trail.

0.5   Climb stairs uphill, with wildflowers lining the trail in season. In 200 feet a trail enters from the left (south). Continue straight (west). This is still the Rockpile Trail (a sign shows the way). There are nice lake views to your right.

0.6   Enjoy a good view of the lake and the city of Florence as you walk under a power line. The trail is thick grass here with wildflowers. In less than 0.1 mile, climb down stairs (about 100 feet).

0.7   Come to the paved Reservation Road. Turn right onto the road to the southwest.

0.8   Pass a bench on the left. The Southport Historical Trail enters the woods to the right of the bench (you'll return to this point later). Continue south on the paved road.

0.9   Come to picnic tables on the right. There is a wide cut through the woods that leads uphill. Turn right (west) and follow the cut uphill.

1.0   Come out at a paved road. Turned right onto the road and head northwest.

1.1   Come to the old railroad bridge. Follow the bridge out across the lake.

1.4   Enjoy great views from the middle of the lake. Turn around and head back the way you came.

1.8   Back at the cut at mile 0.9, turn left and follow the cut back to Reservation Road. When you reach the road, turn left (north) onto the road.

2.0   Back at mile 0.8, turn right onto the Southport Historical Trail, heading uphill using wooden railroad tie and stone stairs. In 175 feet pass a short wooden fence on the left that keeps you from falling into a shallow ravine. In a few feet come to a Y. Take the left fork to the northeast onto the Gunnery Hill Trail.

2.1   Come to a Y. Take the right fork.

2.2   Come to a T intersection with the Southport Historical Trail. Take the left fork and head down more stone steps. After the stairs a seasonal stream is on your right (nice cascades after rain).

2.5   Pass a large area of kudzu.

2.6   Come to a T intersection. There are two signs here: Parking Left and Parking Right. Turn right (south) and continue on the Southport Historical Trail.

2.7   Arrive back at the parking lot.

2 Monte Sano Nature Preserve Loop

Relive some of the early history of old Huntsville by hiking the Monte Sano Nature Preserve Loop. Along this 4.9-mile circuit you will see remnants of the early Huntsville water system on the Waterline Trail, visit an early form of refrigeration for residents of the mountain called the "spring house," and pass an amazing abandoned limestone quarry aptly named Three Caves. Enjoy all of this, of course, within a beautiful northern Alabama landscape.

Start: Hiker's parking lot off Bankhead Parkway NE

Distance: 4.9-mile loop

Hiking time: 2.5 to 3 hours

Difficulty: Moderate to difficult due to length and some steeper climbs at the end of the loop

Trail surface: Dirt and rock footpath

Best seasons: Late fall to late spring

Other trail users: None

Canine compatibility: Leashed dogs permitted

Land status: Land trust property

Nearest town: Huntsville

Fees and permits: None; donation requested at trailhead lockbox

Schedule: Year-round, daily sunrise to sunset

Maps: USGS Huntsville, AL; *DeLorme: Alabama Atlas & Gazetteer*, page 19, D8; trail maps available online at the Land Trust of North Alabama website

Trail contact: Land Trust of North Alabama, 2707 Artie St. SW, Ste. 6, Huntsville 35805; (256) 534-5263; landtrustnal.org

Special considerations: To help protect the trails from erosion, the land trust asks that you do not hike the trails after rain. It is OK to hike if the ground is frozen, but when the temperatures are above freezing, wait a day or two for the trails to dry out.

Finding the trailhead: From Huntsville on I-565 at exit 21, head south on Maysville Road NE 1.4 miles and turn left onto Pratt Avenue NE. In 400 feet Pratt Avenue turns into Bankhead Parkway. Travel 1.4 miles. The parking lot and trailhead are on your right and well marked. GPS: N34 44.610' / W86 32.640'

The Hike

In northern Alabama just south of the Tennessee state line, high atop Monte Sano Mountain and adjacent to the state park of the same name, you will find the largest of the Huntsville Land Trust nature preserves, the aptly named Monte Sano Nature Preserve. Here on this 1,107-acre preserve, you will not only experience some beautiful landscapes but also catch a glimpse of Huntsville history.

Monte Sano has been the center of that history since the early 1800s, when people would flock to the "Mountain of Health" in the belief that the crisp mountain air could cure them of such maladies as yellow fever and cholera.

The preserve sits on the rocky western side of the mountain and has twenty-three trails, each with its own unique history. This hike combines six of them—the

This isn't your everyday Frigidaire. This is what is known as a "spring house." Built on top of the head of a spring, the house was used to store food—the flowing water beneath kept it cool.

Bluffline, Annandale, Waterline, Three Caves Loop, Wagon, and Fagen Springs Trails—to form a loop that I call the Monte Sano Nature Preserve Loop. Pretty clever, huh?

The hike begins on the Bluffline Trail, which meanders beneath a tall limestone bluff, crosses several seasonal streams, and passes a couple of nice little waterfalls. Remember that these are seasonal and in the summer may be small or nonexistent.

The Bluffline eventually reaches the Annandale Trail, which ends at its intersection with the Waterline Trail at a creek. There is a nice seasonal cascade here after a good rain. From here start heading steeply down the rocky slope using the Waterline Trail, which follows its namesake, the old Huntsville water main that was used during the 1950s.

According to locals, in 1935 the Civilian Conservation Corps (CCC) came to the mountain to build Monte Sano State Park. To help the men in their encampment, a water main was constructed that ran from Hermitage Avenue to the top of the mountain. A severe winter soon followed and completely iced up the area's main water tower on top of the mountain. The weight of the ice caused the structure to collapse, leaving residents completely without water. Fortunately they were allowed to tie into the CCC water tank. That connection remained in place for almost twenty years until the city finally laid this water main in 1956. Sections of the pipe can be seen along this narrow path.

Continuing on, come to a three-way intersection with the Waterline, Alms House, and Three Caves Loop. Take the short 0.2-mile Three Caves Loop for a look at the limestone quarry, which, not so coincidentally, has three caves.

The quarry was mined from 1945 to 1955, with the limestone used for steps and foundations, crushed for gravel, and finely crushed for Portland cement. It was the latter that forced the closing of the mine when residents complained of the excessive heavy truck traffic and the thick dust emanating from the operation.

There are several steel fences that you can stand behind to view the quarry, but heed the warning signs and keep children, and yourself, away from the edges of the steep and deep cliffs. As you walk the loop, you will pass a road that leads directly to the caves. Do not go to the caves! Entry is by permission only.

From the quarry take the Alms House Trail. Along this route you will pass what remains of an interesting early refrigeration system called a "spring house." This stone structure was built over a clear, cold spring. The water would cool the meats and vegetables that were stored inside.

And if all this history isn't enough, you will be treated to a beautiful tiered, seasonal waterfall near the end of the hike on the Fagen Springs Trail.

The trails are all very easy to follow since they are well traveled and well worn. They are marked with diamond-shaped markers with HLT (Huntsville Land Trust) and the trail name emblazoned on them. Intersections are clearly marked with signs.

Miles and Directions

0.0 Start from the parking lot on Bankhead Parkway. A sign here indicates where to enter the trail to the northeast. In 100 feet come to a sign that shows the direction of the Bluffline and Old Railroad Bed Trails (the signs are carved wood with red lettering). Turn to the right (southeast). The trail is not blazed at this point, but it is a 2- to 3-foot-wide dirt and rock footpath. The trail has a dense canopy with many pines. In less than 0.1 mile, pass a short side trail to an education pavilion on the right (south).

0.1 Diamond-shaped HLT Bluffline markers begin, tacked to trees. The Old Railroad Bed Trail comes in from the right (west). Continue straight (east) on the Bluffline Trail.

0.2 Cross a stream with a nice cascade when it is flowing. The trail widens to a 4-foot-wide clay and dirt path.

0.3 Cross a power line. There are views of the surrounding mountains and valley (the giant Saturn V that stands at the Space and Rocket Center can be seen in the distance). In less than 0.1 mile, cross a stream (this one is wide and fast after a good rain). There is a bench here. The trail's namesake bluffs begin on the left.

0.4 Cross a small creek.

0.5 Cross an intermittent stream.

0.7 The trail bed is a mix of rock and dirt and can be deep in mud after rain (see "Special considerations"). There are cedars and pines through here and a swift-flowing stream downhill to the right.

0.8 Cross a small creek, followed in less than 0.1 mile by a wider, rocky stream crossing.

1.0 Good view of the bluff on the left.

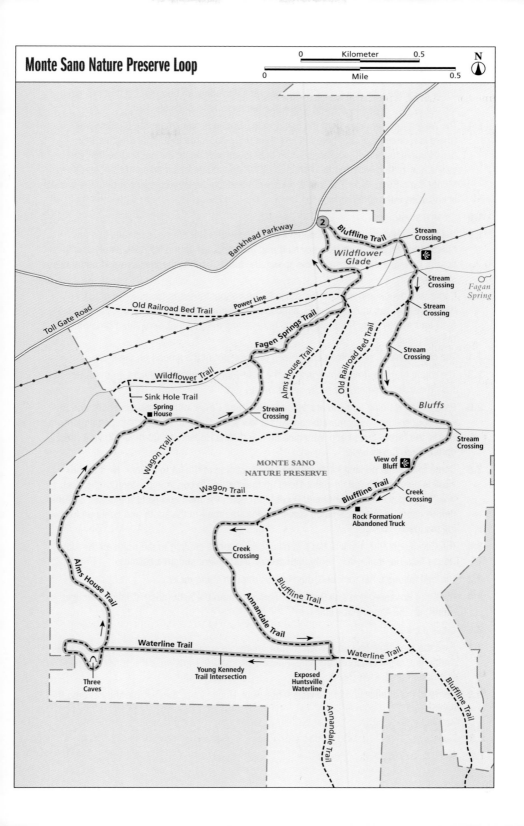

Monte Sano Nature Preserve Loop

Kilometer
0   0.5

Mile
0   0.5

N

Bankhead Parkway

(2) Bluffline Trail

Wildflower Glade

Stream Crossing

Stream Crossing

Stream Crossing

Fagan Spring

Toll Gate Road

Old Railroad Bed Trail

Power Line

Fagen Springs Trail

Alms House Trail

Old Railroad Bed Trail

Stream Crossing

Wildflower Trail

Sink Hole Trail

Spring House

Stream Crossing

Bluffs

Stream Crossing

Wagon Trail

View of Bluff

MONTE SANO
NATURE PRESERVE

Wagon Trail

Bluffline Trail

Creek Crossing

Rock Formation/
Abandoned Truck

Creek Crossing

Alms House Trail

Annandale Trail

Bluffline Trail

Waterline Trail

Waterline Trail

Three Caves

Young Kennedy
Trail Intersection

Exposed
Huntsville
Waterline

Annandale Trail

Bluffline Trail

1.1 Cross a creek.

1.2 A discarded rusty truck is downhill on the right. The bluff continues on the left (southeast). There are some interesting rock formations here, including an outcropping that has been etched by the elements, making it look like the rocks have been stacked.

1.4 The Wagon Trail comes in from the right (north). Continue straight on the Bluffline Trail (there is a directional sign here). In less than 0.1 mile, come to a Y. The Bluffline Trail heads uphill to the left (southeast). Turn right (southwest) onto the Annandale Trail; the trail is now blazed with diamond-shaped MSSP Annandale Trail markers (MSSP stands for Monte Sano State Park). The trail is mostly dirt and can be very boggy after rain. The forest is enclosed with more hardwoods.

1.6 Cross a stream.

1.9 The trail has a deep gully that can fill knee-deep with water after a good rain. In a few hundred yards, pass a whitish gray bluff and outcroppings on the left, with plenty of wild-flowers growing from the tops in the spring. The trail is back in the preserve and out of the state park.

2.0 Come to a bench and a set of log stairs. At the bottom turn right (southwest) onto the Waterline Trail. The trail is elevated, almost like a railroad bed. The trail bed is narrow (1.5 feet) and mostly rock. There are several areas along the trail that have steep drop-offs to the left (south).

2.1 The old Huntsville water line can be seen popping out of the ground on the left.

2.3 The Young Kennedy Trail comes in from the right (north); continue straight on the Waterline Trail. The trail becomes less rocky and is mostly dirt.

2.6 Pass a sign warning that you are approaching Three Caves, with dangerous bluffs, and to keep your children away from the edge. In a few yards come to a Y at a sign pointing the way to the Three Caves Loop, Waterline Trail, and Alms House Trail. Continue straight (west) on the Three Caves Loop.

2.8 Come to a gravel parking lot. Walk along the east side of the lot to a kiosk. Next to the kiosk is a set of railroad tie stairs. Head up these stairs to continue the loop to the west. In a few yards cross a gravel road. Do not turn down the road and go to the caves! Special permission is required. Continue straight across the road to the south and continue follow-ing the loop.

3.0 The Cave Loop ends back at the Y at mile 2.6. Continue straight to the north on the Alms House Trail. The trail is very rocky, with several intermittent stream crossings.

3.2 The trail follows a flat rock bed, then climbs through some rocks.

3.4 The Alms House–Wagon Trail Connector comes in from the right (east). Continue straight (north) on the Alms House Trail.

3.6 Cross a creek.

3.7 Pass the Sink Hole Trail on the left (north). There is a small sinkhole between the two trails. Continue straight (east) on the Alms House Trail. In a few yards pass the spring house foundation on the left (north).

3.9 Come to the intersection of the Wagon and Alms House Trails. Turn left (northeast) onto the Wagon Trail.

4.0 Cross a wide stream.

4.1 Pass the Wildflower Trail. Continue straight on the Wagon Trail. In less than 0.1 mile, cross a wide rocky stream. Just after crossing, start climbing the rocky slope and in a few yards turn right (east) onto the Fagen Springs Trail. The path is not well defined here, so keep your eyes peeled.

4.2 Cross Fagen Springs over a bridge. A nice waterfall is to the right (south).

4.3 Cross the spring again over a 20-foot bridge. Come to an intersection. Turn left (east) onto the Fagen Springs/Wildflower Trail. (A sign here points the way to Toll Gate Road, Railroad Bed, and Owens Drive.)

4.5 Pass a very rocky area of the stream. There is a nice waterfall here. The trail markers are virtually gone through this section. Keep your head up and watch for a green sign with a yellow arrow pointing the way on a tree. In a few yards come to a T intersection with the Alms House Trail. Turn left (northeast) onto the Alms House Trail and in less than 0.1 mile, come to a T intersection with the Railroad Bed Trail. Turn left (northwest), heading toward the falls. (**Note:** A sign here says to take a right, but it appears to be backwards. Take the left. After the sign cross the stream again.)

4.7 Cross under the power line. There is a beautiful, fragrant wildflower glade here in the spring. Start a long, steady, rocky uphill climb.

4.8 A trail comes in on the right (northeast). It looks like the trail that you're on should go straight, but it doesn't; it dead-ends. Turn right onto the unmarked trail, which is still the Alms House Trail. (There are some markers in a few yards, but they are for those heading in the opposite direction.) Very steep climb here over rocks.

4.9 Arrive back at the trailhead.

3 Plateau Loop

Enjoy a pleasant hike through history on this circuitous trail around the top of the "Mountain of Health," Monte Sano. This easy walking path circles the mountain's ridge and leads you to classic Civilian Conservation Corps (CCC) architecture and where the man who helped America land on the moon built an observatory for local schoolchildren that still operates today.

Start: From the hiker's parking lot on Nolen Avenue
Distance: 5.4-mile double loop
Hiking time: About 2.5 hours
Difficulty: Easy over level footpaths
Trail surface: Dirt footpath, minimal asphalt and gravel road
Best seasons: Year-round
Other trail users: Cyclists, joggers
Canine compatibility: Leashed dogs permitted
Land status: State park

Nearest town: Huntsville
Fees and permits: Day-use fee; children 5 and under free
Schedule: Year-round, daily 8 a.m. to sunset
Maps: USGS Huntsville, AL; *DeLorme: Alabama Atlas & Gazetteer*, page 19, D8; trail maps available free at the park office
Trail contact: Monte Sano State Park, 5105 Nolen Ave., Huntsville 35801; (256) 534-3757; alapark.com/monte-sano-state-park

Finding the trailhead: From Huntsville on I-565 at exit 21, head south on Maysville Road NE 1.4 miles and turn left onto Pratt Avenue NE. In 200 feet Pratt Avenue becomes Bankhead Parkway. Travel 2.7 miles and at a sharp bend Bankhead Parkway becomes Fearn Street NE. Travel 0.7 mile and turn left onto Nolen Avenue SE. Follow Nolen Avenue SE 0.7 mile to the entrance gate, where you'll pay your day-use fee. Continue straight on Nolen Avenue SE 0.4 mile. Come to a Y in the road and take the right fork. The hiker's parking lot is immediately on your right. GPS: N34 44.637' / W86 30.676'

The Hike

One of my favorite hiking destinations is Monte Sano State Park in Huntsville. The park has such a wide variety of hiking experiences and beautiful landscapes all within a short drive of the city. But what most people don't realize is the history that surrounds you as you walk the trails of the park.

My favorite route for a quick jaunt around the mountain are the two loop trails, the North and South Plateau Loops. In other editions of my books I have described these two separately, but for this guide I combined them to make a nice, long 5.4-mile trek. Since it's a double loop, you can easily make them into separate 1.9- and 3.5-mile loops. Both trails intersect at the hiker's parking area, the trailhead for this hike.

Whichever way you choose to walk this trail, you will be walking through several decades of mountain history. Start by hiking along the white-blazed South Plateau Loop, a 3.5-mile-long loop that travels down the spine of the mountain to the south.

One of several panoramic views that await you on the Plateau Loop Trail. This one peers down deep into McKay Hollow.

Monte Sano is Latin for "mountain of health," and in the early 1800s thousands flocked to the mountaintop, which quickly become a refuge for those afflicted with yellow fever, cholera, and malaria. They believed the cool, crisp mountain air and crystal-clear mountain streams were the answer to their maladies. Walk this trail on a cool fall or winter morning and you will understand why.

In 1827 one gentleman took this to a new level. Dr. Thomas Fearn built facilities here for these patients and a large, ornate house for himself and his family complete with stables and smokehouse. The colony was highly successful and flourished until the advent of the Civil War, when Union soldiers laid the settlement in ruins. A local newspaper described the incident: "The smokehouse was pilfered by the Yankee Soldiers of its bacon, shoulders, and jowls, but they failed to locate the hams concealed in the cellar."

Immediately after the war the elegant Monte Sano Hotel was built nearby, and again people flocked to the mountaintop in droves. The hotel flourished until the stock market crash and the Great Depression of 1929.

On the far southern end of this trail, where the path loops back to make the return trip, you will come to O'Shaughnessy Point, a beautiful rocky bluff with a panoramic view of the valley below, called Big Cove. The bluff was named for Colonel James O'Shaughnessy. O'Shaughnessy came over from Dublin, Ireland, to supervise the construction of a trunk railroad line from Brunswick, Georgia, to St. Louis, Missouri, with a stop in Huntsville. O'Shaughnessy also helped supervise the building of the Monte Sano Hotel. Upon his arrival in 1890, the colonel purchased an estate on the mountain to house his many guests, plus Dr. Fearn's mansion and sanitarium. Not long after the purchase, the home was destroyed by fire. The colonel rebuilt it in a spectacular Queen Anne style with rich wood paneling, ornate fireplaces, and large wraparound porches, but in only a few short years fire destroyed *that* house too. State park officials tell us that archaeologists return to this area regularly to try and locate the remains of this home.

When you return to the hiker's parking area, you will pick up the blue blazes of the North Plateau Loop. This is a 1.9-mile-long loop that takes you through more recent history. Along this route you will pass the beautiful lodge and picnic pavilions that were hand built stone by stone by the young men of the CCC in the mid-1930s. The park officially opened in 1938 and was called "the showplace of the Tennessee Valley."

This shorter loop will also take you past the Von Braun Observatory. This planetarium and observatory was built by Dr. Wernher Von Braun in 1956. Von Braun was the driving force behind America's space program and the eventual landing of men on the moon. Throughout the 1960s Von Braun and astronaut Alan Shepherd frequently visited the facility to discuss the Apollo program. Today the Von Braun Astronomical Society opens the observatory to the public to view the night sky or maybe hear a lecture by prominent astronomers and NASA scientists and astronauts.

Miles and Directions

0.0 Start from the hiker's parking lot to head southwest. This hike begins with the South Plateau Loop. A sign here shows mileages and blaze colors for the South Plateau Loop (white blazed), Fire Tower Trail (red blazed), and North Plateau Loop (blue blazed). In just a few feet, come to an intersection. The South Plateau Loop heads straight and to the left, while the Bocca Family Trail heads to the left. Continue straight and follow the white blazes. The trail is a 5-foot-wide dirt path.

0.2 Come to a Y intersection. The Fire Tower Trail heads off to the left. Continue to follow the white blazes to the right (south).

0.5 Cross a stream over a 20-foot-long bridge. When the stream is flowing, there is a nice cascade here.

0.6 Cross a stream over a 10-foot-long bridge.

0.9 Come to a rickety old bridge over an intermittent stream and boggy area. It's best to stay off the bridge and walk around the area on the right. Just past the bridge are views through the trees of the valley and farms below to the right (southwest).

1.0 Pass a nice covered trail shelter. Just after the shelter are some outcroppings on the right (southwest).

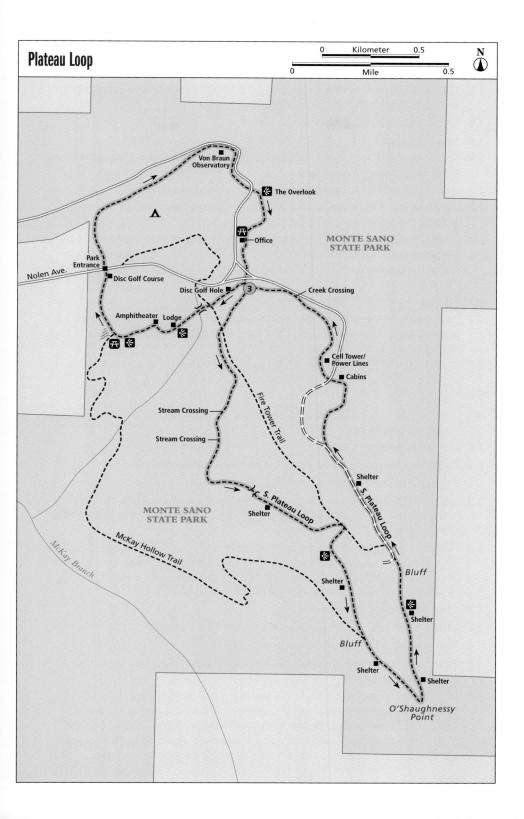

Plateau Loop

0   Kilometer   0.5

0   Mile   0.5

N

Von Braun
Observatory

The Overlook

Office

MONTE SANO
STATE PARK

Park
Entrance

Nolen Ave.

Disc Golf Course

Disc Golf Hole

3

Creek Crossing

Amphitheater

Lodge

Cell Tower/
Power Lines

Cabins

Stream Crossing

Fire Tower Trail

Stream Crossing

Shelter

S. Plateau Loop

S. Plateau Loop

MONTE SANO
STATE PARK

Shelter

McKay Hollow Trail

McKay Branch

Bluff

Shelter

Shelter

Bluff

Shelter

Shelter

Shelter

O'Shaughnessy
Point

1.1 The Bog Trail comes in from the left (northeast). There are also two benches here. Continue straight (southeast) and follow the white blazes.

1.2 Come to a Y. The red-blazed Fire Tower Trail comes in from the left. Take the right fork to the south and continue following the white blazes.

1.3 Enjoy views to the right (southwest).

1.4 Pass a trail shelter.

1.6 The McKay Hollow Trail comes in from the right (there is also a trail shelter here). Continue to the south on the white-blazed trail.

1.7 A short, 100-foot trail to the right (southwest) takes you to a bluff.

1.8 The Bocca Family Trail enters from the left; continue straight (southeast) on the white-blazed trail. There are more views just after the intersection.

1.9 Arrive at O'Shaughnessy Point, with a great view. This is followed by a Y intersection. The Warpath Ridge Bike Trail continues straight to the south; turn left (north) and continue on the South Plateau Loop. In a few feet pass the Mountain Mist Trail on the right, the Bocca Family Trail on the left.

2.1 Pass a trail shelter and view.

2.3 Pass a bluff with a view on the right (east). In less than 0.1 mile, the dirt path merges with a gravel road that comes in from the left (a sign here reads Gravel Road). Continue to follow the white blazes to the north.

2.4 The Fire Tower Trail enters from the left. Continue straight (north), following the white blazes. In 100 yards the Mountain Mist Trail enters from the right (east).

2.6 Pass a trail shelter.

2.7 The gravel road turns to the left; continue to follow the white blazes to the north. The trail is a wide dirt footpath again.

2.9 Pass a trail shelter.

3.0 Pass cabins on the right. The trail crosses a paved road to the northwest.

3.1 Pass a cell tower, cross under a set of power lines, and cross a gravel road to the north.

3.3 The Bocca Family Trail enters from the left. In less than 0.1 mile, come to a Y. The Sinks Trail enters from the right. Continue to follow the white blazes to the west. In 100 feet cross a short bridge over an intermittent creek.

3.5 Arrive back at the trailhead. You can end the hike here and do the North Plateau Loop another day if you wish. For this hike pick up the blue-blazed North Plateau Loop Trail and head southwest. Immediately after passing the kiosk, turn right onto the blue-blazed trail. In 400 feet pass hole #10 of the disc golf course on the right.

3.6 Cross the red-blazed Fire Tower Trail.

3.7 Cross a runoff with a small cascade on a 30-foot-long footbridge.

3.8 Walk behind the lodge to the first spectacular overlook.

3.9 Pass the amphitheater on the right. In 50 feet walk through a picnic area. In less than 0.1 mile, cross a small creek.

4.0 Pass another overlook on the left. In 120 feet pass a CCC picnic pavilion on the left. The McKay Hollow Trail merges here from the right side of the pavilion. Continue to the right (northeast) on the blue trail. (***Option:*** Head down the McKay Hollow Trail for a few short yards to view a waterfall. Be careful, it's steep and slippery.) On the North Plateau Loop in just over 100 feet, the trail leaves the picnic area and heads back into the woods.

4.2 Cross the disc golf course. In 50 feet cross the main park road at the entrance station.

4.3 Pass the red-blazed Fire Tower Trail on the right. You soon pass the primitive campground on the right.

4.4 The trail meanders beneath the campground. Drop off into a ravine on the left. There is a nice little view here in winter.

4.5 Pass the Cold Springs Trail on the left.

4.6 The closest approach to the campground is on the right.

4.8 Pass Von Braun Observatory on the right.

5.0 Arrive at what looks like a T intersection, but the left turn is merely a game trail. Turn right (southeast) and continue on the North Plateau Loop. In 60 feet cross a road to reach the overlook parking lot and arrive at the overlook. In 150 feet the trail heads back into the woods on the south side of the parking lot.

5.2 Cross a paved road to the south.

5.3 Pass a picnic pavilion on the right and come to a trailer that at the time of this writing was being used as a temporary office to register campers. Walk around the left side of the trailer and pick up the blue blazes on the other side, to the south.

5.4 Cross another paved road and arrive back at the hiker's parking lot.

Germans Invade Mexico

In 1985 PBS aired the first of a four-part documentary on the history of space flight in America. This first episode told how German rocket pioneer Wernher Von Braun came to the United States along with twenty assistants to evaluate captured V2 rockets in the New Mexico desert and later transferred to Huntsville to help land a man on the moon.

One of Von Braun's assistants, Krafft Ehricke, described a unique piece of history that occurred during their time in New Mexico: "Our status at that time wasn't prisoners of war but prisoners of peace. One time we had bad luck, we had an accident. A V2 rose from White Sands, its guidance mode failed, and it veered off to the south. Fortunately it was traveling fast enough to arc over El Paso but it did impact a cemetery in Tijuana. We had already been called the only German task force that invaded US territory. Now we were known as the only German team that managed to attack Mexico from their base in the United States."

4 Smokerise Trail

It has been called the "Journey of Injustice," what the Cherokees called the "Trail of Tears." Between the years 1830 and 1840, these Native Americans were forcibly removed from their homes in Tennessee, Georgia, and Alabama and relocated west to Oklahoma. This hike is your chance to walk through a beautiful forest and contemplate this tragic event in US history.

Start: From the kiosk on the southeast end of the parking lot on Cecil Ashburn Drive SE
Distance: 3.0-mile loop
Hiking time: About 2 hours
Difficulty: Moderate with a couple of long, slow climbs
Trail surface: Dirt and rock footpath
Best seasons: Fall–spring
Other trail users: Cyclists
Canine compatibility: Leashed dogs permitted
Land status: Land trust property
Nearest town: Huntsville
Fees and permits: None; donation requested
Schedule: Year-round, daily sunrise to sunset

Maps: USGS Huntsville, AL; *DeLorme: Alabama Atlas & Gazetteer*, page 19, E8; trail maps available online at the Land Trust of North Alabama website
Trail contact: Land Trust of North Alabama, 2707 Artie St. SW, Ste. 6, Huntsville 35805; (256) 534-5263; landtrustnal.org
Special considerations: To help protect the trails from erosion, the land trust asks that you do not hike the trails after rain. It is OK to hike if the ground is frozen, but when the temperatures are above freezing, wait a day or two for the trails to dry out.

Finding the trailhead: From the intersection of US 231 and US 431 in Huntsville, take US 431 south. Travel 1.2 miles and take the Airport Road exit onto the US 231 Frontage Road, which parallels US 231. In 0.4 mile turn left onto Airport Road SW. Travel 1.2 miles; Airport Road becomes Carl T. Jones Drive SE. Travel 1.9 miles and turn left onto Cecil Ashburn Drive SE. In 2.3 miles arrive at the parking lot, which is on your right. GPS: N34 39.423' / W86 31.013'

The Hike

It is one of the most tragic and selfish acts in US history, but one that is rarely talked about or receives recognition like other earth-shaking moments in our history. It is called the "Trail of Tears," a period of time generally between 1830 and 1840 when tens of thousands of Native Americans were forced from the land they had lived on for generations, with thousands losing their lives in the process.

The story of the Trail of Tears began when Europeans first set foot in the New World. Explorer Hernando DeSoto captured natives and used them as slave labor; many were abused and even killed by Europeans, who deemed the native population "savages," as they spread out across this new continent.

Even our founding fathers, beginning with George Washington, saw Native Americans as uncivilized and believed they should be converted to Christianity,

A bit of autumn color splashes on the Smokerise Trail, one of the footpaths used in the infamous and tragic "Trail of Tears."

taught English, and turned into farmers. The main problem was that this new country was beginning to burst at the seams with white European settlers. They needed land and there was only one way to get it.

In 1791 the Cherokee Nation signed several treaties with the US government that recognized the tribe as a sovereign nation complete with their own culture and laws. But it wasn't long before separate treaties began whittling away at the main agreement and Cherokee land was slowly ceded over to the United States. By 1803 a national policy was developed that would relocate all Indians to the newly purchased Louisiana Territory on the western side of the Mississippi River.

During the War of 1812 General Andrew Jackson was fighting a two-pronged war, one against the British, the other against Native Americans, in particular the Red Stick Tribe. Jackson had been an advocate of "Indian Removal" and fought many brutal battles in the Southeast, including the famous Battle of Horseshoe Bend near present-day Alexander City, Alabama.

When Jackson became president, he signed into law a bill called the "Indian Removal Act," which called for the exchange of Indian land on the east side of the Mississippi River for land on the west side. But Jackson often ignored the law and forced tribes to move without compensation. Although the Cherokee had already been losing their land through agreements, the first big relocation came in 1831

The Smokerise Trail passes several interesting rock formations including this boulder that has been worn away by the elements and now resembles a giant bear claw.

when the Choctaw were forced to surrender their land. On foot, many shackled, and with little to no food, water, or other vital supplies, they began the migration westward. Thousands died en route. A Choctaw leader told an Alabama newspaper that it was "a trail of tears and death," and from then on the event had a name.

Later in 1838 President Martin Van Buren continued the tragedy as he began implementation of the Treaty of New Echota. Federal troops rounded up Cherokees and moved them to internment camps in Alabama, Georgia, Tennessee, North Carolina, and Florida and then transferred them west over both land and water routes.

Today not many people understand the devastating impact of the Trail of Tears on Native Americans and our own history, but the Cherokee Nation is trying to change that through public outreach programs with the intention of making the Trail of Tears a national historic trail.

There are only a few places in Alabama where you can walk the actual trail. At the Huntsville Land Trust's Blevin's Gap Preserve, there are actually two preserved sections—one that is closed to the public for trail protection and the Smokerise Trail described here. Note that there is nothing of historic interest to see along this trail. There are no artifacts that say this is where a part of this tragic history occurred. You need to walk this trail armed with the knowledge of the events that occurred here and throughout the Southeast, soak it in, and never forget.

The Smokerise Trail described here uses three trails to form a loop—Smokerise, Sugar Tree, and the Bill and Marion Certain Trails, all of which are dirt and rock footpaths with an excellent canopy that's especially nice in the summer months and beautiful in the fall. By early winter when all the leaves have fallen, you will have a few nice views of the surrounding mountains.

All trails in the preserve are easy to follow with white diamond markers on the trees placed just far enough apart so as not to be distracting. Intersections are well marked with engraved wooden signs showing the trail name and direction.

I highly recommend visiting the Huntsville Land Trust website (see "Trail contact") to check out the event calendar for their Trail of Tears historical hikes. Historians lead the way and describe this tragic tale.

For more information on the Trail of Tears or to help preserve the trail and history, visit the National Trail of Tears Association online at nationaltota.org.

Miles and Directions

0.0 Start from the parking lot on Cecil Ashburn Drive and head southeast. The trail starts at the kiosk. Continue southeast a few yards and turn right (south) onto the narrow dirt Bill and Marion Certain Trail. In about 400 feet come to a Y intersection. A sign points straight ahead to the south for the Bill and Marion Certain Trail and right (west) for the Smokerise Trail. Turn right onto the Smokerise Trail. You can hear the sound of the road off to your right, but for only a short distance as you round the hill.

More on the Trail of Tears

There are many historical markers, depots, and river landings in Alabama that were points along the "Trail of Tears" (TOT), but very few that you can still actually walk. Many sites are either on private property or have been paved over.

When you look at some published online maps of the Blevin's Gap Preserve in Huntsville, you may see a trail marked as a former TOT route. Do not hike that trail! The path is closed to the public for its protection!

If you want to hike another route of the Trail of Tears, drive about 40 miles southeast to Lake Guntersville State Park and walk the Lickskillet Trail, another TOT-identified trail. This is a nice 1.8-mile (one-way) walk around Bailey Ridge. You can make it into a beautiful 4-mile loop by connecting with the Seales and Meredith Trails, with views of the blue-green waters of Town Creek. The western end of Lickskillet was severely damaged by tornadoes several years back, so you may have to do a little bushwhacking to make the link.

Smokerise Trail

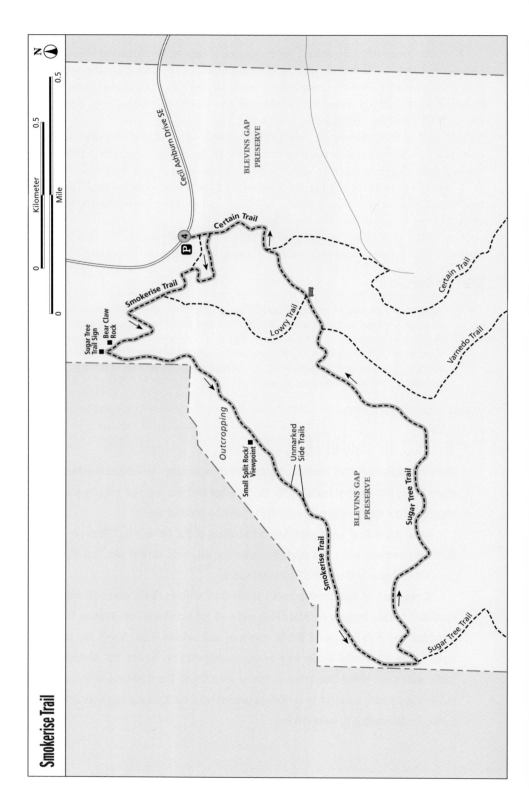

0.2 Come to an intersection with a bench on the right. To the left is the Lowry Trail. Turn right (northeast) to continue on Smokerise. There are some interesting small boulders and outcroppings on the right as you make the turn.

0.3 As the trail bends to the left (southwest), it becomes rockier and starts making its way downhill.

0.6 Pass an interesting rock that looks like a giant bear claw on the right. In less than 0.1 mile the trail bends to the left (south). There is a sign here that reads To Sugar Tree Trail and points back the way you came. Continue to the south. The trail levels out at this point and becomes more dirt than rock.

0.8 Cross a runoff.

1.0 Enjoy a nice view of a small rock outcropping on your left.

1.1 Pass a small split rock on the right, outcroppings on the left, and, when the leaves are down, a nice view of the valley to the right (northwest).

1.2 Pass an unmarked side trail on the right. Continue straight to the south.

1.6 Pass another side trail on the right (southeast). Continue straight to the south.

1.7 Come to the end of the Smokerise Trail at the Sugar Tree Trail. Sugar Tree heads off to the right (south) and to the left (northeast). Turn left onto the Sugar Tree Trail. A large wooden sign here shows the way. This first portion is rocky and looks like a seasonal water runoff.

2.5 Pass an old abandoned car on the right.

2.6 Pass the Varnedo Trail to your right (south). Continue straight to the northeast.

2.8 Come to an intersection with a bench on the right. A sign here shows that the Lowry Trail heads to the left. Turn right (east) to continue on the Sugar Tree Trail. In less than 0.1 mile, the Bill and Marion Certain Trail comes in from the left (north). The Sugar Tree Trail continues straight to the east. Turn left onto the Certain Trail (a sign shows the way and also points this way for the parking lot). Look for the occasional green medallion with silver arrow pointing the way to the parking lot.

3.0 Come to the end of the loop near the kiosk. Continue straight to the north. In less than 0.1 mile, arrive back at the trailhead.

5 Cave Trail

Hike through time to 10,000 BC at Russell Cave National Monument, the site of one of the most complete records of prehistoric cultures in the Southeast. This hike will not only take you to the massive rock shelter itself but also educate you about the everyday life of those who lived here centuries ago, with many informational signs along the way.

Start: From the left rear side of the visitor center

Distance: 1.6-mile lollipop with side trips

Hiking time: About 1.5 hours

Difficulty: Moderate to difficult

Trail surface: Composite boardwalk, asphalt

Best seasons: Year-round

Other trail users: None

Canine compatibility: Leashed dogs permitted

Land status: National monument

Nearest town: Bridgeport

Fees and permits: None; donation requested

Schedule: Year-round, daily 8 a.m. to 4:30 p.m.; closed Thanksgiving, Christmas, New Year's Day

Maps: USGS Doran Cove, AL; *DeLorme: Alabama Atlas & Gazetteer*, page 20, A5

Trail contact: Russell Cave National Monument, 3729 County Road 98, Bridgeport 35740; (256) 495-2672; nps.gov/ruca/

Finding the trailhead: From the intersection of CR 75 and AL 277 in Bridgeport, take CR 75 2.9 miles and turn right onto CR 98. Travel 3.7 miles and turn left onto the park road. Travel 0.3 mile to the visitor center. The start of the hike is at the left rear side of the building. There is also a back exit from the visitor center that is clearly marked Cave Trail. GPS: N34 58.709' / W85 48.579'

The Hike

Russell Cave, which is now part of the national park system as a national monument, was formed tens of thousands of years ago by the action of underground springs in the area. The water slowly chipped away at the limestone on the surface, carving out huge caves and caverns. With plentiful wildlife and plant life, and this formidable shelter, prehistoric Indians formed a civilization here that lasted for 10,000 years. In fact, Russell Cave is recognized as having the most complete record of prehistoric history and culture in the Southeast and provides archaeologists and visitors a glimpse into their everyday lives.

Before heading out on the trail, I suggest you watch the short video at the visitor center, which will give you a little more background of the trail you will be walking and the people who once lived here.

The people who resided here were in a lynchpin period of time between the Paleozoic eras of generally 3 million years ago to 200,000 years ago, when life first appeared and man eventually evolved into tool makers, and the Archaic period from around 10,000 to 4,000 BC, when man learned to be farmers. The people of this time

The Cave Trail at Russell Cave National Monument takes you back in time hundreds of years and traces the history of Native Americans and their survival in the area.

period were hunters and relied heavily on the large animals that roamed the mountains for food, clothing, and other necessities. For example, black bear and white-tailed deer were in abundance during this time, and once hunted they were used for a wide variety of items: meat for food and bones, antlers, and sinew for tools, arrows, and ceremonial pieces. The large foreleg bone of a black bear was hollowed out and packed with bear fat, and the result was a long-lasting torch to light the night.

People of this period were also keen observers of the world around them, especially the native plants of the region. They watched how plants grew, which ones animals ate, and the effect those plants had on animals. With these observations and over thousands of years, they amassed quite a store of knowledge of medicinal uses for plants, many of which are still ingredients in today's vitamins and drugs. For example, the bark of the tulip poplar was used to make an early herbal tea for coughs, fever, and even curing pinworms.

The cave was named for the man that owned the property when it was first mapped, Colonel Thomas Russell. Russell and his family owned the land from 1835 to 1928. It wasn't until 1961 that the land and cave were put under the federal protection of the National Park Service.

BLACK BEAR

The black bear once roamed these mountains when the Prehistoric Indians lived in the cave shelter.

Excavations reveal bones of the black bear. Black bears have migrated back to this area.

The foreleg bones of a bears leg was hollowed out and packed with bear fat and used to make a torch.

The learning never stops along the Cave Trail at Russell Cave National Monument. The trail is dotted with detailed signage pointing out historical facts.

There are actually three trails used for this hike—the Cave Trail, the Nature Trail, and the Hiking Trail. The trek begins, as I said, with a visit to the visitor center. Be sure to speak with the very friendly and knowledgeable rangers about the cave's history. The trail leaves from the very back corner of the building on the left (south) side. Before heading to the cave when you come to the intersection with the Nature Trail, take the Nature Trail up the hillside. Along the route you will learn even more about the fascinating culture that once thrived here through the multitude of informational signage along the way.

The trek is a rather steep climb that is made easier by the use of switchbacks. At mile 0.3 you will come to a Y intersection with the Hiking Trail. Take the right fork onto the Hiking Trail. On this trail in late fall and winter, you will get some nice views of the surrounding mountains and valley. (**Option:** You can cut the trip short by 0.5 mile by taking the left fork and continuing to follow the Nature Trail back to the Cave Trail and the cave itself. Note: Not depicted on map.)

Returning to the first intersection, you will take a right to the south and visit the cave itself. It is an impressive sight as you wind your way around to the entrance on a boardwalk that leads you directly into the cave, where you will find more exhibits depicting early life here. You are asked to stay on the boardwalk that circles the cave's entrance to protect the historic past.

A long boardwalk takes you into the opening of Russell Cave where exhibits of Native American life from centuries ago can be seen.

The Native American Festival

The Native American Festival is held the first weekend of May each year at the Russell Cave National Monument. The two-day event is free to the public and features demonstrations of the life and culture of southeastern Native Americans. Highlights of the festival include hunting, weapon and food preparation demonstrations, as well as native dances, ceremonies, and storytelling. Contact Russell Cave for more information by calling (256) 495-2672, or visit online at nps.gov/ruca/.

Cave Trail

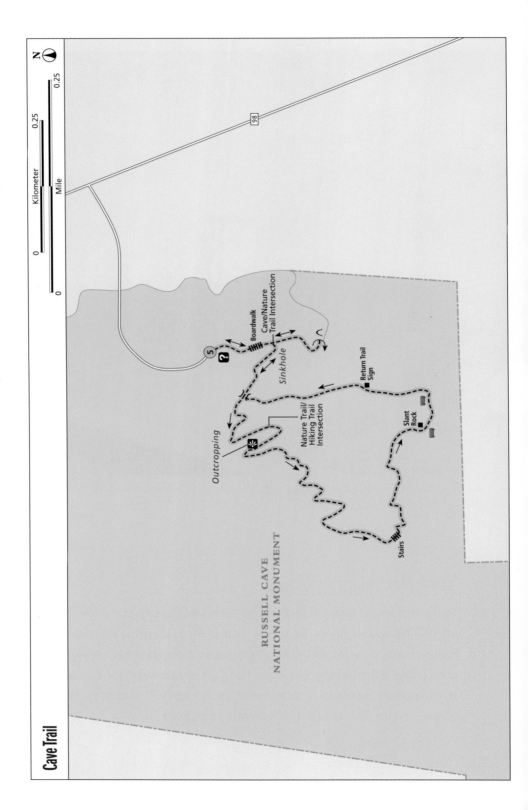

RUSSELL CAVE
NATIONAL MONUMENT

Outcropping

Nature Trail/
Hiking Trail
Intersection

Sinkhole

Boardwalk
Cave/Nature
Trail Intersection

Return Trail
Sign

Slant
Rock

Stairs

Kilometer   0.25

0   0.25
Mile

N

Your first question when you arrive will be, "Are there bats here?" The rangers tell me that brown and northern long ear bats live here, but being nocturnal the chances of seeing them are minimal.

The park holds regular guided tours of the cave daily, but one of the best times to visit Russell Cave is during the Native American Festival, which is held annually the first weekend in May.

Miles and Directions

0.0 Start from the trailhead at the back left side of the visitor center. Follow the composite boardwalk past a picnic area on the left. In less than 0.1 mile come to a Y intersection. A sign points the way to the cave (left) and the Nature Trail to the right. Turn right (northwest) onto the Nature Trail, immediately leaving the boardwalk and climbing a short set of stone stairs. In 200 feet come to an intersection. Turn to the left (south) to view a sinkhole. There is a clever hand-powered kiosk here that tells you about them. When done viewing, turn around and go back to the intersection, but now continue straight to the northwest. The trail is a narrow 2-foot-wide asphalt path.

0.2 Cross a short 4-foot-long cement bridge over a runoff. You will cross twenty-six of these small bridges along this hike. In less than 0.1 mile, come to a Y. An old service road goes off to the right; take the left fork to the west and continue on the asphalt path.

0.3 Come to a Y with a bench on the right. A sign indicates the Nature Trail to the left, Hiking Trail to the right. Take the right fork to the south onto the Hiking Trail.

0.4 View of neighboring mountain to the right (east), rock outcropping on the left.

0.7 Climb down a short set of steps.

0.9 Pass the Slant Rock on the left, a bench on the right.

1.0 Pass a bench on the left.

1.1 Pass a sign that reads Hiking Trail and points back the way you came. Return Trail straight ahead. Continue straight to the north.

1.2 Come to an intersection. Turn right (northeast). In just a few yards arrive back at the boardwalk at the start of the hike. Turn right (southeast) to head to the cave.

1.3 Get your first glimpse of the cave entrance.

1.4 The boardwalk enters the cave and loops around displays depicting Native American life hundreds of years ago. When done, follow the boardwalk back to the visitor center.

1.6 Arrive back at the trailhead/visitor center.

6 King's Chapel Loop

A nice walk in the woods at Lake Guntersville State Park takes you to the King's Chapel Cemetery. Named for one of the families that previously owned the land where the park is now located, the cemetery dates back to the late 1800s. It is the final resting place of the King family and other notable families from the area including Terrell and Rollins.

Start: From the parking area off the Aubrey Carr Jr. Scenic Drive
Distance: 2.3-mile loop
Hiking time: 1.5 to 2 hours
Difficulty: Moderate
Trail surface: Dirt and rock footpath
Best seasons: Fall–spring
Other trail users: Cyclists on Terrell Connector
Canine compatibility: Leashed dogs permitted
Land status: State park

Nearest town: Guntersville
Fees and permits: None; small donation requested at parking lot lockbox
Schedule: Year-round, daily sunrise to sunset
Maps: USGS Columbus City, AL; *DeLorme: Alabama Atlas & Gazetteer*, page 26, A2
Trail contact: Lake Guntersville State Park, 1155 Lodge Dr., Guntersville 35976; (256) 571-5455; alapark.com/lake-guntersville-state-park

Finding the trailhead: From the intersection of AL 227 and AL 79 in Guntersville, take AL 227 south 6.6 miles. Turn left onto Aubrey Carr Jr. Scenic Drive. Travel 7.2 miles and make a left to continue on Aubrey Carr Jr. Scenic Drive (you will pass an entry station that is usually closed). Travel 0.5 mile. The parking lot is on the right. The trail begins across the highway to the south and is well marked. GPS: N34 23.099' / W86 12.388'

The Hike

At Lake Guntersville State Park you will notice trails and features with names like the Terrell Trail, Ellenburg Mountain, and Taylor Mountain. These are all names of families that once settled and lived on the land where the park now resides until the 1930s.

Today you would be hard pressed to find artifacts from these families on the hillsides of Guntersville. Ellenburg Mountain is the home of a nice 3-mile loop trail, the Tom Bevill Trail. Taylor Mountain is now topped with the luxurious Guntersville State Park Lodge. But there is one piece of family history that remains intact to this day and you can still visit—the King's Chapel Cemetery.

The cemetery itself was created by another of the area's families, Andrew King, in 1850. In 1836 King married Mary Ann Rawlings and had six children. His wife's family name, Rawlings, was later changed to Rollins. You will be visiting the graves of some of the Rollinses at the cemetery.

The King's Chapel Cemetery has seen better days. Many of its tombstones have been removed, shattered, or lost over the ages. To their credit the state park has

It's not just the beautiful scenery that draws hikers to the King's Chapel Loop. It's also the King's Chapel Cemetery, which has graves from as far back as the 1890s.

attempted to mark all the graves that no longer have a tombstone, and there are many, with many of the names we just mentioned including King and Terrell.

The lake of Lake Guntersville hasn't always been here—more on that in a moment. The actual town of Guntersville was established in 1785 when John Gunter came down from the Carolinas and became the first white settler here, setting up a homestead on a salt deposit along the Tennessee River that became known as "Gunter's Landing."

Trail intersections at Lake Guntersville State Park, like this one at the King's Chapel Cemetery, are well marked.

Gunter married a Cherokee princess by the name of Ghe-go-he-li, which was later anglicized to Catherine. Because of his marriage and exceptional relationship with local Indian tribes, the landing grew and prospered, and so did Gunter, who became wealthy from his land holdings and slaves. It is quite the twist of fate that while Gunter had a remarkable relationship with the Indians here, his landing would be later used as an embarkation point on the Tennessee River for the forced removal of Indians on the "Trail of Tears."

As a side note, one of Gunter's descendants was the famed humorist Will Rogers.

The town was destroyed by the Union army during the Civil War, but following the conflict it was rebuilt and picked up where it left off, eventually blossoming into a major river port. With the addition of a railroad line through the town, its financial future was secure.

The biggest change to Guntersville came in 1939 when the Tennessee Valley Authority (TVA) completed building Guntersville Dam. With the river blocked off, the valley filled with water, leaving Guntersville as a city on a peninsula. Since that time Guntersville has become a major distribution point for grain and is nationally recognized as the "Powerboat Capital of the South."

You will be using three trails to make this 2.3 mile loop—the King's Chapel, Terrell, and the Terrell Connector. When you arrive at the parking area, note the metal tube on the back side of the parking lot. It is asked that you make a donation to the hiking clubs and the park itself, which maintain these trails.

From the parking lot cross the Aubrey Carr Jr. Scenic Drive and pick up the red-blazed King's Chapel Trail. All the trails are nice 2- to 3-foot-wide dirt and rock footpaths. A thick canopy towers above, making these trails more bearable to hike in the hot, humid summer months. Wildflowers grace the trail as you make your way around the mountain.

The cemetery is located at the intersection of the King's Chapel and Terrell Trails. Quietly pay your respects and take in the inscriptions on the markers that remain. Some descendants of the families buried here still come to visit, so you are respecting them as well.

The Terrell Trail is yellow blazed and meanders along the opposite side of the hill. Notice the remnants of the devastating tornadoes of 2011 and 2013. Many of the downed trees that were cut off the trail lie along its edges. But the forest is resilient and is growing back nicely.

Finally the Terrell Trail spills east of the trailhead on Aubrey Carr Jr. Scenic Drive. You will cross the road here and pick up the white-blazed Terrell Connector to finish out the walk.

Hernando DeSoto in Alabama

Famed explorer and adventurer Hernando DeSoto made his way through what is now Alabama in the mid-1500s. DeSoto came to Peru from his native Spain and became a decorated soldier in Pizzaro's military. In 1538 he amassed a garrison of 600 men and headed north from Cuba to embark on a "great enterprise" in a land that was believed to have more gold than all of South America.

After traveling through what is now the Florida panhandle and up into the future state of Georgia, DeSoto learned that there was an area to the west that had more gold than he could ever imagine. Taking a small group of men, he headed west to what is now called DeSoto Falls at present-day DeSoto State Park in Fort Payne.

After a short stay at the falls, he continued generally toward the west to a place now called Point Rock at Buck's Pocket State Park, which was rumored to have so much gold that it was abundantly visible to the naked eye on the surface of the point.

In 1840 the contingent made it to Point Rock. There was something gold-ish there, and it was definitely in abundance—iron oxide covered the peak, not gold. Records do not show that DeSoto and his men traveled any farther into Alabama.

King's Chapel Loop

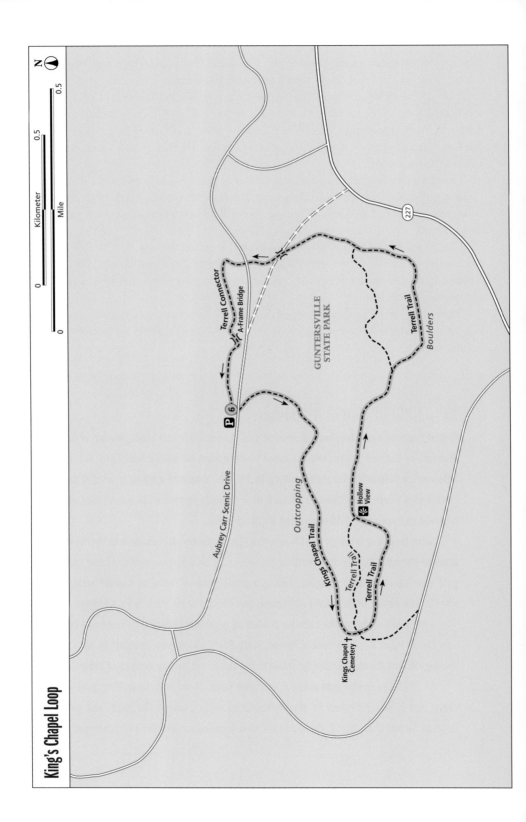

N

Kilometer
0   0.5

Mile
0   0.5

Aubrey Carr Scenic Drive

P 6

Terrell Connector

A-Frame Bridge

227

GUNTERSVILLE
STATE PARK

Outcropping

Kings Chapel Trail

Kings Chapel Cemetery

Terrell Trail

Terrell Trail

Hollow View

Terrell Trail

Terrell Trail

Boulders

Miles and Directions

0.0   Start on the north side of Aubrey Carr Jr. Scenic Drive at the trailhead/parking lot. This is a large gravel lot with room for ten-plus cars. An honor box is located here, and the park asks that you make a small donation to help maintain the trails. From the parking lot cross the road to the south and pick up the red-blazed trail on the opposite side. A sign reading King's Chapel lets you know you're in the right place. Cross the runoff ditch over a short footbridge, then hit the narrow 2-foot-wide dirt trail.

0.4   Pass a short rock outcropping on the right.

0.7   Arrive at the King's Chapel Cemetery. Feel free to explore the cemetery and pay your respects, then walk back to the trail and turn right (south). A sign here shows the way to the Terrell Trail to the right and the King's Chapel Trail back the way you came. Turn right (south) onto the yellow-blazed Terrell Trail. The canopy begins to thin a little through here but is very pretty in the fall. Evidence of the big tornado can be seen along the trail with numerous blowdowns cut and stacked on the sides of the trail.

1.1   View of the hollow to the right (southeast).

1.5   Pass a small boulder field and rock outcropping on the left.

1.9   Cross a 35-foot-long footbridge over a runoff. You start hearing the road as you get closer. In less than 0.1 mile, cross a 30-foot-long footbridge over a runoff ditch next to the Aubrey Carr Jr. Scenic Drive.

2.0   Cross Aubrey Carr Jr. Scenic Drive to the north and pick up the Terrell Trail on the other side (still yellow blazed). In less than 0.1 mile, come to an intersection. A sign here points the way to Taylor Mountain to the right, Terrell Connector to the left. There is also a trail map here. Turn left onto the white-blazed Terrell Connector. This trail is also used by mountain bikes.

2.2   Cross a 30-foot-long, wooden, A-frame-type bridge.

2.3   Arrive back at the parking lot.

7 Cave Mountain Loop

This hike around a Tennessee Valley Authority (TVA) small wild area leads to a cave on the side of the aptly named Cave Mountain. The cave was actually a saltpeter mine that was used for ammunition during the Civil War. The hike takes you to some nice views of Lake Guntersville and a beautiful turtle-filled wetland.

Start: Trailhead on Snow Road/CR 50
Distance: 1.4-mile lollipop
Hiking time: About 2 hours
Difficulty: Moderate to difficult due to a few steep inclines
Trail surface: Dirt and rock footpath, a little rock scrambling
Best seasons: Year-round
Other trail users: Cavers
Canine compatibility: Leashed dogs permitted
Land status: Tennessee Valley Authority small wild area
Nearest town: Guntersville

Fees and permits: None
Schedule: Year-round, daily sunrise to sunset
Maps: USGS Guntersville Dam, AL; *DeLorme: Alabama Atlas & Gazetteer*, page 19, H6
Trail contact: Tennessee Valley Authority Reservation, PO Box 1010, Muscle Shoals 35662; (256) 386-2601; www.tva.gov
Special considerations: See the hike description for a warning about contaminating bats. The cave can be dangerous. You can enter the first 100 to 150 feet; after that special permits are required, and you must be an experienced caver. Contact the TVA for more information.

Finding the trailhead: At the intersection of US 431 and AL 69 in Guntersville, take AL 69 south 6.1 miles. Turn right onto CR 240/Union Grove Road. Travel 2.3 miles and turn right onto CR 50/Snow Road. Travel 2.7 miles. The parking lot and trailhead are on the left. There is a yellow steel-pole gate here, gravel parking area, and enough room for at least 20 cars. GPS: N34 25.116' / W86 24.276'

The Hike

This Tennessee Valley Authority small wild area is only 34 acres in size, but within its boundaries high above Lake Guntersville you will find a spectacular little 1.4-mile lollipop loop, the Cave Mountain Loop, that features rock bluffs, tupelo swamps, and, no surprise here, a cave.

The property itself is owned and managed by TVA and is only a short distance from Guntersville Dam, which forms the lake. All in all TVA has thirty-one such "small wild areas" scattered throughout the region. The areas were developed as part of the National Heritage Project in 1976. Along with The Nature Conservancy, the project sought ways to protect threatened and endangered species of wildlife and plant life in environmentally sensitive areas; one of those studied was Cave Mountain.

This rocky loop trail travels just below the summit of Cave Mountain through a mixed hardwood forest that is gorgeous in the fall. As you round the northern end of the hike, the trail drops down and parallels a beautiful tupelo swamp. Box turtles line

Cave Mountain's namesake stands wide open facing a beautiful wetland. The cave was once the site of saltpeter mining operations during the Civil War.

up on logs to sun themselves, and as you near the halfway point, the sound of frog song in the evening echoes off the mountain. You will be walking a 1- to 2-foot-wide footpath wedged between the swamp on your left and a large limestone bluff on your right. The trail can be a bit muddy and treacherous through here, as water seeps off and out of the rock wall and gushes down its face during a hard rain.

This rock wall is where the highlight of the hike comes in, the mountain's namesake, the cave itself. It is not a massive cave like the rock shelter at Russell Cave or Kinlock but a neat hole in the wall that was a small water channel centuries ago; rains widened the tunnel to its present-day size.

At one time the cave had an enormous bat population, but that proved to be their own demise. A high concentration of bat guano created something of value to the Confederate army during the Civil War—saltpeter. When processed, this becomes potassium nitrate, which is a key ingredient of black powder.

During the war the Long Hollow Nitre Works set up shop here and began mining the crystallized chemical. The constant activity at the site eventually drove the bats from the cave, and they haven't been back since.

Mining the cave was backbreaking work. At its peak the operation was hauling 1,000 pounds of the mineral from the mine each day by hand. Many times the miners

As you wind around the top of Cave Mountain, be sure to turn around for a beautiful view of Lake Guntersville and the dam.

would have to crawl through narrow openings dragging heavy bags full of the material with them.

The cave has a semicircular opening with a flat rock floor. Sadly graffiti "artists" have added their own history to the walls. The entrance goes in about 300 feet and turns pitch black. It is a sheer vertical drop after that, so only experienced spelunkers are allowed to continue into the cave.

Having said that, a statement released in June 2015 by the TVA requested that hikers stay out of the cave until further notice. A disease called white nose syndrome has been reported in other caves in northern Alabama. While this cave has been "bat free" for some time, the cave itself could harbor the disease. It is not harmful to humans, but it is to bats, so a person walking in an infected cave and then visiting another cave with bats could contaminate the colony.

Miles and Directions

0.0 Start from the trailhead/parking lot on CR 50/Snow Road to the northeast. A kiosk here has a large map of the route and photos of some of the plants and reptiles you could see on the trek. The trail has large, white paint blazes and at this point is a 3- to 4-foot-wide dirt path, but soon becomes rocky as it heads through rock outcroppings and boulders. Several species of trees are identified throughout the hike.

Cave Mountain Loop

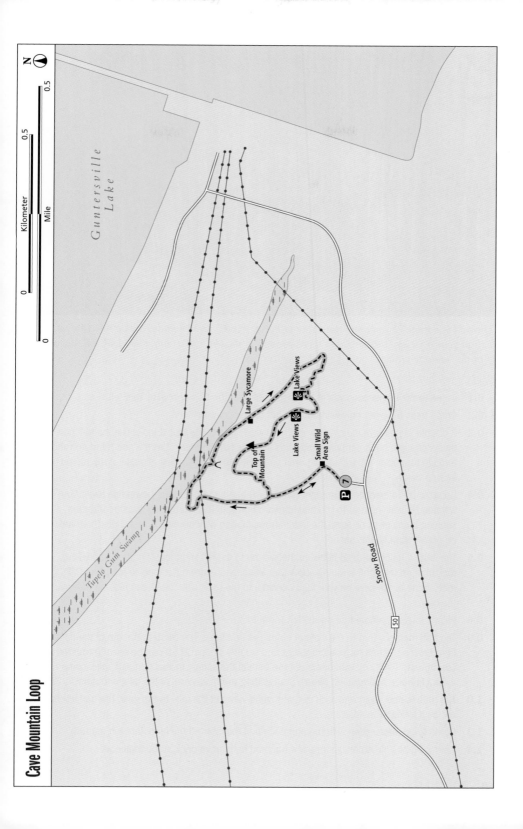

Guntersville Lake

Tupelo Gum Swamp

Large Sycamore

Top of Mountain

Lake Views

Lake Views

Small Wild Area Sign

P

Snow Road

50

N

0   0.5   Kilometer
0   0.5   Mile

The trail is narrow as you make your way to the cave at Cave Mountain, with a towering rocky bluff to your right and this amazing tupelo swamp to the left. On a sunny day look for dozens of turtles sunning on logs.

0.1 Come to the intersection where the loop portion of the hike connects. Turn left (west).

0.2 Some trees have not only white blazes but orange as well.

0.3 A double white blaze indicates a left (northwest) turn in the trail. It looks like the trail continues straight, but it actually dead-ends in a few hundred feet. Turn left and head downhill through the rocks. You will see a power line tower and get your first glimpse of the tupelo swamp below.

0.4 Come to a T intersection. Turn right (northeast) and head under the power line tower. You will now be walking next to the tupelo swamp on your left (northeast). Watch for turtles sunning themselves on logs. The trail narrows here to only about 1.5 feet wide. There are no blazes through this section.

0.5 The narrow trail is wedged between the swamp to the left (northeast) and an impressive rock bluff on the right, towering above you. Water seeps down the face. In less than 0.1 mile, come to the cave on your right carved into the rock wall. The blazes resume following the cave.

0.6 Pass a large sycamore tree on the left (northeast).

0.9 The trail makes a turn to the west at double white blazes. The climb to the top of the ridge from here is through rock outcroppings and is fairly steep. CR 50 can be seen to your left (southwest). Plenty of wildflowers dot the path in the spring. In less than 0.1 mile, come to a double blaze and turn left (west). Start getting your first views of the lake and dam.

1.0 The path is now a dirt and rock mix, with good views of the lake to the east. The trail levels out as it follows the ridgeline.

1.3 Come to an intersection with the approach trail that started the loop. Turn left (south).

1.4 Pass a Small Wild Area sign. In a few hundred feet, arrive back at the trailhead.

8 Kinlock Shelter

This is a short hike, only a mile long, but the history is astounding. The massive Kinlock Shelter towers above the valley floor. The shelter has been used by Native Americans for centuries as a place of spiritual worship and ceremony. Petroglyphs from ancient times adorn the walls, but this is not simply a historic site. The shelter is still used today, and therefore it is asked that you visit it with reverence.

Start: From the parking lot on Kinlock Road
Distance: 1.0 mile out and back
Hiking time: About 1 hour
Difficulty: Moderate with a short but steep rock climb near the shelter
Trail surface: Dirt and rock footpath
Best seasons: Fall and spring
Other trail users: None
Canine compatibility: Leashed dogs permitted

Land status: National forest
Nearest town: Haleyville
Fees and permits: None
Schedule: Year-round, daily sunrise to sunset
Maps: USGS Kinlock Spring, AL; *DeLorme: Alabama Atlas & Gazetteer*, page 23, B8
Trail contact: Bankhead National Forest, 1070 Hwy. 33, Double Springs 35553; (205) 489-5111; www.fs.fed.us/

Finding the trailhead: From the intersection of AL 13 and AL 195 in Haleyville, take AL 195 south 8.5 miles. Turn left onto Kinlock Road. Drive 3.6 miles and cross the Hubbard Creek Bridge. Continue north on Kinlock Road, driving up a short hill. In 0.5 mile come to the parking area at the top of the hill on the left. It is a small, gravel parking area with a historical marker on the left side of the lot. Start the hike from here. GPS: N34 18.797' / W87 30.525'

The Hike

I arrived at the trail that leads down into the ravine at the Bankhead National Forest on a cool fall morning. Slowly I made my way down the sandstone rock wall, minding my steps on the damp, leaf-covered path, not once looking up.

The trip down was shorter than I expected (having talked to locals before heading out), and I quickly reached the bottom. As I started walking on the now level ground, I finally looked up. My jaw dropped when I saw it, and all I could say under my breath was "wow!"

Peeking out above the trees was the yawning opening of the Kinlock Shelter. Just this first initial impression was enough to cause that reaction, and immediately I understood why Native Americans have used this location for centuries as a place of spiritual worship.

Before telling you about the history of the Kinlock Shelter and this hike to it, keep in mind that, as with all historic landmarks and sites, it is unlawful to remove artifacts or deface the site. Here at Kinlock you are asked to treat this spiritual site with the utmost respect and reverence.

Photos do not do justice to the mammoth entrance of the Kinlock Shelter, a Native American spiritual and ceremonial site.

This mammoth rock shelter, carved into the sandstone rock wall over the centuries by the weathering action of the elements and streams, has seen human activity for thousands of years. Evidence of that history can be seen etched in the rock walls. Without a guide you may have trouble finding them, but look hard and you will see centuries-old petroglyphs depicting turkey tracks and straight cuts in the wall in succession where tools were sharpened.

The Yuchi Tribe is believed to have been the first to use the cave, then later the Cherokee and other tribes. The cave is still used by Native Americans for spiritual ceremonies; one is the Winter Solstice Sunrise Ritual marking the longest night of the year.

Besides human activity the plant world is well represented here as well. Be careful where you tread, and look for the rare filmy fern, which has made its home here for 35 million years. It is believed that these are descendants of a species of fern that thrived here when the climate was tropical.

The shelter was named for a tract of land approximately 480 acres in size that was purchased by brothers David and Greene Hubbard, who named the tract "Kinlock." No one is quite sure why they named it that or what the name signifies. In 2000 this

The Free State of Winston

Not all Southerners were loyal to the Confederacy during the Civil War. In fact, there were pockets throughout the South that remained true to the Union. One of those was Winston County in Alabama.

It can be debated whether or not the Civil War was fought solely on the abolition of slavery, but slavery was a driving force in the conflict. In 1860 Winston County only had fourteen slave holders and 122 slaves total. For them the abolition of slavery wasn't a reason to leave the Union.

Immediately following Abraham Lincoln's election, states began to secede. In December 1860 Alabama held a conference to discuss secession. One of the delegates, Chris Sheats, along with twenty-two other delegates, refused to sign the secession resolution that was drafted.

When he returned to Winston, a mass meeting was called to discuss the decision. Held at Looney's Tavern in the town of Houston, 2,200 people attended, and in the end they drafted their own document stating that no state can legally leave the Union, but if a state did leave the Union, then any county had the right to leave a state. The county vowed to remain neutral during the Civil War, to the point where Confederate soldiers imprisoned the men of the county and threatened to shoot them in the back if they didn't fight for the Southern cause, which only stoked their resolve to stay a free county.

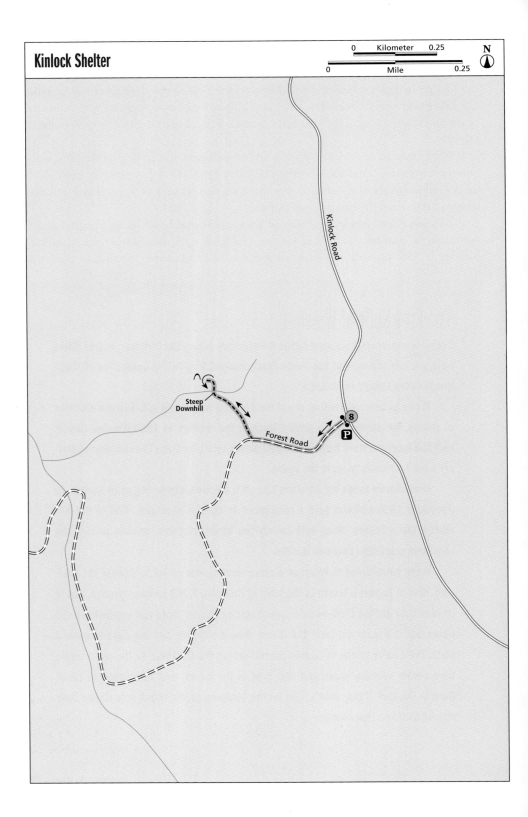

Kinlock Shelter

As you make your way into the enormous Kinlock Shelter, the rocky grays and brown give way to a multicolored wall of sandstone.

area, including the rock shelter, the old mill built by Hubbard, their namesake creek, and the remains of the plantation, was added to the National Register of Historic Places.

The trail to the shelter is short, only 0.5 mile (1 mile total), and begins at a small gravel parking area just past three white columns that mark the location of the old

Hubbard Plantation. The plantation was used by the Civilian Conservation Corps' Company 1403 in 1933 as a camp when they worked in the area, but was destroyed by fire in 1935. From the parking lot take a short walk to the west up the dirt Kinlock Road that you drove in on, and you will come to a gated forest service road on the left. Take the service road about a quarter mile; the trail to the shelter ducks into the woods to your right. It isn't blazed but is clearly visible.

The scamper down the rock bluff is only about 100—maybe 200 feet—but fairly steep, so watch your footing, especially in wet weather.

Miles and Directions

0.0 Start from the parking lot on Kinlock Road. This is a narrow gravel lot with room for about five cars comfortably. Head west/northwest on the dirt road about 200 feet and come to a gated forest service road on the left. Turn here to the southwest onto the dirt road. Walk around the gate and follow the road uphill.

0.2 At the top of the hill, look for the trail to the shelter on your right. It is unmarked but easy to see and follow. Turn right here (northwest) onto the trail.

0.3 Pass a side trail, possibly a deer trail, to the right. Continue straight to the northwest. In less than 0.1 mile the trail begins a steep, rocky climb downhill. Be careful, especially after a rain or on damp mornings. The trail down can be slick.

0.4 After the climb down the trail levels out. Look up to get your first amazing view of the rock shelter. The trail is covered with large bigleaf magnolia leaves. In a few yards cross a small creek that can be boggy.

0.5 Arrive at the Kinlock Shelter and its massive tall, wide entrance. Feel free to explore, but for safety reasons it is not recommended going into the narrow back chambers. When done exploring, turn around and retrace your steps to the trailhead.

1.0 Arrive back at the trailhead.

9 Dismals Historic Gorge

History greets you at every turn along this trail through the Dismals Canyon. The high, green moss covered canyon walls and rock shelters were home to Cherokee, Chickasaw, and Paleo Indians as far back as 10,000 years ago. Remnants of an old water mill and its old mill stone can be seen as well as the hiding place of robbers. Oh, and did I mention the scenery is absolutely breathtaking?

Start: From the back deck of the park's general store and restaurant
Distance: 1.1-mile double lollipop
Hiking time: About 1 hour (varies depending on exploring)
Difficulty: Easy
Trail surface: Dirt and rock footpath
Best seasons: Year-round
Other trail users: None
Canine compatibility: Leashed dogs permitted
Land status: Privately owned

Nearest town: Phil Campbell
Fees and permits: Day-use fee
Schedule: Year-round, Mon to Thurs 11 a.m. to 5 p.m., Fri 11 a.m. to 6 p.m., Sat 9 a.m. to 9 p.m., Sun 9 a.m. to 5 p.m.; check times before arriving, as they change frequently
Maps: USGS Phil Campbell, AL; *DeLorme: Alabama Atlas & Gazetteer*, page 23, B6
Trail contact: Dismals Canyon, 901 Hwy. 8, Phil Campbell 35581; (205) 993-4559; www.dismalscanyon.com

Finding the trailhead: From the intersection of AL 13 and AL 237 in Phil Campbell, take AL 237 0.5 mile. Turn right onto CR 12/College Road. Travel 3.2 miles and turn left onto US 43 South. In 1.1 miles turn right onto CR 8 and travel 0.9 mile. The entrance to the park is on your left. Turn into the entrance and small parking lot. Park and walk 400 feet to the south to the country store. After paying your fee and signing a liability waiver, begin the hike through two French doors in the left center of the building. GPS: N34 19.568' / W87 46.907'

The Hike

Up in northwest Alabama you can explore some interesting canyons with a rich geologic and human history dating back thousands of years ago, such as those found in the Sipsey Wilderness or Cane Creek Preserve. Today I'll be taking you to another canyon in that corner of the state that also has a rich history and offers an excellent, easy walk for the entire family, Dismals Canyon.

The canyon is a privately owned property that has been granted National Natural Landmark designation by the National Park Service. That doesn't mean it is a national park, just that it is a location of historical and environmental significance that needs to be protected.

The gorge here was once a primeval swamp. Over 300 million years ago, during the Paleozoic era, the land was lifted up, the swamp drained, and the resulting action of the water flowing through the rock weathered it away to form the gorge you see today. As you walk beneath the towering bluffs, you get a sense that the canyon, with

One of the many geologic and historical features of Dismals Canyon, "Weeping Bluff" is reflected in a pool along the trail.

its dark, green mossy tones and dark passageways, hasn't really changed much since that time. You will pass evidence of this tumultuous period of geologic history at what is called "The Grotto," where house-size boulders formed natural bridges after the large earthquakes of the time.

Through dating of artifacts found in the many caves and rock shelters, archaeologists believe that humans first inhabited the canyon 10,000 years ago. These Paleo Americans left behind a fairly complete record of their past through spear points and other relics. (Remember, this is a federally protected site; if you come across any relics, look, don't touch, and report them and their location to the staff.) At mile 0.3 you will visit Temple Cave, where these ancient people once lived. The large flat rock outside the cave was used for grinding food, and the flat rock along the back of the cave was where they built fires. The heat would radiate outward off the rock wall.

This rock cave at the Dismals was formed when two large blocks fell from the gorge walls.

Later Native Americans, including Chickasaw and Cherokee Indians, called this canyon home, living here and conducting ceremonial rituals. You will see the "Kitchen" where the tribes cooked. A split in the rock acted as a natural chimney for the smoke and is called the "Stove Pipe."

Once again we cross paths with the infamous "Trail of Tears" here at the Dismals. In 1838 US soldiers rounded up Chickasaw Indians and interned them in the canyon for two weeks before "herding them off like cattle" to Muscle Shoals and eventually to land west of the Mississippi. In all, 90 percent of the Chickasaw who were forcibly relocated died on the Trail of Tears.

At mile 0.4 and again on the return trip, you will pass Weeping Bluff, a beautiful, picturesque high rock wall with a bridge and a pool in front of it where the scene is reflected. It is said that if you look at the wall at the right angle you can see the face of an Indian maiden; the water seeping down makes it look as if she's crying for the loss of the canyon's only true friend, the Chickasaw.

Dismal Canyon also holds some modern history. As you first enter the canyon, you will pass Rainbow Falls. At one time the falls powered an old gristmill that stood here until a flood hit in the 1950s. Along this section you can see a few of the old mill wheels next to the trail. When the sun is at the right angle, you can see a rainbow in the spray of the falls, hence the name.

Besides all the fun exploring the beauty and history of the gorge itself, families will have a chance to refresh themselves at a wonderful little soda shop and restaurant inside the general store. Everything from hamburgers to root beer floats can be had here. There is also a nice picnic area if you decide to bring your own lunch.

And just because you have explored the canyon during the day doesn't mean the fun stops there. Visit the Dismals Canyon website for times when they do their night tours of the canyon. Knowledgeable guides lead flashlight-armed visitors down the trail to see the dismalites, small larvae that live in only a few select places in the world, in conditions like those found here at Dismals Canyon. Dismalites are glowworms of sorts that cling to the rock walls and produce a dazzling blue glow.

Miles and Directions

0.0 Start from the country store at the French doors to the left in the middle of the building. On the landing outside the door, turn right and follow the stairs and cement path to the bottom. In less than 0.1 mile, arrive at a platform, passing a restroom on the right. Turn left and climb down the stairs to a lower platform. At this platform turn right and head down some narrow, steep stairs.

0.1 Arrive at the gorge. Huge rock bluffs are on your right and a nice view of Rainbow Falls on the left. Notice the old mill wheels from the old gristmill. In less than 0.1 mile, pass a swinging bridge across the creek on the left. Continue straight (south). Pass Phantom Falls—the echo produced by Rainbow Falls makes you "think" there is another falls behind you. Keep going straight and walk through a cave over a wooden bridge.

0.2 Come to a side trail on the right that leads to the top of Phantom Falls. When done visiting, continue straight to the south. In less than 0.1 mile, pass Indian Head Rock on the right. The creek is directly next to the trail on the left; just after this pass a wooden bridge on the left. Continue straight to the south. In less than 0.1 mile arrive at the Kitchen and Stove Pipe. Keep going straight to the south, passing stepping-stones in the creek to the left.

0.3 The path Ys. When I walked it, the right fork was blocked with a sign that read "snake den." If it's walkable you can go either way. It links up again on the opposite side of an outcropping. The left fork takes you through a narrow "squeeze." In less than 0.1 mile, come out of the "squeeze" and to an intersection with three possible routes. The middle and right trail both go around an outcropping and join up again on the opposite side. In a few yards the two paths reconnect and you walk under a rock shelter called Temple Cave.

0.4 A very picturesque scene is across a pool on your left with a view of a wooden footbridge beneath the towering rock wall called Weeping Bluff.

0.5 Pass an amazing rock bluff on your left. Continue straight to the south. In less than 0.1 mile, cross a footbridge over the creek and turn left (north). The return trip is on the opposite side of the creek.

0.6 Come to a Y intersection. The left fork takes you along the creek. The right takes you to the Champion Tree. If you take the right fork, just past the trees are a set of stairs that leads back to the creek and rejoins with the left fork. In less than 0.1 mile, walk through stone cuts. A set of stairs made with wooden, 4-by-4-inch water bars leads the way.

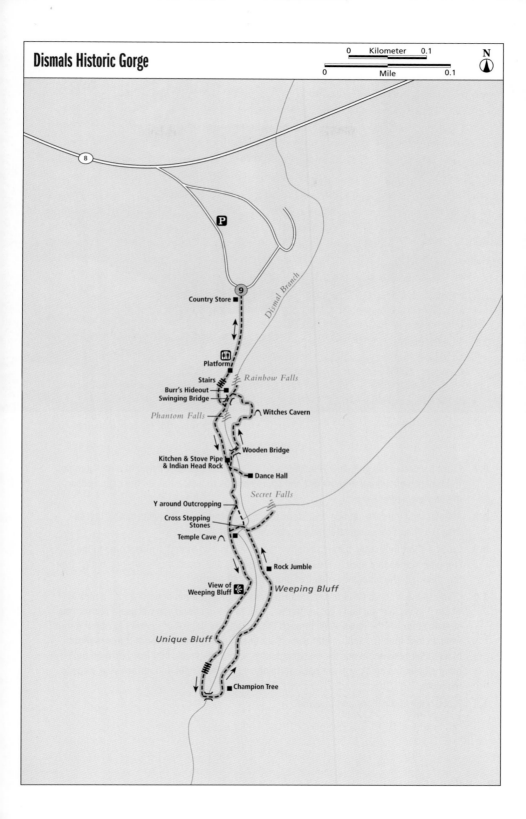

Dismals Historic Gorge

0 — Kilometer — 0.1

0 — Mile — 0.1

N

8

P

9

Country Store

Dismal Branch

Platform

Stairs

Rainbow Falls

Burr's Hideout

Swinging Bridge

Phantom Falls

Witches Cavern

Wooden Bridge

Kitchen & Stove Pipe
& Indian Head Rock

Dance Hall

Secret Falls

Y around Outcropping

Cross Stepping
Stones

Temple Cave

Rock Jumble

View of
Weeping Bluff

Weeping Bluff

Unique Bluff

Champion Tree

At the entrance to the gorge at the Dismals, you are treated to a beautiful view of Rainbow Falls.

0.7 Cross a wooden bridge below Weeping Bluff. In less than 0.1 mile, come to a rock jumble. The trail moves around it to the left and shortly comes to a side trail on the right. Follow this to view Secret Falls.

0.8 After viewing the falls, retrace your steps to the main trail and turn right (north). In less than 0.1 mile, cross eight stepping-stones over the creek.

0.9 Cross a short footbridge through another "squeeze." In less than 0.1 mile, come to the stepping-stones that lead to the Dance Hall. After visiting, cross a 50-foot-long bridge over the creek. On the other side make an immediate left (north).

1.0 Come to the Witches Cavern. Keep walking straight until you run headlong into a rock wall where it looks like you can't go any farther. Look to the right and you will see a narrow passageway through the rocks. Walk through the winding passage that narrows to about a foot wide. In less than 0.1 mile, climb a short set of stone stairs and arrive at Burr's Hideout. Make a left here and cross the swinging bridge across the creek. In a few yards, on the other side of the creek, you are back at Rainbow Falls. Turn right and retrace your steps to the store.

1.1 Arrive back at the store and trailhead.

10 Noccalula Falls Historic Gorge Trail

Part legend, part ancient history. That's what's in store for you as you walk to—and under—Noccalula Falls. The falls were named for Cherokee Indian princess Noccalula and the legend of her tragic love story that ends at the bottom of this 90-foot-deep gorge. The trail into the gorge takes hikers past towering rock bluffs, small caves, and a mammoth rock shelter that allows you to walk beneath the falls.

Start: From the trailhead 0.3 mile northwest of the park entrance
Distance: 0.8 mile out and back
Hiking time: About 1.5 hours
Difficulty: Easy to moderate with slippery rocks at the falls and a moderate climb out
Trail surface: Dirt and rock footpath, cement ramp down to canyon
Best seasons: Year-round, better in spring and fall when the falls are running
Other trail users: None

Canine compatibility: Leashed dogs permitted
Land status: City of Gadsden park
Nearest town: Gadsden
Fees and permits: Day-use fee
Schedule: Year-round, daily 9 a.m. to 7 p.m.
Maps: USGS Gadsden West, AL; *DeLorme: Alabama Atlas & Gazetteer*, page 26, F3
Trail contact: Noccalula Falls Park, 1500 Noccalula Rd., Gadsden 35904; (256) 549-4663; cityofgadsden.com/Facilities/Facility/Details/3

Finding the trailhead: From the intersection of I-59 at exit 188 and AL 211, take AL 211 south 2.6 miles. The park is on your right. Pay your admission fee and follow the paved walk through the park, crossing the train tracks and passing the petting zoo and pioneer village buildings. At 0.2 mile from the entrance, cross the train tracks one last time. The trailhead is 100 feet straight ahead. GPS: N34 02.323' / W86 01.542'

The Hike

How many love stories with tragic endings have been written over the centuries? *Romeo and Juliet, Anna Karenina, Wuthering Heights.* All with basically the same ending—a love dies, literally. Another lesser known love story took place at Noccalula Falls in the city of Gadsden, and it, too, had a tragic ending. And that is what brings us to the park of the same name, to hike a trail and gorge named in honor of the Indian princess who, as legend has it, lost her life here because of love.

Before Princess Noccalula, of course, there is the geologic history of the falls. The falls were created by Black Creek, which flows through what is now the city of Gadsden. As with all Alabama rivers and streams, the creek is seasonal with low, almost trickling water in the heat of summer and thundering cascades in fall and spring after soaking rains.

Over the centuries Black Creek began eroding away the land and eventually created a beautiful 90-foot waterfall and the gorge we will be walking. As time went by,

A couple stands under a massive rock shelter beneath Noccalula Falls for a look at the falls from the other side.

the water's action at the bottom of the falls, a plunge pool, and the water's action at the top of the falls began to erode the rock wall underneath until finally the overhang that had formed collapsed. Today it is an impressive rock shelter that the trail actual travels through directly behind the falls.

But that was a long time ago in geologic history. In more recent history the legend of Noccalula began. The story was originally penned by famed female composer Mathilde Bilbro. Bilbro was a prolific Alabama composer of the late 1800s and early 1900s, so much so that she was recognized in the world-renowned orchestral publication *Etude Magazine* as one of the world's best-known musicians. Between 1890 and 1900 Bilbro moved to Gadsden, and it was here that she first heard the story of the Indian princess and later penned the story.

As the story goes, a tribe of Cherokee Indians lived near what was then called Black Creek Falls. The tribe's leader was a powerful chief in early northeast Alabama. His daughter, Princess Noccalula, was said to have been the most beautiful in the land and was famed for her "lovliness of character."

Through the years many men, all gallant warriors in their own right, vied for the hand of the young princess, but her father denied them all. There was only one man that Noccalula's father approved of, a young warrior from a powerful neighboring tribe. As you might imagine, this warrior had it all—money (or wampum) and horses. He had social standing.

But Noccalula had other plans for her life. She told her father that she was in love with another brave from their own tribe. Unfortunately this brave had no material possessions or wealth. He was a brave man, but not "worthy" in her father's eyes. To him a union of two powerful tribes and wealth was more important than his daughter's true happiness. Noccalula's lover was banished from the tribe and the wedding arrangements were made.

Before long it was the wedding day. According to the story Noccalula awoke that morning to the birdsong she loved so much. Attendants helped her dress in wedding attire and then escorted her to the wedding feast.

Sometime during the feast the princess, who was grieving for her lost love and the fact that her own father would use her to build his power, slipped away unnoticed into the woods. Some say the soothing, rushing sounds of Black Creek Falls drew her to the falls. She stood at the edge for a moment, then with one leap jumped over the edge to the gorge floor below.

Upon receiving word of his daughter's death, Noccalula's father went into grieving and at that moment renamed the falls Noccalula Falls. Some say if you look closely at the spray of the falls into the plunge pool, you will see the image of the princess. A statue of the princess peers down from high above the gorge.

The hike through the princess's gorge is a beautiful walk along the lower section of Black Creek below the falls, but the real treat of this hike is the falls themselves. The trail works its way over a rock- and boulder-strewn path into the giant rock shelter that was formed by the falls thousands of years ago, directly behind the falls.

Be very careful walking here, though. When the falls are rushing, the rocks can be very slippery. You can also walk through this rock shelter to the opposite side of the falls, then carefully walk down to a small beach in front of the falls for an even more impressive view.

Noccalula Falls Historic Gorge Trail

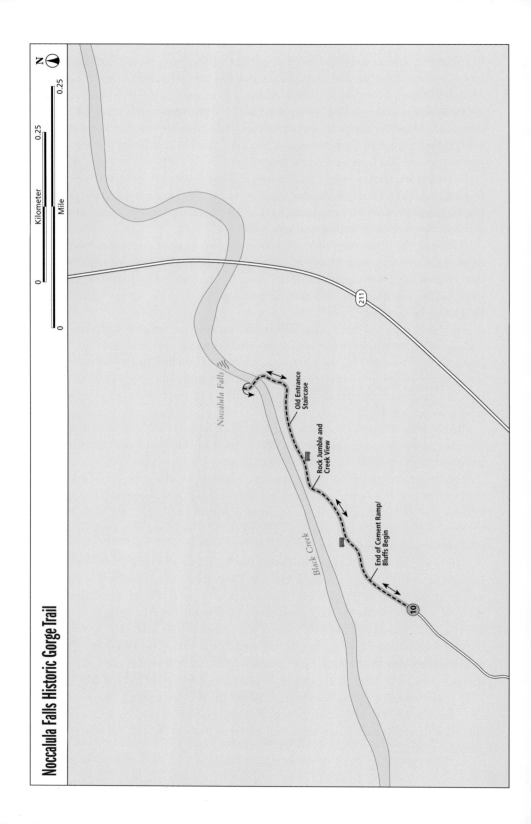

Noccalula Falls

Black Creek

Old Entrance Staircase

Rock Jumble and Creek View

End of Cement Ramp/ Bluffs Begin

211

10

N

Kilometer
0   0.25

Mile
0   0.25

You can make this into a loop hike by walking a narrow trail on the north (opposite) side of the creek after crossing behind the falls. When I visited, it was overgrown and quite slick, so I only describe the main trail here as an out and back.

Also remember that when the creek is high, it is a dangerous place to be. The park will shut it down during times of floods.

Miles and Directions

0.0 Start at the Historic Gorge trailhead on the far northwestern side of the park. The trail starts out as a rather steep downhill walk on a wide cement ramp. In about 400 feet you arrive at the gorge. The trail is dirt and strewn with rocks and boulders the remainder of the trip. The rock walls of the gorge tower above you.

0.1 Pass a bench on the left.

0.2 Walk through a rock jumble with some nice views of Black Creek on the left. In less than 0.1 mile, pass a bench on the right.

0.3 Pass the original entrance to the gorge, a set of metal stairs, on the right.

0.4 Arrive at the falls. Feel free to walk behind them in the huge rock shelter, but be careful! It can be very slippery here. And remember, swimming and wading in the plunge pool or creek is prohibited. When you're done, turn around and retrace your steps to the trailhead. (**Option:** It is possible to make this into a loop hike by following the north bank of Black Creek back to the southwest. I recommend you talk with the staff at the main entrance before venturing on this route.)

0.8 Arrive back at the trailhead.

11 Horse Pens 40

Over 15,000 years of human history echo through the magnificent rock outcroppings and boulders of Horse Pens 40. This hike will allow you to explore these rock formations where Cherokee and Creek tribes once lived, seeking sanctuary and spiritual renewal. The rocks were also used to corral horses, and during the Civil War by locals to hide their valuables and livestock. The trail will also take you to the edge of the plateau for magnificent views from this southern Appalachian mountain.

Start: From the park's country store
Distance: 0.9-mile loop (varies depending on exploring)
Hiking time: About 1 hour
Difficulty: Easy
Trail surface: Dirt and rock footpath
Best seasons: Fall–spring
Other trail users: Rock climbers
Canine compatibility: No pets permitted

Land status: Privately owned
Nearest town: Ashville
Fees and permits: Day-use fee
Schedule: Year-round, daily 8 a.m. to sunset
Maps: USGS Steele, AL; *DeLorme: Alabama Atlas & Gazetteer*, page 25, G10
Trail contact: Horse Pens 40, 3525 County Rd. 42, Steele 35987; (256) 538-7439; horsepens40.tripod.com

Finding the trailhead: From the intersection of I-59 at exit 166 and US 231 in Ashville, take US 231 north 3.2 miles. Turn right onto CR 35. In 0.2 mile CR 35 turns into Gallant Road. Travel 1.6 miles and turn right onto CR 42. This is a winding uphill drive, so drive carefully. In 0.2 mile come to the country store. Park here, pay your fee, and begin your hike. GPS: N33 55.333' / W86 18.461'

The Hike

Many historic sites in Alabama have a centuries-old history where prehistoric inhabitants first lived in an area, then Europeans arrived creating a town or village, then that town dies out for whatever reason—floods, yellow fever, and so forth. Horse Pens 40 is different in that it can brag of an almost 15,000-year history and 8,000 years of constant human occupation.

The park is currently privately owned by a local family, but because of its rich Native American history, it is protected under federal laws. That history dates back at least 12,000 years to the Paleozoic era. Along this craggy landscape archaeologists have discovered evidence of sacred rituals, ceremonies, and burials dating as far back as 12,000 years ago. The large rock overhangs provided the perfect setting for these ceremonies.

One interesting feature of Horse Pens 40 is that researchers believe it is the only site in the country with the last remaining example of an ancient leaching pit. Normally tribes would dig a hole in the clay ground, place food items such as acorns and

The amazing rock outcroppings of Horse Pens 40, used by Native Americans to corral livestock and where local residents hid valuables, and themselves, during the Civil War

hickory nuts in the hole, and run water through the pit to remove the tannin and make the nuts edible. At Horse Pens 40 there is a natural stone cavity that appears to have been used for this purpose and could have made 150 pounds of edible meal from nuts a day.

Later Indian history shows that this "mountain fortress" was part of the border between the Cherokee and Creek Nations. For hundreds of years the two tribes fought over this land. Eventually they signed a peace treaty, the only one between the two nations, at this location.

As you drive in to the park, you will see large cleared areas. These are called "Cherokee Old Fields," which were cleared by the tribe and used for growing crops. In the 1830s many Cherokee families flocked to these rocks and used them as hiding places from the US military during the period of Indian removal from their land known now as the "Trail of Tears."

The rocks and shelters proved to be a good hiding place for settlers of the area as well. During the Civil War families would hide valuables, horses, and even children here to protect them from advancing Union troops and "bushwhackers." Mostly from Missouri, bushwhackers were guerrillas that fought Union occupation by ambushing patrols and even murdering Union-loyal farm families. Horse Pens 40 was the perfect staging area for such "raids." Later, when the Confederacy discovered the outcroppings, they used them as hiding places too, making this a highly concealed supply depot.

Today the park continues to be the center of activity for the region. To this day Native Americans still use Horse Pens 40 for spiritual ceremonies, and the large rock amphitheater makes the perfect music venue. Each year notable artists like Emmylou Harris (who made her first paid performance here at age 16), Charlie Daniels, and Allison Krause make appearances.

The trail described here winds through all of these amazing outcroppings and boulders. Highlights include Little Elephant Rock, which really does look like a baby elephant. Just past the elephant is a beautiful cathedral-like cut in the outcroppings that tower above you. And don't miss the view from "The Point." A short wooden span bridges the gap between an outcropping and the main bluff, and the view is wonderful, especially on a morning where a light fog, or "smoke," is rising from the surrounding mountains.

Don't be surprised if you round a bend and find yourself in a throng of people bouldering. Armed only with their bouldering mat, it is fascinating to watch as they attempt to make some technical climbs up the rocks, and most are happy to share their knowledge of the sport with you.

There are few to no blazes on this trail, only the occasional wooden arrow tacked to a tree that you will probably miss if you don't look up, but that's OK. The route I describe here is only one of several ways you can hike through this maze of rock outcroppings and boulders. Take your time, meander about, make your own route, and enjoy the splendid beauty and history of Horse Pens 40.

Miles and Directions

0.0 Start from the country store and follow the wide gravel road to the west.

0.1 Come to a Y intersection as you near the campground. Take the left fork to the south, passing some portable toilets and a Purell station for cleaning your hands on the left.

0.2 Pass two wooden barricades at the southwestern end of the campground. No Parking signs are attached to the barricades. Just after passing them you will be standing next to some impressive rock outcroppings. Two signs are posted here: One points to the left and says Nature Trail; the other points straight ahead and reads Lookout Point. Continue heading straight to the west, and head to the point by following along the base of the rock outcroppings. In less than 0.1 mile, a picnic area is on your right. Also to your right (west) is a sign that reads Lookout Point. Follow the arrow to the west. The trail becomes a narrow 2-foot-wide dirt and rock path.

0.3 Approaching Lookout Point the trail bed is flat rock. A short 6-foot bridge crosses the gap between the rock outcropping and the point. Walk across the bridge for an amazing view of the surrounding mountains and valley. Re-cross the bridge and turn right (south) and continue on the path.

0.4 There is a side trail to the right with a red wooden arrow. You can easily mistake this as a turn. Instead continue straight to the southeast around a large and impressive boulder field. In less than 0.1 mile, turn left (west) and head through the boulder field. In a few

Horse Pens 40

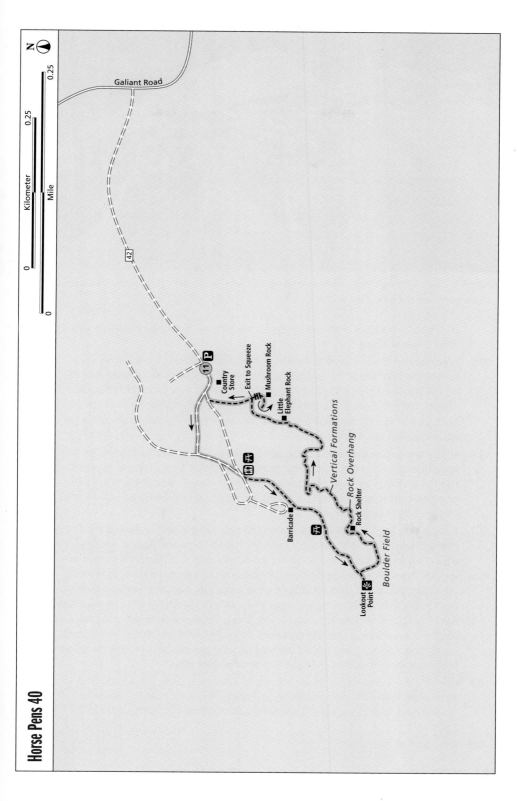

Galiant Road

Kilometer
0   0.25   0.25

Mile
0   0.25

N

42

P

11

Country Store

Exit to Squeeze

Mushroom Rock

Little
Elephant Rock

Vertical Formations

Rock Overhang

Rock Shelter

Barricade

Boulder Field

Lookout
Point

Beautiful clumps of purple American beautyberry add color to the drab grays of the surrounding rock outcroppings of Horse Pens 40.

yards pass a small rock shelter on the right. A few feet past the shelter you will be walking under a rock overhang.

0.5 Take a look up at some very impressive rock formations. The trail Ys here, but will rejoin itself on the other side of an outcropping. Take the right fork for an easier route; take the left fork (you'll see a red arrow on the rocks) to the north to walk under the rocks and through a little squeeze. In less than 0.1 mile, come to an intersection. You can see a picnic area to your left. Turn right (east) onto the narrow path; the outer edges of the trail are demarcated with a line of rocks.

0.6 At an interesting weathered rock outcropping, come to a Y. Turn right (northeast). The trail winds through some weathered "pillow" rocks. In less than 0.1 mile, come to another Y. Take the left fork to the east and continue through the outcroppings (the right fork will reconnect in a few dozen yards). The path is sandy through here, and 4x4 posts are used as water bars to prevent erosion.

0.7 Arrive at Little Elephant Rock, which is identified by a sign and really does look like a baby elephant. Continue straight through a cathedral formed by the outcroppings towering around you. In less than 0.1 mile, you exit the outcroppings. A performance stage is on your left. Turn right (east) and climb a short, grassy hill on railroad tie stairs. In about 20 yards turn right down a short set of stairs under a sign that reads Entrance and make your way through a small, narrow rock squeeze. When you exit, you will be inside an amphitheater of rock. Continue straight (south). In less than 0.1 mile, you come out of the outcroppings and arrive back at Little Elephant Rock. Turn right (north) and retrace your steps to the right back up the grassy hill, but this time pass the entrance sign. In a few yards pass Mushroom Rock on your left and come to a set of wooden stairs.

0.8 Climb the stairs to the top of the outcropping. In a few yards come to a wooden deck with an excellent view of the outcroppings you just passed through at mile 0.7. When done viewing, climb back down and at the bottom head straight to the north to return to the trailhead.

0.9 Arrive back at the trailhead.

CENTRAL REGION

I ron and steel. That's what made the Central Region of Alabama. The Birmingham area is one of the few places in the world where the three ingredients for making iron—iron ore, coal, and limestone—can be found all in one place, and shrewd businessmen capitalized on this fact from the 1800s to the 1960s.

You can explore much of this rich history on the trails in Red Mountain Park, where much of the iron ore was mined from the ground and shipped to local foundries. In fact, the trails here still have the red tint of the ore. You will visit several of the old mines, long since sealed, at Red Mountain and view an actual ore crusher buried deep in the woods at Ruffner Mountain Nature Preserve, which was used to pulverize huge chunks of rock, preparing it for shipping. Then it's on to Tannehill Historic State Park to see an actual furnace from the late 1800s that has been restored.

But it's not only about mining in the Central Region. You will also explore one of the earliest communal cultures in the region at Moundville Archaeological Park, where you will have your best view of ancient Indian mounds built over 10,000 years ago and learn how their culture influenced modern man.

You will also climb the rocky Smith Mountain and learn about the fire tower that stands tall above Lake Martin and was loving restored by a local group of hikers.

The Central Region of Alabama holds an amazing wealth of history to explore, so let's get started.

12 Fossil Trail

Take a walk back in time, I mean a *long* time, when the Earth was still a work in progress and much of Alabama was covered by an ancient sea. The Fossil Trail at Rickwood Caverns State Park is a rock- and boulder-strewn path where you will find the fossil records of that time in the form of leaf and seashell imprints embedded in these rocks.

Start: At the parking area 500 yards east of the park office on the left-hand side of Rickwood Park Road
Distance: 1.2-mile lollipop
Hiking time: About 1 hour
Difficulty: Easy to moderate with some rock scrambling
Trail surface: Dirt and rock footpath
Best seasons: Year-round
Other trail users: None
Canine compatibility: Leashed dogs permitted
Land status: Alabama state park

Nearest town: Warrior
Fees and permits: Day-use fee; additional fee to tour the cavern
Schedule: Year-round, daily 8 a.m. to sunset
Maps: USGS Warrior and Blount Springs, AL; *DeLorme: Alabama Atlas & Gazetteer*, page 24, H5
Trail contact: Rickwood Caverns State Park, 370 Rickwood Park Rd., Warrior 35180; (205) 647-9692; alapark.com/ rickwood-caverns-state-park

Finding the trailhead: From the intersection of AL 160 and US 31 in Warrior, take US 31 North/AL 160 west 0.2 mile and turn right onto Skyline Drive. Travel 2.5 miles and turn right onto Rickwood Caverns Road. Travel 1.4 miles and turn right onto Rickwood Park Road. In 0.2 mile come to the entrance gate and pay station. After paying your day-use fee, continue straight 0.2 mile. The parking area is on your left. GPS: N33 52.492' / W86 51.691'

The Hike

While the cave at Rickwood Caverns is spectacular in and of itself, there is still more exploration to do at the park that bears the cave's name. There is a sweet little trail here that your family—from the oldest to the youngest—will love, called the Fossil Trail. Along this 1.2-mile loop, kids, and adults, will find themselves scouring the rocks looking for signs of prehistoric leaves and invertebrates.

As the name implies, the history found on this trail goes back a few years, about 360 million years, as a matter of fact. This region of Alabama is an area of limestone, shale, coal, and sandstone that actually runs from north-central Alabama through Tennessee, Kentucky, Pennsylvania, and western New York. In the north it's called the Appalachian Plateau. Here in the south it's the Cumberland Plateau.

The story of how the fossils got here begins in the Mississippian period between 360 and 320 million years ago. During this time what we now know as Alabama was under an ancient, shallow sea. Slowly, very slowly, the land began to rise through

Right from the beginning the Fossil Trail has an unworldly appearance.

geologic processes. During the Pennsylvanian period (320 to 296 million years ago), a series of ice ages took place where the Earth's glaciers would thaw and cause the oceans to rise then refreeze and cause the oceans to recede, leaving behind dead organic material such as leaves in swamps. Some of this material converted to coal, while others decayed but left an impression in the sediment that, when it dried and hardened, became known as a fossil.

Sometimes the ocean would submerge a swamp as it was rising, and a small marine environment developed. This continual ocean/swamp dance left layers of sediment thousands of feet deep, and much like the leaves of early years, the remains of tiny shelled sea creatures left behind a fossil record of their existence.

By 285 million years ago the land was really pushing up, and now rivers, streams, and runoff from the receding oceans eroded the land and formed many of the features we see today. Rickwood Caverns is a perfect example; the water hollowed out this massive cave but left behind a record of its geologic history. Besides caves this erosion created chimneys, natural arches, and rock shelters throughout the plateau.

Fossil Trail

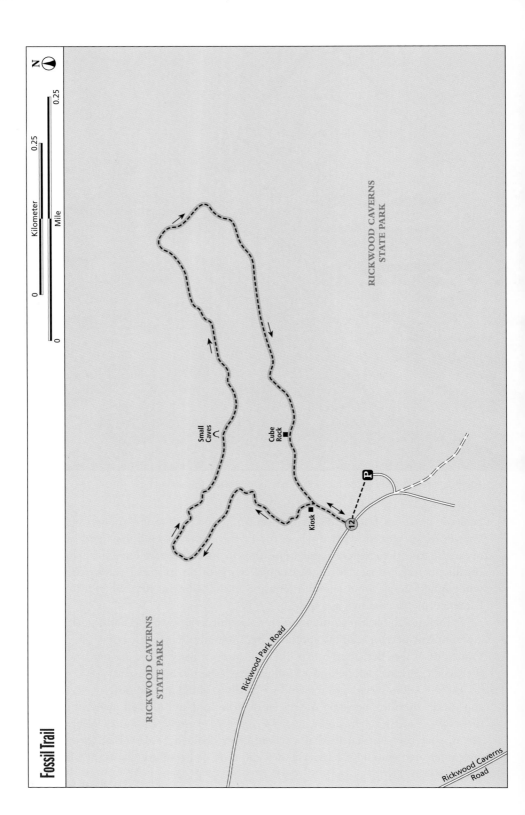

The Fossil Trail is aboveground through a field of boulders and outcroppings. It's just a great romp through the woods and over, around, and through these rocky bluffs. I will admit the fossils are hard to find, and I'm sure you will have your head down searching every rock for them. Don't keep it down too long, though; enjoy the beauty of the rocky landscape.

I rated this hike as an easy to moderate 1.2-mile loop. There are some small climbs, but they really aren't that steep. This rating is on the low side of moderate.

The path is well marked with paint blazes. The rocks are covered with moss and lichen, and you never know what little animal might scurry from the crevices. If you do bring smaller children, be careful around mile 0.4. There are sinkholes on each side of the trail with short but dangerous drop-offs. The more adventurous may want to poke around these, but be very careful!

Miles and Directions

0.0 Start from the parking area just a few yards past the park office on the left. Follow the road to the west about 500 yards to the trailhead on your right. A sign that reads Hikers Only, No Vehicles marks the entrance. The trail is well marked with yellow paint blazes on the rocks. For the first 0.1 mile, you will be walking through a rather open area with rocks all around giving an unworldly appearance.

0.1 Come to a Y at a kiosk. This is where the loop connects. Take the left fork to the northwest. A yellow arrow marks the way.

0.4 Look for small caves along the sides of the trails that have been formed by the jumble of rocks. The trail becomes less rocky for a bit after this section.

1.0 Pass an interesting boulder sitting on top of a rocky pedestal. The rock has weathered almost into a cube shape.

1.1 Arrive back at the loop intersection you began the trip on at mile 0.1. Turn left (southwest) here.

1.2 Arrive back at the trailhead.

13 Mine Ruins/Crusher Trail

Ruffner Mountain near Birmingham once played an important role in making that city an important iron town, and that history is showcased on the park's Mine Ruins/ Crusher Trail. This hike uses three different trails to wind you through mine ruins and an amazing ore crusher that appears out of the woods like an ancient Mayan ruin.

Start: North side of Ruffner Mountain Nature Center parking lot under wooden trailhead entrance
Distance: 2.1-mile lollipop
Hiking time: About 1.5 hours
Difficulty: Moderate with some short climbs
Trail surface: Dirt and rock footpath
Best seasons: Year-round
Other trail users: None
Canine compatibility: Leashed dogs permitted
Land status: Nonprofit nature center
Nearest town: Birmingham

Fees and permits: None; donation requested
Schedule: Trails open year-round, daily sunrise to sunset; visitor center open Tues to Sat 9 a.m. to 5 p.m., Sun 1 p.m to 5 p.m; closed Thanksgiving, Christmas Eve, Christmas Day, New Year's Day
Maps: USGS Irondale, AL; *DeLorme: Alabama Atlas & Gazetteer*, page 31, D7; trail maps available at trailhead kiosk
Trail contact: Ruffner Mountain Nature Center, 1214 81st St., Birmingham 35206; (205) 833-8264; ruffnermountain.org

Finding the trailhead: From the intersection of I-65 and I-59/I-20 in Birmingham, take I-59/I-20 east 6.4 miles. Take exit 131 (Oporto Madrid Boulevard) and in 0.2 mile turn right onto 77th Street North/Oporto Madrid Boulevard. In 0.6 mile turn left onto Rugby Avenue and travel 0.7 mile. Turn right onto 81st Street South and in 0.4 mile arrive at the nature center. Drive past the visitor center. The road loops around past parking for special events, and you will come to another parking lot on the uphill side near the gift shop/visitor center. The trailhead is here on the north side of the parking lot. GPS: N33 33.516' / W86 42.429'

The Hike

This hike delves into the mining history of the "Magic City," Birmingham, for a trip to the Ruffner Mountain Nature Preserve. You will travel into the woods on the southeastern slope of the mountain to visit some very heavy machinery that made the mining operation more efficient—the giant ore crusher of the Ruffner #2 Mine.

The history of the #2 Mine and all the mines on the southeast side of the mountain begins with Colonel James Withers Sloss, a railroad man and plantation owner who, like many of the day, came to Birmingham to make a fortune in the iron and steel industry. In 1882 he opened the first of two blast furnaces in the area under the company he founded, the Sloss Furnace Company, and began producing pig iron.

The future, however, wasn't in pig iron but steel, which was stronger but more pliable and better suited for building rails for the rapidly expanding railroad lines of the day. Unable to acquire rights to use the processes to transform the area's raw materials

Rounding a bend in a small switchback, the enormous ore crusher appears in the woods like an ancient Mayan temple.

into high-grade steel, Sloss sold the company in 1886, and in 1899 it reorganized as the Sloss Iron and Steel Company, or SISC. In 1886 SISC opened the #2 Mine at Ruffner, which remained in operation until 1953.

The work of the miners was backbreaking to say the least. All the mining was done by hand, mostly by African Americans under contract to the company, who used pickaxes, wedges, and on occasion explosives to break up chunks of the ore, then load it into ore cars that they pushed, by hand, to the surface on a small tramline to the crusher. Historical records show that in 1892 the workers were making 60 cents per car load. A few years later, when scales were introduced, wages were based on actual tonnage hauled (60 cents per ton).

The ore crusher was located in a shallow ravine between two ridges where the ore could be more easily dumped into the top of the machine. At full operation the crusher could pulverize 100 to 180 tons of ore per hour.

I call this hike the Mine Ruins/Crusher Trail, but in reality we use four trails to make this into a lollipop loop and to access the trail to the ore crusher—the Quarry, Mine Ruins, Crusher, and Ridge and Valley Trails.

As you walk along the Mine Ruins Trail, keep your eyes peeled for signs of those long-gone mining days, such as stone retaining walls and hundred-year-old foundations.

Rounding a ridge near the far end of the loop, you will begin walking steeply down the hillside into a ravine. As you walk through the lush green forest (in spring and summer), you will see it rising up like an ancient Mayan ruin—the ore crusher itself.

The trail winds down to the bottom of the ravine where you will cross a small creek (this area could be deep in water and mud after a good rain) and come right up to the base of the structure. Including the stone base the crusher stands a good 30 to 40 feet tall. A set of wooden stairs on the right side allows you to walk to the top to take a look inside.

For the most part the trails along this trek are well maintained. The Quarry Trail is a good 3 to 4 feet wide with the brush trimmed well back. When you get onto the Mine Ruins/Crusher Trail, the path narrows to a 2-foot-wide dirt and rock path, a little less maintained and somewhat overgrown in sections at times but not impassable. All the trails are well marked: The Quarry Trail is painted with white blazes, the Mine Ruins/Crusher Trail with blue blazes, and the short section of the Ridge and Valley Trail that we will use with orange blazes.

In the summertime you will appreciate the thick hardwood canopy that covers all the trails at Ruffner Mountain, making for a cooler hike. Along the Crusher Trail, as you near the ore crusher itself, in the wet months of spring and summer, the dark greens of the moss and leaves on the trees are striking. In the fall the color burst is exhilarating.

Miles and Directions

0.0 Start from the trailhead at the north end of the parking lot next to the gift shop and office building. The white-blazed trail begins under a small wooden portal and is a narrow dirt path with excellent canopy. In less than 0.1 mile, come to a Y intersection. A sign points to the right fork and the Quarry Trail; the left fork is the Geology Trail. Take the right fork to the south.

0.2 Cross a paved road to the south. A kiosk with information about The Nature Conservancy and the preserve is on the opposite side. Just after passing the kiosk, come to a Y. A sign points to the right to the Trillium Trail and the Nature Center and to the left to the Quarry Trail. Take the left fork to the south and continue on the Quarry Trail. In another 20 yards pass the trail that leads to the Buckeye/Wetlands Trails on your left. Continue straight to the south.

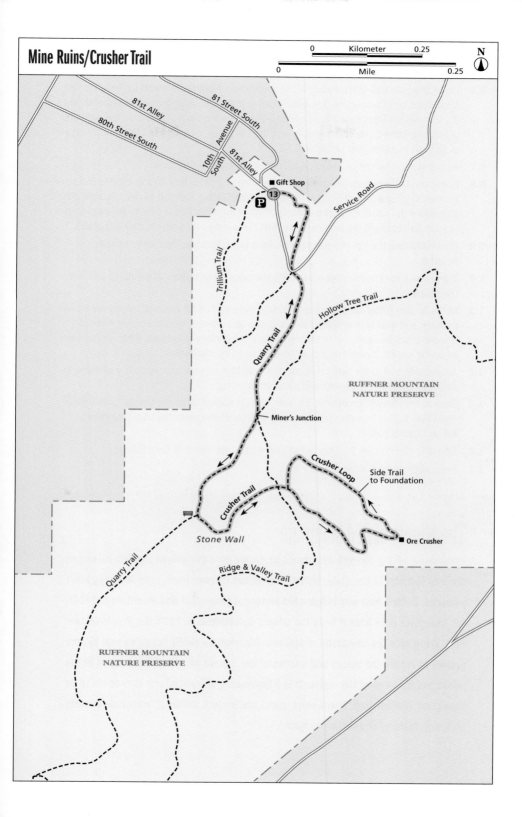

Mine Ruins/Crusher Trail

0   Kilometer   0.25

0   Mile   0.25

N

81st Alley

81 Street South

80th Street South

10th Avenue South

81st Alley

■ Gift Shop

13

P

Service Road

Trillium Trail

Quarry Trail

Hollow Tree Trail

RUFFNER MOUNTAIN
NATURE PRESERVE

Miner's Junction

Crusher Loop

Side Trail
to Foundation

Crusher Trail

Stone Wall

Quarry Trail

Ridge & Valley Trail

Ore Crusher

RUFFNER MOUNTAIN
NATURE PRESERVE

0.4 A trail with a sign reading Miner's Junction comes in from the left. Continue straight to the south on the Quarry Trail.

0.6 Come to a side trail with a bench at the intersection. A sign here points to the left for the Mine Ruins and Crusher Trail. The Quarry Trail continues straight. Turn left (southeast) onto the blue-blazed Mine Ruins/Crusher Trail. The trail narrows to a 2-foot-wide dirt path and is less maintained than the others. In less than 0.1 mile, look for a cut stone retaining wall to your left in gullies next to the trail.

0.7 Pass a stone structure on the left. Continue straight to the northeast.

0.8 Come to a trail junction. The orange-blazed Ridge and Valley Trail (simply labeled Trail on a wooden sign) crosses left to right. The blue-blazed Crusher Trail can be seen straight ahead and will be the return route of the loop portion of this hike. Turn right onto the blue-blazed Crusher Trail to begin the loop (a sign points the way and reads To Crusher—0.6 mile).

0.9 The trail follows the top of a narrow ridge for a short distance, then starts heading downhill.

1.0 The massive ore crusher appears through the trees at the bottom of the hill to your left (northeast).

1.1 At the bottom of the hill cross a small creek. The area can be very wet, maybe even deep in water, and muddy after a hard rain. It is here you arrive at the ore crusher. A set of wooden stairs takes you up to the top of the machine for a good look. When you're done exploring, continue past the crusher on the trail to the northwest.

1.2 A short side trail to the right takes you to an old stone foundation. Retrace your steps to the main trail, turn right (northwest), and continue on.

1.3 Back at the intersection at mile 0.8, turn right (northwest) onto the orange-blazed Ridge and Valley Trail. In less than 0.1 mile, turn left (southwest) onto the blue-blazed Mine Ruins/Crusher Trail.

1.5 Turn right (north) onto the Quarry Trail and retrace your steps to the trailhead.

2.1 Arrive back at the trailhead.

The Miners of Red Mountain

Throughout *Hiking through History Alabama*, we have discovered the rich history of the iron industry in the state, visiting mines, old railroad lines, even towering blast furnaces. But the best way to learn the history of places like Red Mountain and Ruffner Mountain is to hear it from the miners themselves. In 2009 the Red Mountain Park along with the University of Alabama Birmingham (UAB) began an oral history project to record the voices and images of the miners who lived and worked in the mines and furnaces of the region. It is a fascinating story—and one that needs to be heard and remembered. Learn more about the project online at www.redmountain park.org/history/oral-history-project/.

14 Quarry Trail

Take a walk along an old mining road for a glimpse at Ruffner Mountain's mining past along the Quarry Trail. This easy to moderate walk takes you through a beautiful mixed hardwood forest that culminates in a spectacular view of the mountain's old limestone quarry.

Start: North side of Ruffner Mountain Nature Center parking lot under wooden trailhead entrance
Distance: 2.7 miles out and back
Hiking time: About 1.5 hours
Difficulty: Easy to moderate with some short climbs
Trail surface: Dirt and rock footpath
Best seasons: Winter to late spring
Other trail users: None
Canine compatibility: Leashed dogs permitted
Land status: Nonprofit nature center
Nearest town: Birmingham

Fees and permits: None; donation requested
Schedule: Trails open year-round, daily sunrise to sunset; visitor center open Tues to Sat 9 a.m. to 5 p.m., Sun 1 p.m to 5 p.m; closed Thanksgiving, Christmas Eve, Christmas Day, New Year's Day
Maps: USGS Irondale, AL; *DeLorme: Alabama Atlas & Gazetteer*, page 31, D7; trail maps available at trailhead kiosk
Trail contact: Ruffner Mountain Nature Center, 1214 81st St., Birmingham 35206; (205) 833-8264; ruffnermountain.org

Finding the trailhead: From the intersection of I-65 and I-59/I-20 in Birmingham, take I-59/I-20 east 6.4 miles. Take exit 131 (Oporto Madrid Boulevard) and in 0.2 mile turn right onto 77th Street North/Oporto Madrid Boulevard. In 0.6 mile turn left onto Rugby Avenue and travel 0.7 mile. Turn right onto 81st Street South and in 0.4 mile arrive at the nature center. Drive past the visitor center. The road loops around past parking for special events, and you will come to another parking lot on the uphill side near the gift shop/visitor center. The trailhead is here on the north side of the parking lot. GPS: N33 33.516' / W86 42.429'

The Hike

Before it became a hot spot for education and outdoor recreation, the area now protected by the Ruffner Mountain Nature Preserve in Birmingham was a hot bed for mining. The reason was simple—this area had a rich supply of three minerals: limestone, coke (coal), and hematite, the three key ingredients to make iron and steel. It turns out that central Alabama is one of the few places in the world where all three of these ingredients can be found together. As a result a town that was little more than a dot on the map almost overnight became a financial success story—Birmingham.

In 1882, while mining operations were picking up steam on the south end of Red Mountain, geologist William Henry Ruffner documented the geology and minerals of the area which is now the home of the Ruffner Mountain Nature Preserve. At about the same time, a north Alabama merchant and railroad man, Colonel James Sloss, came

This large depression in the earth is the site of a former limestone quarry. Today hikers search for fossil records from ancient times on its walls.

into the picture. Sloss was one of the first to mine and sell high-grade coking coal mined in the city, as well as limestone. In 1881 he formed the Sloss Furnace Company and began constructing the city's second blast furnace, Sloss Furnace.

Sloss convinced the L&N Railroad Company to route their rail line through Jones Valley, which is located just below the mountain. This meant that Sloss was able to mine the mountain of both minerals and ship it directly to his own furnace more efficiently. In its first year of operation, the furnace sold over 24,000 tons of iron. After being sold in 1886, it remained in operation until 1953.

Following the closure of the mine and quarry, the land was reclaimed by nature, but remnants of Birmingham's glorious iron past still haunt the woods here with the gaping quarry, abandoned mines, and giant rusting ore crushers lurking in the dense forest, many of which can still be seen when you hike the park's many trails, including the Crusher Trail.

The Quarry Trail is called the backbone of the preserve. It runs down the spine of the mountain—with many side trails branching off—taking visitors not only to the mining history of the area but also to beautiful wetlands and hardwood forests. You can create a wide variety of hiking experiences just by starting on this trail.

The Quarry Trail is white blazed and runs the length of the park from north to south. Intersections are well marked with unique wooden signs pointing the direction to each trail. They resemble the old "hometown signs" you see in movies about

An Oasis of Trails and History

There is so much more to see at the Ruffner Mountain Nature Preserve that you should plan a full day to explore. The nature/visitor center features excellent displays about the mining history of the mountain and the natural beauty and landscapes found here in this suburban park. They also have live animals that the kids will love to see. Over 12 miles of trails on this 1,038-acre property lead hikers to beautiful wildflowers, wetlands, fossil-finding adventures, and more of the mountain's fascinating mining history. Admission to the park is free, but please help keep it open and the trails maintained by making a donation at the nature/visitor center.

World War II or the Korean War—you know, the large wooden signs with one end tapered, pointing the direction to "San Francisco 2,000 miles" or "New York 5,000 miles." And there are plenty of informative signs dotting the path that are easy to read and help you identify plants and history along the way.

The Quarry Trail ends 1.1 miles from the trailhead and joins the Possum Loop Trail and the red-blazed Overlook Trail for a short distance. There is a quick scamper up a short hill near the turnaround to the Cambrian Overlook, where you will get some good views of the deep cut and impressive limestone walls of the quarry that helped make Birmingham what it is today.

The overlook is your turnaround for the trip described here, but there are plenty more trails, and history, to discover at Ruffner Mountain. Spend the day and explore.

Miles and Directions

0.0 Start from the north side of the parking lot. The trailhead is a large wooden gateway that you walk under. In 100 feet pass the kiosk (with maps) to the left. In another 300 feet come to a Y intersection. The Geology Trail goes straight to the east, the Quarry Trail to the right (south). Turn right onto the Quarry Trail.

0.2 Cross a paved service road to the south and pass another kiosk with a trail map and Forever Wild sign. The Trillium Trail branches off to the right. Continue straight to the south. In 100 feet pass the Hollow Tree Trail on the left, going straight up a set of stairs.

0.4 Come to Miner's Junction. The Ridge and Valley Trail comes in from the left; continue straight to the south.

0.6 Pass the Mine Ruins/Crusher Trail. There is also a bench here. This section can be very muddy and hold some good-size puddles after a heavy rain. In 50 feet pass the Jimmie Dell Wright Overlook/Winter Overlook Trail on the right.

0.8 Pass the Silent Journey Trail on your right. The blazes are white and yellow here as the Possum Loop begins. There is also a Don't Pick the Flowers sign here.

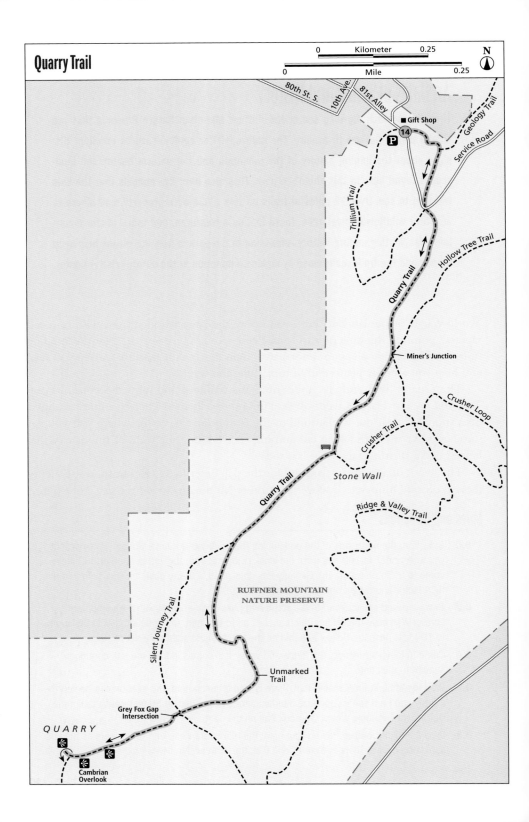

Quarry Trail

0   Kilometer   0.25

0   Mile   0.25

N

80th St. S.

10th Ave.

81st Alley

Geology Trail

Gift Shop

14

P

Service Road

Trillium Trail

Quarry Trail

Hollow Tree Trail

Miner's Junction

Crusher Loop

Crusher Trail

Stone Wall

Ridge & Valley Trail

Quarry Trail

Silent Journey Trail

RUFFNER MOUNTAIN
NATURE PRESERVE

Unmarked
Trail

Grey Fox Gap
Intersection

QUARRY

Cambrian
Overlook

A wooden trellis-like structure with a hint of an Asian influence marks the entrance to the Quarry Trail.

1.0 Pass an unmarked trail on your right.

1.1 Arrive at Grey Fox Gap. There is an information kiosk here with a map. The Quarry Trail ends at this major trail intersection where the Silent Journey, Possum Loop, and Ridge and Valley Trails all converge. Continue straight on the red-blazed Overlook Trail to the southwest. In 50 feet you pass two signs at a Y: One points to the right (northwest) and the Quarry Entrance Trail; the other points to the left (west) and the Possum Loop. Take the left fork to the west. The trail is now blazed red and yellow.

1.3 Start getting views to your right of the quarry, especially when the leaves are down in late fall and winter. In 150 feet climb down a steep set of rock stairs. At the bottom is a Y intersection. The left fork is the Possum Loop. Take the right fork to the north and follow the sign to the Cambrian Overlook. In only 50 feet come to a short, rocky side trail on the right. Turn onto that trail to the northwest (a small sign reads Cambrian Overlook).

1.4 Arrive at the Cambrian Overlook. Enjoy the view, but be very careful on the dangerous, steep bluff. Turn around and retrace your steps to the trailhead.

2.7 Arrive back at the trailhead.

15 Vulcan Trail

The Roman god Vulcan is the god of fire and forge, a symbol of iron and steel, so it is no wonder that a statue of Vulcan stands high about the "Magic City" of Birmingham. And just below the statue is the Vulcan Trail, which follows the route of the old Birmingham Mineral Railroad (BMRR) that used to transport ore to nearby furnaces. Along this paved multiuse trail, you will see the remnants of the old trestle and have nice views of the city.

Start: From the Vulcan Trail parking lot off Richard Arrington Jr. Blvd South, just below the Vulcan Park and Museum
Distance: 2.2 miles out and back
Hiking time: About 1 hour
Difficulty: Easy
Trail surface: Asphalt
Best seasons: Year-round
Other trail users: Joggers, cyclists
Canine compatibility: Leashed dogs permitted

Land status: City-managed rail-trail
Nearest town: Birmingham
Fees and permits: None; small fee to get a view from the statue
Schedule: Year-round, daily sunrise to sunset
Maps: USGS Birmingham South, AL; *DeLorme: Alabama Atlas & Gazetteer*, page 31, E6
Trail contact: Vulcan Park and Museum, 1701 Valley View Dr., Birmingham 35209; (205) 933-1409; www.visitvulcan.com

Finding the trailhead: From the intersection of I-20 at exit 125 and US 280 East/US 31 South in Birmingham, take US 280 East/US 31 South 1.2 miles south. Take the University Boulevard exit and travel 0.2 mile, then make a right onto 8th Avenue/University Boulevard. Travel 0.3 mile and turn left onto 22nd Street South. In 0.5 mile turn right onto Highland Avenue South. In 0.1 mile the road becomes 21st Way South. In 0.3 mile 21st Way South bends to the right and becomes 16th Avenue South. In 0.2 mile turn left onto Richard Arrington Jr. Boulevard South and travel 0.3 mile. The trailhead parking is at the bend on the right. GPS: N33 29.552' / W86 47.727'

The Hike

Vulcan is the Roman god of fire and the patron of metal working—smithing. So it was only fitting that high atop Red Mountain, where the city of Birmingham's economic future was born with the iron ore mining industry, a statue to Vulcan was erected.

The statue is impressive in itself. Standing 56 feet tall, it is the largest cast-iron statue in the country. Depicting the burly, bearded Roman god with a spear in one hand and a blacksmith's apron, he stands overlooking the city and the trail you're about to walk, the Vulcan Trail.

The Vulcan Trail follows the former route of the Birmingham Mineral Railroad. The BMRR line was officially opened in March 1884 as a division of the L&N Railroad Company. Several branches and spurs were constructed off the main line, one of which ran all the way to present-day Hoover and what is now Red Mountain Park

The only remaining trace of the old BMRR line along the Vulcan Trail are two old stone trestle supports.

(the BMRR Trail there was part of this rail line), as well as to various ore crushers scattered across the area.

In 1885 the rail line expanded again, this time with a closed loop track that circled the mountain. This expansion was done under the direction of another major railroad company, the Tennessee Coal and Iron Railroad Company (TCI). TCI agreed to the deal with the understanding that L&N would grant them an exclusive contract to haul ore.

By the mid–1920s the booming iron industry was slowing in Birmingham, and all of the various ore hauling rail lines began shutting down, including the L&N and TCI lines. The tracks and bridges were removed and the beds left abandoned.

Jump ahead to 2003 when the city took a portion of the line just beneath their famous Vulcan Park (where the statue stands), paved it, and created the Vulcan Trail, where you can walk the former backbone of the iron industry in Birmingham.

Kudzu is King

As you walk the Vulcan Trail, you will notice nice, green, leafy foliage clinging to, well, everything! This is kudzu, a plant that has its roots in Japan. During our nation's one hundredth birthday celebration at the 1876 Centennial Exposition, the Japanese government honored us by constructing a garden exhibit featuring their native plant. Americans loved the oversize leaves and the smell of the grape-like blossoms.

In the 1920s things got out of hand. In Chipley, Florida, Charles and Lillie Pleas discovered that livestock loved the plant too, and they began selling plants to farmers across the country. In the mid-1930s the Civilian Conservation Corps found the plant was useful in controlling soil erosion. And in the 1940s farmers were paid $8 an acre to distribute what was by then called the "Miracle Vine."

By 1953 the plant was running rampant across the South. In the summer kudzu can grow 60 feet a year, killing competing vegetation beneath it as it blocks out the sun, so in the "sunny South" you can see how the plant ran rough-shod over the countryside. The government stopped promoting it that year, and in 1973 it was officially categorized as a weed.

The Vulcan Trail is an easy-walking 2.2-mile out-and-back multiuse trail, meaning that you can expect bikers and joggers most any time of the day. The footpath is paved, and as mentioned is routed just below the ridge of the mountain. At the trailhead the statue of Vulcan looms above you. The trail is not blazed, but you won't need them. It runs 1.1 miles and dead-ends with obvious signs telling you to turn around.

The path meanders around the mountainside with some nice views of the city just before mile 0.5. Just past this you will come to the first of two trestle supports. This and another at mile 0.8 are the only remaining artifacts that remind us of the city's glorious mining railroad past on Red Mountain.

When you're done, be sure to drive just a short half mile and visit Vulcan Park and Museum to get a more in-depth look at the iron history of the city and ride the elevator to the top of the statue for a bird's eye view.

And a word of caution: The Vulcan Trail trailhead is located on a sharp bend on Richard Arrington Jr. Boulevard. If you're heading north on the road to get to it, you will have to make a left turn into the parking lot right at the bend, crossing two lanes of traffic. Just be careful when turning and watch for oncoming traffic.

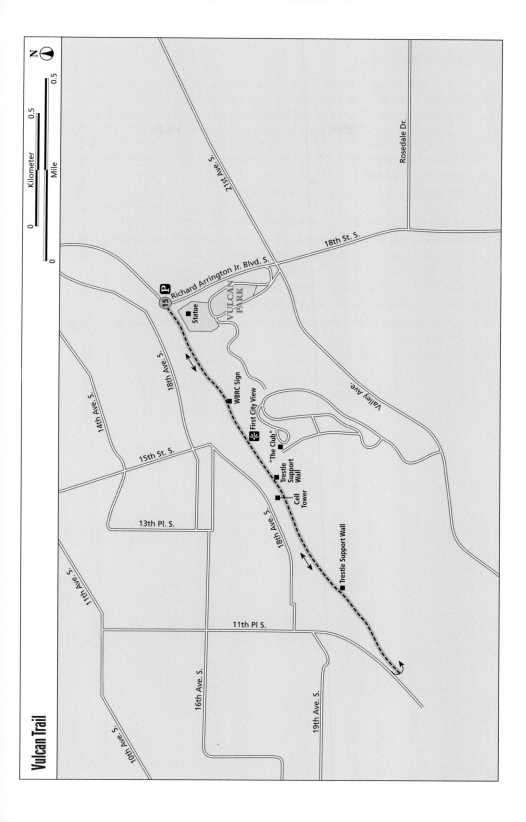

Vulcan Trail

N

Kilometer
0   0.5

Mile
0   0.5

18th Ave. S.

14th Ave. S.

11th Ave. S.

10th Ave. S.

16th Ave. S.

13th Pl. S.

11th Pl S.

19th Ave. S.

15th St. S.

18th Ave. S.

P

15

Richard Arrington Jr. Blvd. S.

Statue

VULCAN PARK

18th St. S.

21st Ave. S.

Rosedale Dr.

Valley Ave.

WBRC Sign

First City View

"The Club"

Trestle Support Wall

Cell Tower

Trestle Support Wall

Miles and Directions

0.0 Start at the trailhead on the southwest side of the Vulcan Trail parking lot on Richard Arrington Jr. Boulevard. An informative sign gives a brief history of the route. To your left and up the hillside is Vulcan Park and statue. To your right is a drop-off behind a fence that is covered with kudzu. The trail starts as a wide cement sidewalk but turns into asphalt a few yards in. The left (southeast) side of the trail is a rock bluff for most of the hike. Unfortunately many of the rock formations and remnants of the old railroad line have been swallowed up by kudzu.

0.3 Pass beneath the neon WBRC radio sign on the left.

0.4 First good view of the city to the right (northwest). The James Bond–esque building known as the Club (a private member restaurant) sits high atop the hillside on the left.

0.5 Look for the first of two old trestle support walls on the left (southeast). This one, sadly, has been adorned with colorful graffiti. To your right there are apartment buildings just down the hillside, and through the trees you get excellent views of the city.

0.6 Pass the chain-link fence surrounding a cell tower on the right.

0.8 Pass the second, and better looking, train trestle support on your left.

1.1 Turn around and retrace your steps to the trailhead. You'll have better views of the city on the return trip.

2.2 Arrive back at the trailhead.

16 Ike Maston/BMMR Loop

Another fascinating hike through Birmingham's glory days as an iron giant, the Ike Maston/BMMR Loop climbs up ridges and leads to the beautiful mission-style architecture of the Redding Shaft Mine and Hoist House, then follows a section of the old Birmingham Mineral Railroad (BMRR) back to the trailhead.

Start: Trailhead on Frankfurt Drive
Distance: 3.2-mile lollipop
Hiking time: About 2 hours
Difficulty: Moderate to difficult due to a steep incline
Trail surface: Dirt footpath, gravel road
Best seasons: Year-round
Other trail users: Cyclists, joggers
Canine compatibility: Leashed dogs permitted
Land status: Red Mountain Park land
Nearest town: Hoover

Fees and permits: None; fee for Iron Ore Zip Line and Segway tour (reservations required)
Schedule: Year-round, daily 7 a.m. to 7 p.m.
Maps: USGS Bessemer, Bessemer Iron District, and Birmingham South, AL; *DeLorme: Alabama Atlas & Gazetteer*, page 30, F5; trail maps available at information kiosk (free but donation requested)
Trail contact: Red Mountain Park, 277 Lyon Ln., Birmingham 35211; (205) 202-6043; redmountainpark.org

Finding the trailhead: From I-65 in Birmingham take exit 255 and head west on West Lakeshore Parkway. Travel 3.2 miles and turn right onto Frankfurt Drive. The trailhead is at the bend as Frankfurt Drive becomes Lyon Lane. Park anywhere along Frankfurt Drive. GPS: N33 26.747' / W86 51.735'

The Hike

Red dust. Iron ore. This red powder is what made a little dot on the map in the middle of Alabama a major southeastern city.

Birmingham is nicknamed the "Magic City." It rose, almost overnight, to become a major iron and steel producing city, and it was all due to the fact that the Birmingham area was one of the few places in the world that had all three of the key ingredients needed to make iron and steel: hematite (iron ore), limestone, and coke (coal).

The center of this activity was Red Mountain, where iron ore was mined and then shipped to foundries throughout the area, including Tannehill, the Bibb furnace at Brierfield, and Sloss. Today Red Mountain is bustling again, but this time with hikers, joggers, and bike riders. They come for an array of outdoor recreational activities like zip lines and Segway rides, but the trails here at Red Mountain Park can take you back to those glory days of iron and steel.

The story of iron ore in central Alabama dates back centuries ago to the region's Native Americans, who used the red dust to dye clothes and pottery. In the early 1800s a local farmer, Baylis Earle Grace, realized that Alabama had all the natural

One of the highlights of this hike is the beautiful mission-style remains of the Redding Shaft Mine and Hoist House.

resources needed to make iron and steel, and soon people were flocking to the area to scrape the land and sell the minerals to a nearby foundry.

Speculators began buying up large tracts of land on and near Red Mountain in the mid-1800s in an attempt to capitalize on the burgeoning iron-mining industry. The area's first commercial mine was opened in 1863 on what is now the eastern side of Red Mountain Park. It was called Eureka 1, and with its opening the mining boom was on at Red Mountain. By 1871 the population was rapidly increasing, and the city of Birmingham was founded.

The boom lasted for over a century until economic conditions forced its collapse. In 1962 the last active mine, which at the time was owned by US Steel, shut down. After that Red Mountain stood virtually untouched, being reclaimed by nature, until 2007 when a local resident, Ervin Battain, and a group of enthusiastic volunteers, with an amazingly generous donation by US Steel of 1,200 acres of land on the mountain, began work on Red Mountain Park, a place for recreation but also a place to remember what made Birmingham the city it is today.

The Ike Maston-BMMR Trail described here is a 3.2-mile lollipop loop that uses three trails: the Ike Maston, a short section of the Songo, and the BMRR South Trail. The steep, rocky climb up the Ike Maston Trail is rated "most difficult," but from there the going is easier. The easy, flat trails such as the BMMR can be crowded on weekends, but the Ike Maston will get you away from the crowds. As you walk the path, notice the trail bed—it's red, the "gold" of these parts, iron ore dust.

The Ike Maston Trail was named for one of the last miners to work on the mountain when it closed. You can hear Mr. Maston tell his story in his own words on the Red Mountain website: www.redmountain.org/park–overview/oral–history–project.

The highlight of this trek is the Redding Shaft Mine and Hoist House where the Songo Trail leaves the Ike Maston Trail for the return trip back. Like all mines in the park, the Redding has been sealed off for safety reasons. This 400–foot–deep shaft mine was in operation from 1917 to 1927. Across from the mine is the hoist house, a beautiful mission–style structure that at one time hauled the ore from the mine to the surface.

The return trip uses the wide, flat BMMR South Trail. The trail is a long since abandoned railroad bed that used to run all the way up to the location of the present-day Vulcan Park. This path is now a favorite of joggers and morning walkers.

The trails are not blazed here at Red Mountain but are easy enough to follow, and intersections are well marked with signs.

Miles and Directions

0.0 Start at the trailhead at the bend in the road where Lyon Lane and Frankfurt Drive meet. The trail, a dirt and gravel road, heads up a short hill to the northeast and then turns north.

0.2 Come to the welcome kiosk with information about the park and its trails. Maps are available here. Please drop a dollar or two into the lockbox for the map, and remember to pack it out with you. Two very nice Port-a-Johns are located to the right. Turn left (west) here. The path is still a dirt and gravel road at this point and unmarked.

0.4 Come to the intersection with the BMRR South Trail. Turn left (southwest) onto the BMRR. The trail continues to be a dirt and gravel road. In less than 0.1 mile, come to a sign indicating that the Ike Maston Trail is to the northwest and the BMRR continues to the southwest. Turn right (northwest) onto the unmarked gravel connector trail.

0.5 A chain blocks the road to the north. Turn left (southwest) onto the Ike Maston Trail. Shortly after the turn a small sign warns that the trail is "most difficult." The trail is now a dirt footpath and begins a steady and steep climb.

0.7 Cross an intermittent creek. The dirt has a red iron hue here.

0.8 In a hollow to the left (southwest), you can see a clearing for a petroleum pipeline.

0.9 Come to a sign indicating that the Smythe Trail connects from the left (south). In less than 0.1 mile, cross the petroleum pipeline clearing (the pipe is underground).

1.1 Enjoy a view of the valley to your left (east).

1.2 Cross an intermittent stream with a stone water bar, then climb a hill to the west on some old wooden stairs made from railroad ties.

1.6 The Songo Trail joins the Ike Maston Trail from the right (north). Continue straight to the northwest on the Ike Maston Trail. In a few hundred feet, cross a stream over a nice wooden bridge.

1.7 Pass an old 4-by-4-inch cement post on the right.

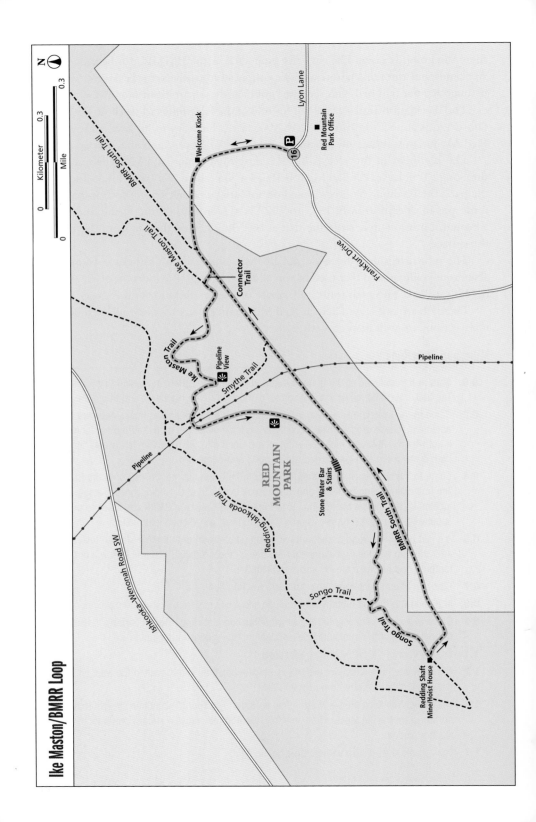

Ike Maston/BMRR Loop

N

Kilometer
0   0.3   0.3

Mile
0   0.3

Ishkooda-Wenonah Road SW

BMRR South Trail

Ike Maston Trail

Welcome Kiosk

Connector Trail

Lyon Lane

Red Mountain Park Office

P
16

Frankfurt Drive

Ike Maston Trail

Pipeline View

Smythe Trail

Pipeline

Pipeline

Redding-Ishkooda Trail

RED MOUNTAIN PARK

Stone Water Bar & Stairs

BMRR South Trail

Songo Trail

Songo Trail

Redding Shaft Mine/Hoist House

1.9 Arrive at the Redding Shaft Mine and Hoist House. There are interesting signs here telling the story of the hoist and the mine. Turn left (southeast) onto the Songo Trail, which is now a gravel and dirt road. In less than 0.1 mile, turn left onto the BMRR South Trail. A frog pond is here at the bend, and the frog song is marvelous. (*Option:* At the Hoist House, continue straight on the Ishkooda Trail to visit the SkyHy Treehouse and Ishkooda Overlook, then follow the Smythe Trail back to mile 2.6 of the hike.)

2.5 Cross the petroleum pipeline clearing again.

2.6 Pass the Smythe Trail to the left (north).

2.8 Pass the connector trail to the Ike Maston Trail to the left (north).

3.0 Arrive back at the welcome kiosk. Turn right (south) onto the dirt and gravel entrance road and head back the way you came to the trailhead.

3.2 Arrive back at the trailhead.

17 Red Mountain Mine Trail

Hidden away on the ridges of Red Mountain are several old iron ore mines, long since abandoned and sealed off, that provide a fascinating look back at the rich mining history of this area. The Red Mountain Mine Trail uses several of the trails at Red Mountain Park to visit three of these mines.

Start: From the trailhead on Frankfurt Drive
Distance: 2.5-mile lollipop
Hiking time: About 1.5 hours
Difficulty: Moderate
Trail surface: Gravel and dirt service road, dirt footpath
Best seasons: Year-round
Other trail users: Cyclists, joggers
Canine compatibility: Leashed dogs permitted
Land status: Red Mountain Park land
Nearest town: Hoover

Fees and permits: None; fee for Iron Ore Zip Line and Segway tour (reservations required)
Schedule: Year-round, daily 7 a.m. to 7 p.m.
Maps: USGS Bessemer, Bessemer Iron District, and Birmingham South, AL; *DeLorme: Alabama Atlas & Gazetteer*, page 30, F5; trail maps available at information kiosk (free but donation requested)
Trail contact: Red Mountain Park, 277 Lyon Ln., Birmingham, AL 35211; (205) 202-6043; redmountainpark.org

Finding the trailhead: From I-65 in Birmingham take exit 255 and head west on West Lakeshore Parkway. Travel 3.2 miles and turn right onto Frankfurt Drive. The trailhead is at the bend as Frankfurt Drive becomes Lyon Lane. Park anywhere along Frankfurt Drive. GPS: N33 26.747' / W86 51.735'

The Hike

You won't have to look very hard to see it—the red dirt covering the trail. It's iron ore, the mineral that Native Americans used to dye clothes and pottery, and the same ore that eventually made Birmingham a major Southern iron producing city. You'll have another chance to follow the red path and explore this rich mining history on what I call the Red Mountain Mine Trail at, where else, Red Mountain Park.

This route uses four trails—the BMMR South Trail, Eureka Mines Trail, #14 Mine Trail, and the #14 Mine Trail Connector—to form a loop that will take you to not one, not two, but three of the old mines that date back to the 1800s. Many of these trails are old mining tramways, roads specifically cut for the mines, where tracks were laid to haul the ore out for processing.

Remember, all mines in Red Mountain Park have been sealed off for safety reasons. Still, be careful around the entrances. It goes without saying that you shouldn't climb on them. Loose rocks or tailing dumps lie near the mines and could cause injury. Please use caution.

In the 1800s speculators from around the country flocked to the area, which at the time was just a simple dot on the map, to capitalize on a new discovery—the

One of three abandoned mines you will visit on this hike. This is the #14, which was active from 1895 to 1941.

region held all three ingredients to build a successful iron producing industry: limestone, coke (coal), and hematite. The bulk of the mining was established right here on Red Mountain.

In 1862 two of those speculators, John T. Milner and Frank Gilmer, purchased the first land on the slopes of Red Mountain for just that purpose and opened the first mines here, calling them Eureka 1 and Eureka 2. By 1892 seven new mines had been dug into the slope. This grouping was known as the Ishkooda Group; the oldest of those seven was Ishkooda Mine #13, which was dug in 1873 by the Tennessee Coal and Iron Company (TCI). The #13 mine is the first you will come to on this hike.

TCI created a close-knit community on the slopes of Red Mountain. They constructed houses, schools, churches, even a commissary for the workers and their families. At the height of its operation in the early 1920s, the Ishkooda Mines had a community of over 1,500 residents.

The entrances to the #13 mine and the rest of the mines in the park, were plugged by TCI with cement when they were abandoned. The mines' birth and death dates are stamped on their "tombstones." For #13 the inscription reads "1873–1933."

When you arrive at any of the mines, take a close look around. You may be surprised at what you find—maybe the carriage from an old coal cart or old railroad spikes. Remember, these are historic artifacts and must remain where they lie.

Moving on, you will come to the second mine, Ishkooda #14, which was originally called Eureka Mine #2. This mine was in operation from 1895 to 1941 before being abandoned and plugged.

The final mine, East #2 Mine, belonged to the Woodward Iron Company. The Woodward Iron Company was established in 1881 by brothers William and Joseph Woodward. By the 1920s the company was one of the largest sellers of pig iron in the country.

The trails at Red Mountain are a joy to walk, and I'm sure you will agree once you've taken this trek. The landscape is a rich hardwood forest with a thick canopy, the perfect answer for hot summertime hiking. The trails on this route are not blazed, but you won't need them. They are well used and easy to follow. Intersections are well marked with directional signs. And as with all paths that clamber up the hillside here, the dirt path is tinted red from iron ore.

Miles and Directions

0.0 Start from the park entrance on the north side of Frankfurt Drive as it bends to the east. Climb a series of railroad tie stairs uphill. At the top of the hill, pick up the wide gravel road to the north. In less than 0.1 mile, pass the south entrance to the 0.11-mile-long Remy's Dog Park Loop trail on the right. Continue straight to the north.

0.2 Come to an intersection with a short connector trail at the park kiosk and main trailhead. You can pick up maps here and make a donation to help keep the park operating. To the left (west) the trail takes you to the BMMR South Trail. Turn right (east) onto the gravel road. In less than 0.1 mile, come to a Y intersection. The right fork is the north entrance to the Remy's Dog Park Loop. Take the left fork to the east. In a few yards come to another Y. The right fork takes you through a picnic area that reconnects to the main trail in just a few dozen yards. Right now take the left fork to the north and stay on the gravel Eureka Mines Trail.

0.4 A side trail comes in from the right (east). Continue straight to the north.

0.5 Pass a sign on the right that reads Red Ore Zip Tour/Hugh Kaul Beanstalk Forest, with an arrow pointing straight ahead to the north. Continue straight. In less than 0.1 mile, come to a Y. Take the right fork to the north.

0.6 Pass a short trail to the zip line and Segway tour on the left, a motivational obstacle course on the right. Continue straight to the northeast. In less than 0.1 mile, come to a Y. A sign here points the way to the #14 mine (right fork) and the #13 mine (left fork). This is the south end of the loop portion of this hike. Take the left fork to the northwest.

0.7 A narrow trail comes in from the right with a footbridge over a ditch. Turn left here onto a wide gravel path.

0.8 Pass a footbridge and a side trail on your right. Continue straight to the north a few yards to reach the #13 mine. Once you're finished exploring the mine, turn around and head back to the footbridge. Turn left (northeast) and cross the footbridge. This is the Ike Maston Trail.

0.9 Come to a Y. A sign here points to the right and the Eureka Mines Trail. Take the left fork to the southeast onto the #14 Mine Trail. The trail is a narrow red-dirt path again. Look for zip line platforms high above in the trees.

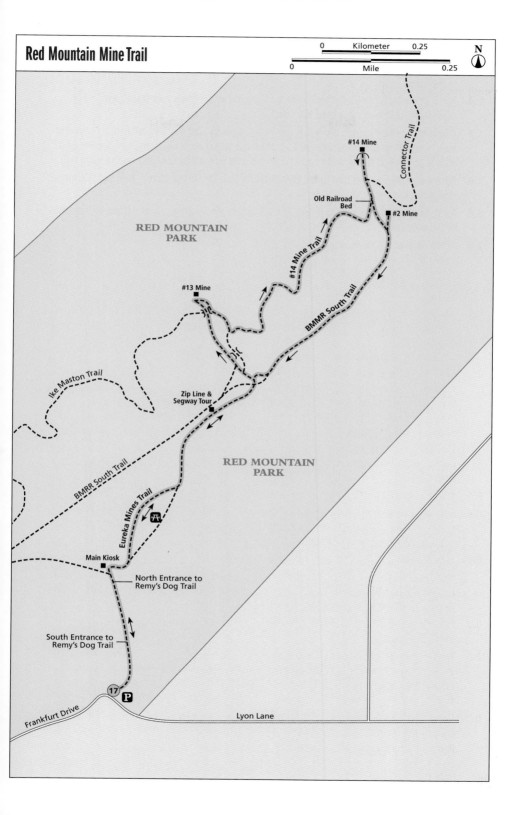

Red Mountain Mine Trail

0 Kilometer 0.25

0 Mile 0.25

N

RED MOUNTAIN PARK

RED MOUNTAIN PARK

Connector Trail

#14 Mine

Old Railroad Bed

#2 Mine

#14 Mine Trail

#13 Mine

BMMR South Trail

Ike Maston Trail

Zip Line & Segway Tour

BMRR South Trail

Eureka Mines Trail

Main Kiosk

North Entrance to Remy's Dog Trail

South Entrance to Remy's Dog Trail

17

P

Frankfurt Drive

Lyon Lane

1.3 Come to a T intersection. Turn to the left (north). In less than 0.1 mile, pass a trail with steps leading up a hill on your right. That is the #14 Mine Connector Trail. Continue straight to the north.

1.4 Arrive at the #14 mine. After exploring, turn around and retrace your steps to mile 1.3. Once there, continue straight to the south.

1.5 A side trail comes in from the left. A sign here points to East #2. Turn left (north) onto this trail. In less than 0.1 mile, arrive at East Mine #2. When done exploring, turn around and retrace your steps to the main trail at mile 1.5 and turn left to continue on the main trail.

1.6 Pass a sign on your left that reads BMMR South Trail. This is the start of that trail. Continue straight to the south.

1.9 Arrive back at the Y at mile 0.6. Take the left fork to the southwest and retrace your steps to the trailhead.

2.5 Arrive back at the trailhead.

18 Tannehill Historical State Park Loop

Follow this loop trail through Tannehill Historical State Park and travel back to the iron age of the Birmingham area. As you wander through the mixed hardwood forest, you will have a chance to see the lovingly restored furnace and the blue-green waters of Roupes Creek, which once powered the foundry. The trail also uses an old stage-coach road that was heavily traveled in the mid–1800s, and you can pay your respects to those who are interred at the Slave Cemetery.

Start: Behind the Iron and Steel Museum of Alabama

Distance: 4.1-mile lollipop

Hiking time: 2 to 2.5 hours

Difficulty: Moderate with some short climbs

Trail surface: Dirt footpath, gravel road

Best seasons: Year-round

Other trail users: Cyclists

Canine compatibility: Leashed dogs permitted

Land status: Alabama historic state park

Nearest town: McCalla

Fees and permits: Day-use fee; Iron and Steel Museum fee

Schedule: Year-round, day use daily sunrise to sunset; visitor center open Mon to Fri 8:30 a.m. to 4:30 pm, Sat 9:30 a.m. to 4:30 p.m.; Iron and Steel Museum open Mon to Fri 8:30 a.m. to 4:30 p.m., Sat 9 a.m. to 4:30 p.m., Sun 12:30 p.m. to 4:30 p.m.

Maps: USGS McCalla, AL; *DeLorme: Alabama Atlas and Gazetteer*, page 30, H3; trail maps available at country store

Trail contact: Tannehill Ironworks Historical State Park, 12632 Confederate Pkwy., McCalla 35111; (205) 477-9400; tannehill.org

Finding the trailhead: From the intersection of I-459 and I-20 West/I-59 South, take I-20 West/I-59 South 5 miles. Take exit 100 (Abernant/Bucksville) and turn left onto AL 216 East. (Shortly after turning onto AL 216, it becomes Bucksville Road.) Follow AL 216/Bucksville Road 0.6 mile and make a slight right onto Tannehill Parkway. Travel 1.9 miles and turn right onto Eastern Valley Road. In less than 0.1 mile, turn left onto Confederate Parkway/Tannehill Park Road. The park entrance is ahead in 0.7 mile. GPS: N33 14.970' / W87 04.297'

The Hike

Tannehill Historical State Park is the perfect place to visit to get a true feel for the history of the iron and steel industry of Alabama. A series of four trails linked together will lead you through some of this history up close, including a towering restored blast furnace.

The story of Tannehill, like most of the mining and furnace operations in central Alabama, dates back to the 1800s, when the city of Birmingham was a mere dot on the map but would soon become a mecca for the iron and steel industry in the South.

In 1830 a Pennsylvanian, Daniel Hillman, came to Alabama to capitalize on this rapidly growing industry. As soon as he arrived, he constructed a forge along Roupes Creek, where the current Tannehill Historical State Park resides. Two years after

The centerpiece of a hike at Tannehill, the lovingly and painstakingly restored iron furnace

setting up the operation and long before he had a chance to see the fortune the forge would eventually make, Hillman passed away, and a local farmer, Ninian Tannehill, purchased the forge.

With the use of slave labor, Tannehill had three tall furnaces built on this site. Sandstone bricks were laid skillfully by hand by the laborers, and in 1862 the iron-works began full production of pig iron, much of which was used by the Confederacy.

Three years later, on March 31, 1865, the Eighth Iowa Cavalry of the US Army moved in and laid the foundry to waste by shelling it and setting fire to the structure. Just a few miles up the road, Union troops torched the slave quarters.

Following the war a businessman purchased the ironworks and tried several times to rebuild it, but this was the era of Reconstruction and times were tough for the South; the facility was eventually abandoned and soon reclaimed by nature.

Almost a century later the State of Alabama along with several colleges resurrected the site. Archaeological digs uncovered the old blower house and the main furnace, which was rebuilt to its former glory and is an impressive sight to see. It is now listed on the National Register of Historic Places.

This loop trail begins at the Alabama Iron and Steel Museum, which is located in the park and well worth the visit. Take your time to view the artifacts in the museum while you visit the park.

From here the trail comes to a Y intersection, or actually the junction with three trails. Take the left fork. This is the Iron Works Trail, with beautiful views of the roiling

The sun glints off the rushing waters of Roupes Creek, which once powered the mighty blast furnace at Tannehill.

rapids of Roupes Creek that once powered the furnace, which leads you to the massive furnace and blower house itself.

Cross the creek here and start up the Slave Quarters Road Trail where, as the name implies, the housing for the slaves who built the furnace was located and later burned by the Union army. You will have to look hard through the brush, but you might be able to see an old foundation or two just off to the right.

Next swing to the east on the Old Bucksville Stage Road. This wide dirt road was the main highway into the area in the mid-1800s. Today the road takes hikers to the next trail on this loop, the short Cemetery Trail, which leads to the slave cemetery. At one time a few crudely carved stones with some of the names of those buried here could be seen. As of my last visit, the stones were gone.

Lastly, the loop joins up with the Iron Haul Road Trail, which, you guessed it, was a road used for hauling loads of material to the furnace.

In addition to the furnace and historic sites found along the trails at Tannehill, be sure to visit the many historic structures of the period from 1830 to 1870 that have been brought in and restored for the public to view. Local craftspeople demonstrate the making of quilts, furniture, and pottery at the site each year between March and November.

Alabama Iron and Steel Museum

Located at the start of the Tannehill Historical State Park Loop trail, the Alabama Iron and Steel Museum is a comprehensive interpretive center that brings to life the rich mining and iron producing history of the region. The 13,000-square-foot museum has artifacts from the thirteen main iron companies, their mines, and the furnaces of the area that made central Alabama a booming iron region. You can see some of the actual parts of the Bibb Furnace (Brierfield Historical State Park), which are now used to demonstrate early iron making processes; the Dotterer Steam Engine, similar to the one used at the Tannehill furnace; and interactive displays that will teach you about the processes needed to make iron.

Miles and Directions

0.0 Start from behind the Alabama Iron and Steel Museum. Head down a set of cement stairs toward the creek to the southeast. Cross the creek on a small wooden bridge (a playground is on the opposite side of the creek on your right; a picnic area is to the left). There is a Y intersection after the bridge. Take the left fork to the east (a sign here reads Iron Works Trail). This trail takes you behind the craft buildings and to great views of the creek.

0.4 Come to the furnace. Cross the creek to the left (east) over the wood and steel Jim Folsom Bridge. On the other side come to the intersection with the Iron Haul Road Trail. A sign here points to the left (northeast), showing the way to the cemetery and Stagecoach Road. Turn left here onto the Slave Quarters Road Trail.

0.5 Pass a short pier that juts into a pond to the left (west).

0.9 Cross a stream that flows under the road.

1.2 Come to the intersection with the Old Bucksville Stage Road Trail. A sign here points to the cemetery (to the right) and furnace (the way you just came). Turn right (southeast) onto the Old Bucksville Stage Road Trail.

1.9 Come to the intersection of the Iron Haul Road Trail and Cemetery Trail. Turn right (southwest) onto the Cemetery Trail.

2.0 Arrive at the slave cemetery. A chain-link fence encircles the site. You can enter through a gate that is tied shut with a rope. (**Option:** From the cemetery the trail continues to the southeast another 0.1 mile, where it connects with the Iron Haul Road Trail [mile 2.3 below]. On my visit this section of trail was underwater from a runoff stream. I opted to turn around at the cemetery and return to the intersection of the Old Bucksville Stage Road and Iron Haul Road Trails.)

2.1 Back at the intersection of the three trails, turn right (southeast) onto the Iron Haul Road Trail.

Tannehill Historical State Park Loop

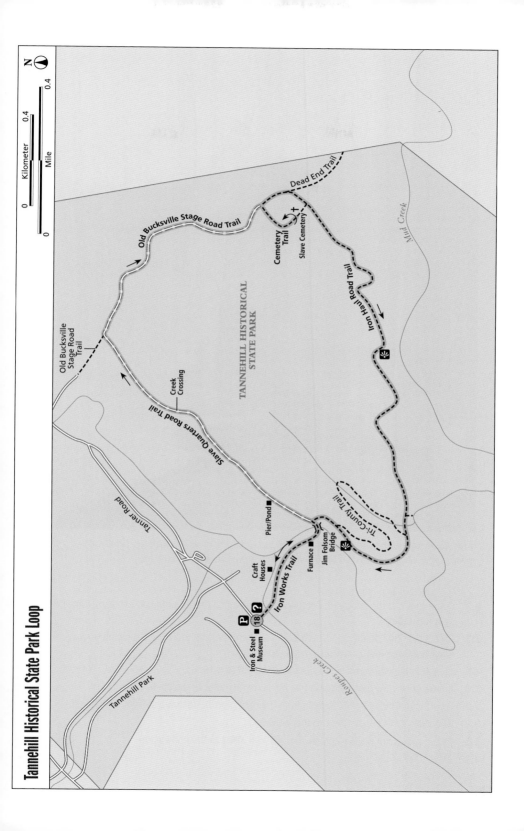

N

0   0.4 Kilometer
0   0.4 Mile

Old Bucksville Stage Road Trail

Dead End Trail

Cemetery Trail

Slave Cemetery

Iron Haul Road Trail

TANNEHILL HISTORICAL STATE PARK

Old Bucksville Stage Road Trail

Creek Crossing

Slave Quarters Road Trail

Mud Creek

Tanner Road

Pier/Pond

Tri-County Trail

Craft Houses

Furnace

Jim Folsom Bridge

Iron Works Trail

Iron & Steel Museum

P

18

Tannehill Park

Roupes Creek

This stone monument, made with some of the same bricks as the furnace, stands as a memorial to the workers who built and operated the furnace at Tannehill.

2.2   Come to a Y. To the left (southeast) is a dead-end trail (and it's marked as such). Take the right fork (south).

2.3   Pass a side trail on the right (north). This is where the side trail from the cemetery joins the Iron Haul Road Trail. Continue straight (southwest).

2.8   Start seeing good views of Mud Creek to the left (south).

3.3   A nice, grassy, 30-foot-long side trail leads to the banks of the creek.

3.4   Pass the Tri-County Trail coming in from the right (north). Continue straight to the west.

3.6   Good views of Roupes Creek to the left (west).

3.9   Return to the Jim Folsom Bridge. Retrace your steps to the parking lot.

4.1   Arrive back at the parking lot.

19 Moundville Archaeological Park

An amazing day of exploring awaits you at Moundville Archaeological Park. This 2.8-mile loop allows you to walk among some of the twenty-eight mounds built by Native Americans of the Mississippian period centuries ago, even climb to the top of two of them. As you walk, you will be fascinated by how the mounds were built, basketful by basketful of dirt, and by the civilization that was carved out here.

Start: From the parking lot at the entrance building
Distance: 2.8-mile loop with out and back
Hiking time: About 1.5 hours
Difficulty: Easy
Trail surface: Grass, pea gravel, minimal cement sidewalk, asphalt
Best seasons: Year-round
Other trail users: None
Canine compatibility: Leashed dogs permitted
Land status: University land

Nearest town: Moundville
Fees and permits: Day-use fee, includes tour of museum
Schedule: Year-round, daily 9 a.m. to sunset; Jones Museum daily 9 a.m. to 5 p.m.
Maps: USGS Fosters, AL; *DeLorme: Alabama Atlas & Gazetteer*, page 35, D9
Trail contact: Moundville Archaeological Park, PO Box 870340, Tuscaloosa 35487; (205) 371-2234; moundville.ua.edu

Finding the trailhead: From the intersection of AL 69 and CR 50 in Moundville, take AL 69 north 0.5 mile. Turn left onto Mound Parkway. In 0.7 mile arrive at the entrance to the park. Park behind the building and go inside to pay your admission and see the orientation video. Begin the hike from the parking lot. GPS: N33 00.177' / W87 37.692'

The Hike

Political center, religious center, economic center—Moundville, near present-day Tuscaloosa, was the hub of activity for the region during what is called the Mississippian period of human existence. The lifestyle and culture of these people is a fascinating study and best experienced at Moundville Archaeological Park, where this loop trail is found.

As I said, the area was called Moundville because of the Native Americans who lived here around AD 1120. It is called the Mississippian period because these tribes were first established along the Mississippi River. These people were known as mound builders, and the culture and community they built was quite sophisticated. Here on this 185-acre site, for example, the tribes built what archaeologists describe as a "planned community." The land was first leveled by filling it in with hand-delivered dirt, then twenty-eight mounds were built, all by hand, one basket of dirt at a time, over hundreds of years—hence the name, Moundville. The mounds were built in a circle with a large open area in the middle, almost like a square in a modern town or city.

Ancient Native American mounds dating back to somewhere between AD 1000 and 1450 are reflected in the watery pond that was once a borrow pit.

The mounds were as small as 3 feet to almost 60 feet tall, all level at the top. The two largest mounds, identified in the park as Mound "A" and the Chieftan Mound, are at the northern end of this loop hike. Mound "A" is believed to have been used as a ceremonial mound, while the Chieftain Mound was where the elites or tribal leaders lived. The latter mound is one of only two you can climb to the top of. A representation of the house that would have been there awaits you at the top.

And yes, there are burial mounds here. These smaller mounds were usually located near the family home. The deceased were buried with stones, shells, or fragments of copper or, in the case of the elite population, copper axes. As with today's society there were three tiers of social status—the workers and farmers, elites, and chiefs.

No one knows why the population began to move away from Moundville. Archaeologists believe the population started declining between AD 1300 and 1450. We do know that by 1540, when the Spanish arrived, the town was virtually deserted.

The park is the product of the University of Alabama Archaeology Department, which has been doing research here since 1869 when onetime university president Nathaniel Lupton first mapped the property. Excavations didn't begin until 1905, with small diggings by independent archaeologist Clarence Moore. The first major research performed here began in 1929 when the director of the Alabama Museum of Natural History, Walter Jones, teamed up with archaeologist David DeJarnette to uncover a wealth of artifacts and further advance the understanding of this early culture. Jones went on to establish Mound State Park, later called Mound State Monument, in 1933 with a museum to house those artifacts. The museum was built with the help of the Civilian Conservation Corps. The University of Alabama renovated the museum in 1999 and then did a further update in 2010, renaming it the Jones Archaeological Museum.

The museum displays an amazing collection of artifacts, with state-of-the-art imagery such as a holographic tribesman who narrates a bit of the culture's history. You will pass the museum on this hike, and it is well worth spending some time there. Exiting the back of the museum, you will be able to walk up to the top of Mound "B" for a panoramic view. There's even binoculars there.

This is a trail that you could drive, but it is best experienced on foot. Pay your admission fee and park behind the entrance building. From there cross the road and begin your hike in a counterclockwise direction following the edge of the huge, grassy field. You will be walking between and next to several smaller mounds that you probably wouldn't visit on a drive through the park, and also pass a couple of borrow pits where the tribe dug some of the dirt used to build the mounds. One in particular is next to the Jones Museum and has become a beautiful little pond with the mounds in the distance reflecting off its surface.

Miles and Directions

0.0 Start from the parking lot behind the entrance building where you pay your fee. Be sure to check out the 15-minute video before heading out to get an orientation about what you will be seeing. From the parking lot head across the street to the north into the large, grassy area. Start walking across the huge, grassy field counterclockwise to your right (north). For most of the trip you will be paralleling the road. Come to two small mounds on your right. Walk to the left of them and see the borrow pit on your left.

0.1 Pass a smaller mound to your right.

0.2 Pass another small mound to your left.

0.3 Start approaching the larger Mound "A" on your left. The largest of the mounds, the Chieftain Mound, is to your right across the road. Cross the road to the north and head to the mound.

0.4 Arrive at the Chieftain Mound. You can walk up to the top for a good view and information about the significance of the mound including a replica hut. When done exploring, climb down and walk straight to the north.

0.5 A sign marks the entrance to the Douglas Nature Trail. Take the pea gravel footpath to the north.

0.6 A long boardwalk begins. When I visited, the structure was under repair and you had to walk next to the boardwalk. Either walk the boardwalk (if it's repaired) or next to it to the northeast.

0.7 If you are walking next to the boardwalk, you can get on it here. Turn right and head northeast on the boardwalk. If you have been walking on it, continue straight to the northeast.

Moundville Archaeological Park

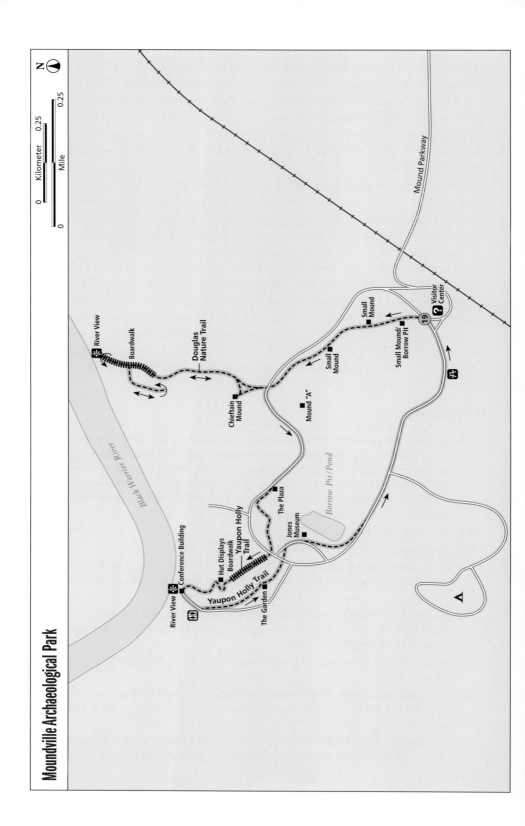

N

0   Kilometer   0.25

0   Mile   0.25

Black Warrior River

River View
Boardwalk
Douglas Nature Trail
Chieftain Mound
Mound "A"
Small Mound
Small Mound
Small Mound/ Borrow Pit
Small Mound
Visitor Center
19
Mound Parkway

Conference Building
River View
Hut Displays
Boardwalk
Yaupon Holly Trail
The Plaza
Jones Museum
Yaupon Holly Trail
The Garden
Borrow Pit/Pond

In less than 0.1 mile, arrive at a great view of the Black Warrior River. Once again when I visited for the book, it was impossible to walk farther on the boardwalk. Turn around and retrace your steps to the Chieftain Mound at mile 0.4.

1.2 Back at the Chieftain Mound cross the road to the southwest and resume the walk to the right along the grassy field, passing the large Mound "A" on the left.

1.5 Pass the large, grassy area known as "The Plaza." Walk between the two mounds before you as you head toward the Jones Museum.

1.6 Just before arriving at the museum, turn right (northwest) and cross the street using the crosswalk. This is the beginning of the Yaupon Holly Trail, which is a boardwalk through the woods.

1.7 Come to the end of the boardwalk. A picnic area is to the left. Continue straight to the northwest toward the replica village. In less than 0.1 mile, arrive at the village, a series of four huts with displays inside depicting life at Moundville centuries ago. The first hut depicts "fruit from the river," the second burial ceremonies, the third Moundville artisans, and the fourth manufacturing. From here head straight to the northwest toward the conference building and river.

1.8 Walk around the right side of the conference building for a stroll and view high above the banks of the Black Warrior River, then walk back around the building to the southwest, heading toward the picnic area you passed at mile 1.7.

1.9 Pass a restroom across the road to the right.

2.0 Walking on the opposite side of the picnic area, arrive at "The Garden," a representation of what inhabitants once grew here. Continue to the southeast, back to the road heading toward the museum.

2.2 Arrive at the Jones Museum. Three mounds are located here, one of which is accessible by visiting the museum and heading out the back exit. This is the second of two mounds you can climb, with more informational signage and binoculars on top so you can survey the scene. When done visiting, exit the museum and turn left (southeast) to follow the grassy field once again. Be sure to see the borrow pit next to the museum that is filled with water now and reflects the sky and surrounding mounds.

2.4 Pass Campground Road and the park's campground on the right.

2.7 Pass a picnic area on the right.

2.8 Arrive back at the parking area.

20 Furnace Trail

Visit the remains of the Bibb Furnace, another one of the productive iron furnaces from central Alabama's past. The Furnace Trail takes you past the remains of the furnace, both from the front and the back, as well as the reservoir that once fed water to the massive structure.

Start: From the parking area just past the main entrance at the park office
Distance: 1.4-mile lollipop
Hiking time: About 1 hour
Difficulty: Easy
Trail surface: Dirt and gravel footpath, minimal asphalt
Best seasons: Year-round
Other trail users: None
Canine compatibility: Leashed dogs permitted

Land status: Alabama state historic site
Nearest town: Montevallo
Fees and permits: Day-use fee
Schedule: Year-round, daily sunrise to sunset
Maps: USGS Aldridge, AL; *DeLorme: Alabama Atlas & Gazetteer*, page 37, C6
Trail contact: Brierfield Ironworks Historical State Park, 240 Furnace Pkwy., Brierfield 35035; (205) 665-1856; brierfieldironworks .org

Finding the trailhead: From the intersection of AL 195 and AL 25 in Montevallo, take AL 25 south 6.6 miles. Turn left onto Frederick Pass Road. Travel 0.4 mile and turn left onto Furnace Parkway. Travel 0.4 mile and turn left onto Furnace Parkway. In 0.1 mile come to the entrance gate and pay station. If no one is manning the gate, deposit your day-use fee in the honor box. Continue straight another 0.1 mile and find a parking spot. The hike starts from here. GPS: N33 02.313' / W86 56.902'

The Hike

So far on these treks across Alabama, retracing its long history, you have encountered several hikes to old mining operations and one to a blast furnace, Tannehill. The last visit to the mining history of the state is at Brierfield Ironworks Historical State Park and the Furnace Trail. Brierfield is the site where the Bibb Furnace once stood, a major supplier of pig iron to locals and later the Confederate military.

Bibb Furnace was a unique venture. When speculators came to Alabama to make their fortune in the burgeoning iron industry, they usually had some semblance of knowledge about the business. Bibb was bankrolled and built by a group of men who called their venture the Bibb County Iron Company. The company was led by Caswell Campbell Huckabee, who admittedly had no clue about the iron industry. With the exception of a forge operator from Six Mile, Alabama, Jonathan Smith, Huckabee's partners were either farmers or gristmill operators.

In 1862 the stone furnace was completed and actually began producing high-grade iron. The Confederacy took notice but, as history writes, the partners weren't interested. They would much rather sell their iron to the highest bidders. Later that

The remains of the old Bibb Furnace stand stoically beneath a protective roof at Brierfield Ironworks Historical State Park.

year the Confederate States of America (CSA) passed a law that required furnaces like Bibb to produce a certain quantity of iron for the war effort. In 1863 Huckabee agreed to produce 1,000 tons of pig iron for the military in exchange for an advance of $20,000 in Confederate bonds.

The Civil War was heating up in 1963, and the need for armaments by the Confederacy was growing rapidly. The CSA gave Huckabee a "choice" of options for the furnace: give the CSA all the iron produced at the furnace, sell or lease the furnace to the government, or have the entire operation confiscated. Huckabee chose to sell the furnace for $600,000, nine slaves, twenty carts, twenty wheelbarrows, two hundred axes, forty-one oxen, and seventy mules. This would be the only furnace owned by the Confederate government.

Following the purchase the CSA made considerable upgrades to the furnace, including adding a "rolling mill" and connecting it directly to the Alabama and Tennessee River Railroad line. By the time the expansion was complete, the furnace and the rolling mill were producing 10 tons of iron a day. By late 1864 the site was producing large Brooke cannons for the Confederate navy, one of which was recovered from the CSS *Tennessee*, which fought in the Battle of Mobile Bay and can be seen in downtown Selma.

In March 1865, however, the walls came tumbling down, literally, as the Union army, vowing to destroy the South's "power to make war," laid the furnace complex to waste.

After the war several attempts were made to resurrect the facility, but in 1894 an accidental blowout was the death knell for the furnace. Scavengers made off with bricks from the furnace, further reducing it to rubble. It wasn't until 1976 that the site was put under the protection of the Bibb County Historical Society, which erected a protective cover over the remains of the site and opened Brierfield Ironworks Historical State Park.

Almost immediately after entering the park, you will see a sign marked Furnace Trail on your left, and you may wonder why I didn't start the trail there at the official trailhead. In all my visits to Brierfield, I encountered campers set up for the weekend in front of the trailhead, so instead of trampling through their campsite I opted to start on the far northern end of the campground where a side trail leads in.

You will first walk past the park's centerpiece, the remains of the Bibb Furnace. The remaining stones and foundation lie in a pile next to the trail and are covered with a steel roof to protect them from further deterioration. The furnace is roped off, so do not hop the line and touch the artifacts. Even though the furnace is only a shell of its former self, you can see vestiges of the main opening and walls, still an impressive sight.

From here it is a beautiful walk up and down hills on the narrow dirt footpath through a hardwood forest. In the fall the colors are magnificent. A few pines are interspersed in the scene.

The trail makes a big swing from north to west to south. Here you will come to a depression on the top of a hill. This is the old furnace reservoir that once provided water for furnace operations. You can climb down into the depression and on the south side see the stone channel where the water would flow out and down to the furnace.

Finally you will swing around to the back side of the furnace. From this vantage point, which is cordoned off with a fence, you can get a sense of how big the furnace once was as you look down at it from above.

The trail is not marked but is easy to follow, although at several intersections you may get confused about which way to go. Don't worry, most of these side trails simply loop around back to the main trail.

Before heading out, you should check the park's calendar online or contact the office to make sure there isn't a special event going on. I have come here to hike on a couple of occasions and ran into bow hunters having a competition weekend on the trail. The trail was still open for hiking, but with arrows flying I thought better of it.

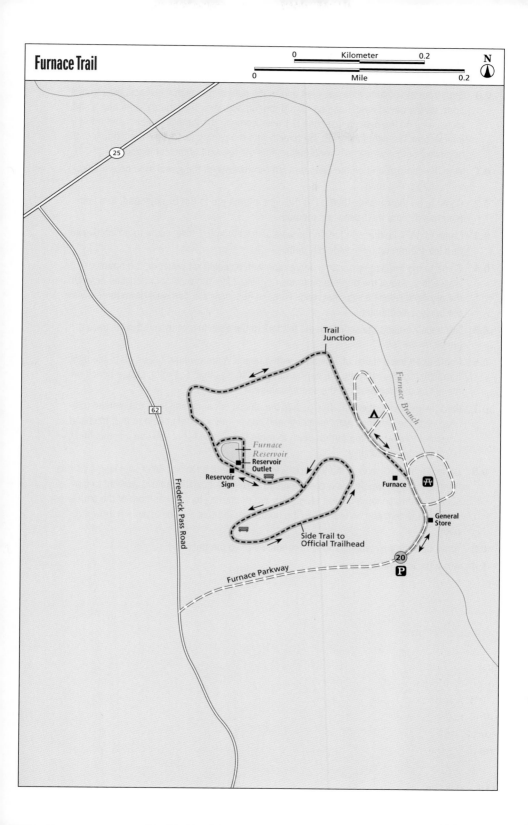

Furnace Trail

0   Kilometer   0.2
0   Mile   0.2

N

25

62

Trail Junction

Furnace Branch

Furnace Reservoir

Reservoir Outlet

Reservoir Sign

Furnace

Frederick Pass Road

Side Trail to Official Trailhead

General Store

20

P

Furnace Parkway

Miles and Directions

0.0 Start from the parking area just past and to the right of the entrance shack. Walk to the north on the paved road, heading toward the furnace. Pass the country store and a small picnic area on the right. In less than 0.1 mile, come to the furnace remains and a Y intersection. The right fork takes you directly into the campground. Take the left fork to the northwest onto a wide gravel road that rounds the left side of the campground.

0.1 With the campground on the right, turn left (northwest) off the gravel road onto an old, wide, dirt service road.

0.2 Come to an intersection. The trail to the right returns you to the campground. Turn left (southwest) onto the narrow dirt footpath.

0.3 Come to a Y. Take the right fork to the west. In less than 0.1 mile, come to an intersection. Turn left (south) onto the wide dirt path.

0.4 Come to the furnace reservoir, a depression with a sealed-off outlet on the opposite side. Walk either side of the depression to the opposite side. There are four benches here. On the opposite side is a sign that reads Furnace Reservoir. You can walk down here to view the brick-sealed outlet.

0.5 Two trails Y behind the sign. Take the left fork to the east. In less than 0.1 mile, pass a bench on the left.

0.6 Come to an intersection at a clearing with a bench. A narrow path heads off to the right. Turn right (southwest) onto the narrow dirt path. In less than 0.1 mile, pass a bench on the left as the trail winds to the south/southeast.

0.7 Pass a side trail to the right. This path is the official entrance trail from the marked trail-head near the entrance gate. As mentioned earlier, many people camp at that trailhead. I decided to start the trip farther down to avoid the campers, but you can use this trail to begin your hike if you like.

0.8 Come to the back side of the furnace. A fence here with a Do Not Enter sign keeps visitors from venturing down. This is a good angle to better see how the state is working to preserve the furnace remains and where they are excavating to uncover more of the structure. When ready continue on the trail to the northwest. The trail is once again a narrow dirt path.

0.9 Arrive back at the clearing and retrace your steps to the trailhead.

1.4 Arrive back at the trailhead.

21 Flagg Mountain Loop

Time has virtually stood still atop Flagg Mountain. It was here that the Civilian Conservation Corps (CCC) began work on another state park complete with stone fire tower and beautifully hand hewn log cabins. The project was never completed, and today you can hike to this site and view the cabins that remain virtually untouched since the late 1930s. While this trail currently does not lead to the fire tower, you can still view it on a short dirt–road walk or drive.

Start: From the northern Yellow Trail trailhead on Weogufka Forest Road
Distance: 2.4-mile loop with out and back
Hiking time: About 2 hours
Difficulty: Moderate
Trail surface: Dirt and rock footpath, some old dirt road
Best seasons: Year-round
Other trail users: Hunters (see "Special considerations")
Canine compatibility: Leashed dogs permitted
Land status: State forest

Nearest town: Weogufka
Fees and permits: None
Schedule: Year-round; overnight backpacking permitted
Maps: USGS Flag Mountain, AL; *DeLorme: Alabama Atlas & Gazetteer*, page 38, D2
Trail contact: Alabama Hiking Trail Society, PO Box 235, Rockford 35136; hikealabama.org
Special considerations: Hunting is permitted on this state forest property. Visit outdoor alabama.com/hunting/ for dates.

Finding the trailhead: From the intersection of CR 56 and CR 29 in Weogufka, take CR 56 west 3.2 miles. Turn left onto CR 55. Travel 0.8 mile and turn left onto Weogufka Forest Road (formerly CC Camp Road). Travel 1.3 miles. The trailhead is on the left tucked away in the woods just off the road. A diamond-shaped yellow and green AHTS sign is here. A narrow shoulder where you can park is only a few yards ahead on the right. GPS: N32 59.084' / W86 21.274'

The Hike

Flagg Mountain has always been one of my favorite hiking destinations in the state, for many reasons. First, it's just a beautiful walk in the woods with its hardwood forest blazing with color in the fall or maybe a light blanket of snow on the ground in the winter. Then there is its solitude. Not many people hike the mountain (of course, writing about it might change things). But most importantly I love it because of its Civilian Conservation Corps history. It's almost as if the mountain is stuck in time back in the mid– to late 1930s. Not much has changed.

It has been a while since I last hiked the mountain. In two editions of my book *Hiking Alabama*, I told of the trail and its CCC past, but soon after, the property was leased and access was blocked, so I removed mention of it from the fourth edition and haven't been back. Only recently has the lease expired, and hikers are now encouraged by the Alabama Forestry Commission to hike the area. So here we are.

One of several cabins hand built by the Civilian Conservation Corps (CCC) in the late 1930s.

Flagg Mountain stands 1,152 feet tall and is one of the southernmost mountains in the Appalachians. It's a very nondescript mountain when it comes to history. No Civil War battles were fought here, although some argue that it may have been used as a lookout position for the Confederate army, which used signal flags to communicate—hence the name—but then why the two "gs" in the name?

The real history of Flagg Mountain began in 1927 when the Alabama state legislature passed the State Land Act that authorized the development of state parks for its residents. In 1933 an advance group of fifteen young men from the CCC arrived in Weogufka, Alabama, from New York to begin the process of clearing the land for a new state park. It was said that Flagg Mountain was home to the largest yellow pine forest east of the Rockies and that the park would be "one of the most scenic in the state."

CCC Company 260 was directed to build roads to the summit of the mountain, hiking trails to points of interest, cabins for tourist lodging, a dam on a stream to supply water, a museum to house Indian artifacts, and a 52-foot-tall observation tower for panoramic views of the surrounding mountains. On a clear day from the top of the tower, you can see 60 miles in all directions.

Flagg was located in an extremely remote location, which forced the company to rely on the natural resources they had at their disposal and lots of help from the locals. This gave rise to the company motto, "We Can Take It!"

The skill of these young men is astounding. The cabins, many of which still stand today and which you will see on this hike, were made of hand-hewn logs that fit together almost seamlessly. And the fire tower is a true work of art. Built completely out of carved stone, the tower itself has walls 2 to 3 feet thick. The cabin atop is 12 feet by 12 feet in size and fully enclosed with glass windows. Next to the fire tower is another building just as impressive, the recreation hall, which again highlights the magnificent stonework of the CCC.

After the 200 men of Company 260 were replaced with Company 4498 in 1935, work continued on the park until they were disbanded in 1936; World War II broke out soon after. Historian Bob Pasquill in his wonderful book, *The Civilian Conservation Corps in Alabama 1933–1942: A Great and Lasting Good*, correctly described the park as "the greatest state park that never was." The park never opened. Instead the Alabama Forestry Commission took over and used the fire tower as a lookout until 1989, when they abandoned it and the cabins, leaving them all to nature.

The CCC in Alabama

It has been called the greatest work program in history, one that not only provided jobs for countless thousands of young men during the depths of the Great Depression but also left a legacy of conservation that resulted in thousands of amazing national and state parks and forests across the country—the Civilian Conservation Corps (CCC).

Almost immediately after taking office in 1933, President Franklin D. Roosevelt enacted a new program that would spur the economy by creating a virtual army of young men to bolster the nation's infrastructure as well as build exciting new places of recreation for the public.

At its height the CCC employed 500,000 men, all in their late teens to early twenties, to build dams, state parks, and more. The men were provided food, shelter, clothing, and $30 a month in pay with $25 of that sent home to their families.

Most of the state parks in Alabama were built by the CCC. Their amazing handiwork can be viewed at places like Cheaha, Monte Sano, and Chewacla State Parks as well as in state forests like Weogufka, where a massive stone fire tower tops the summit of Flagg Mountain, all hand built by the CCC.

According to historian and author of the book *The Civilian Conservation Corps in Alabama 1933-1942: A Great and Lasting Good*, Robert Pasquill says that the program employed 20,000 men in the state between 1933 and 1942, creating thirteen state forests and seven state parks.

You can see the CCC in action in Alabama online through rare historical movies (see appendix B, "Additional Resources," for URLs).

A beautiful example of CCC stonework is the lookout tower atop Flagg Mountain. A new trail is being built in 2016 to make a hike to the tower easier.

Since then, through the efforts of local residents who leased the property from the state, the cabins have been stabilized and prevented from deteriorating. And now groups like the Alabama Hiking Trail Society (AHTS) are working with state forestry to help reenergize the mountaintop and hope to someday soon open the tower and cabins to the public, as it was supposed to be all those years ago.

The hike uses two brand-new trails built by AHTS—the Yellow and White Trails—to create a loop, and an old CCC road that leads to the cabins. The trail is your standard 1- to 2-foot dirt and rock footpath blazed with either white or yellow paint blazes. At the southern intersection of these two trails, instead of heading back on the White Trail to the trailhead, you will use the CCC road to visit the cabins.

As mentioned before this trail does not lead to the fire tower—not yet anyway. It does go to the cabins, and in the "Miles and Directions" section I give you options on how to get to the tower to see it. Remember, do *not* climb the tower! As of this writing extensive work needs to be done to shore it up, so climbing it is dangerous.

Miles and Directions

0.0 Start at the northern Yellow Trail trailhead on Weogufka Forest Road (formerly CC Camp Road). The trail is a dirt and rock footpath covered with pine straw or leaves and is generally 1 to 2 feet wide. In less than 0.1 mile, come to a trail kiosk where there is a large map

Flagg Mountain Loop

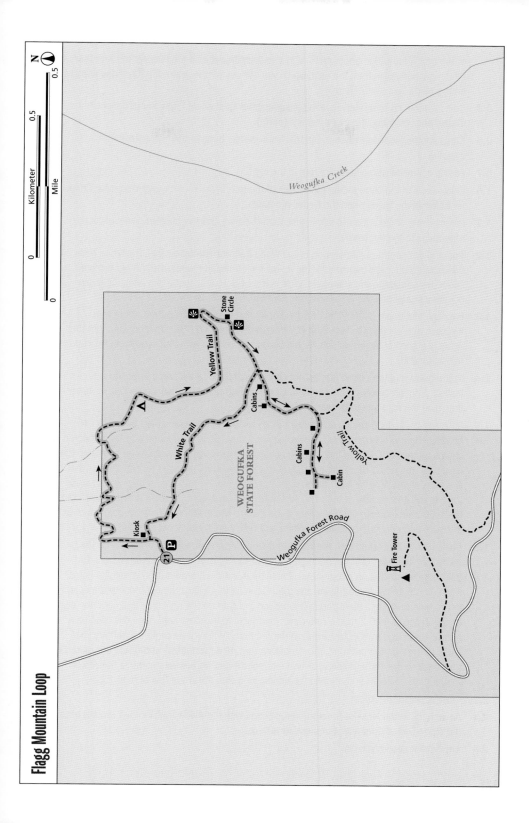

of the trail, information about AHTS, and a registry. This is also the intersection with the White Trail coming in from the east, which you will use for the return trip. Continue straight on the Yellow Trail to the north.

0.3   Cross a short 15-foot bridge over a seasonal creek built as an Eagle Scout project. Immediately after crossing, the trail turns left (north).

0.5   Cross another seasonal stream. The trail immediately turns to the left (north) after crossing.

0.7   Pass a campsite with a steel fire ring to the right.

1.0   Enjoy views of the surrounding mountains to the left (east). You may see Weogufka Creek far below in the valley when the leaves are down.

1.1   Pass a circle of stone on the left. In less than 0.1 mile, there is another nice view of the mountains to the left (east).

1.2   Come to the southern intersection of the White Trail with the Yellow Trail. The White Trail heads off to the right (northwest). The Yellow Trail turns left (southeast). An old dirt road continues straight to the southwest. We'll come back to this spot again later. Right now continue straight on the unmarked dirt road uphill to the southwest.

1.3   Pass the first cabin built by the CCC to your right. It is simply a rundown frame with fireplace and chimney. In less than 0.1 mile, pass a second CCC cabin on your right that again is a shell of its former self. At this second cabin turn left (southwest) and head down the power line.

1.4   At the bottom of the power line, do not continue straight up the steep opposite side. Instead turn left (south) onto a wide dirt road. In less than 0.1 mile, come to a Y intersection. Take the right fork to the west.

1.5   Pass one of the CCC cabins on the right that has been partially restored and shows the beautiful handiwork of the CCC. In less than 0.1 mile, pass the second and third restored cabins on the right. To your left (west) you can see the Flagg Mountain tower high atop the mountain. You could climb the power line to get there, but I wouldn't recommend it—that is a long, steep slog. We'll get there. Right now turn around and start retracing your steps back to the intersection at mile 1.2. Just after you turn around, there is a side dirt road to the south that leads to another cabin if you care to see it. When done exploring, return to this spot and continue back to the White and Yellow Trails intersection.

1.9   Back at the intersection with the White and Yellow Trails, turn left (northwest) onto the White Trail. (**Option:** One option to get to the fire tower is to turn right (south) here and follow the Yellow Trail an additional 0.7 mile to its southern terminus on Weogufka Forest Road. Turn right (west) and follow the road 0.5 mile to a Y. Take the right fork to the east. In 0.1 mile come to a steel gate. Walk around the gate on the right side and continue east on the dirt road. In 0.2 mile a rutted old road forks to the west (left). Take this road past a radio tower and in 300 feet arrive at the fire tower. When done exploring, retrace your steps to the Y on the dirt road. You can either turn right (northeast) and follow the road 0.8 mile back to the north trailhead or turn left (south) and retrace your steps to the Yellow Trail's south trailhead and back to the intersection with the White Trail at mile 1.2.)

2.2   Cross a seasonal stream.

2.3   Arrive back at the kiosk at the north intersection with the Yellow Trail. Turn left (south) onto the Yellow Trail and retrace your steps to your car.

2.4   Arrive back at your vehicle.

22 Confederate Memorial Park Nature Trail

The Nature Trail at the Confederate Memorial Park is more than just a nice walk in the woods. The trail meanders around the grounds of what was once a retirement home established by the state to assist the wounded and aging Confederate soldiers who had fought for their cause. The trail passes many sites that were important to the home.

Start: Museum parking lot
Distance: 1.4-mile lollipop
Hiking time: 1 to 1.5 hours
Difficulty: Easy on a wide, flat trail
Trail surface: Dirt and gravel footpath, some pavement near end
Best seasons: Sept to May
Other trail users: None
Canine compatibility: Leashed dogs permitted
Land status: Alabama state historic park
Nearest town: Verbena

Fees and permits: None to hike; small museum fee
Schedule: Year-round; park open daily 6 a.m. to sunset; museum open daily 9 a.m. to 5 p.m.
Maps: USGS Marbury, AL; *DeLorme: Alabama Atlas & Gazetteer*, page 38, H1; brochures with map available at museum gift shop
Trail contact: Confederate Memorial Park, 437 CR 63, Marbury 36051; (205) 755-1990; www.preserveal.org/confederatepark.aspx

Finding the trailhead: From exit 200 on I-65 in Verbena, take CR 59 south 2.4 miles. Turn right onto US 31 South. Travel 2.3 miles and turn left onto CR 23. Travel 0.7 mile and make a right onto CR 63. The park entrance is straight ahead in 0.5 mile. The museum and parking is on the right, just after the entrance. GPS: N32 43.122' / W86 28.449'

The Hike

Hiking through the many parks of the Southeast, you will undoubtedly run across plenty of Civil War history. Most of the time this takes the form of a battlefield hike. But this time we're going to walk through some post–Civil War history at Confederate Memorial Park.

As with all wars, soldiers returning home needed care either monetarily, physically, or emotionally. The same occurred at the end of the Civil War, when thousands of veterans returned from the battlefield without families, jobs, money, or a place to live.

The park you will be hiking in for this trek was the former site of the Alabama Old Soldiers Home. Unlike their Northern counterparts who received a fairly decent pension from the federal government, Confederate soldiers received little to nothing. Many had severe physical disabilities and were living in poorhouses.

In response several Southern states reached out and established veterans' homes to fill the need. In Alabama the effort was spearheaded by Montgomery attorney and Confederate veteran Jefferson Manly Falkner. Falkner donated 102 acres of land for the cause and then began a fund-raising drive where he traveled the state asking for

Time has stood still for the reservoir and pump house that originally furnished water to the retirement home.

donations. In an article from the *Montgomery Advertiser* in 1902, one trip brought in "$125 cash, $50 worth of 'dressed lumber', and 25,000 of the best shingles."

Construction began in April 1901, and one year later enough was completed to allow the first residents to move in. As long as you were a Confederate veteran who had lived in Alabama for at least two years, you were eligible to apply. Eventually the home included twenty-five buildings and a twenty-five-bed hospital. At its height the facility housed 104 Confederate veterans and their wives. It ceased operation in 1939 when the last remaining residents, five surviving widows, were placed into the care of the state welfare department.

Soon after its closure the buildings were dismantled and the land all but forgotten, except for the two cemeteries where the remains of many former residents are buried as well as the man who started it all, Jefferson Falkner.

The land officially opened as a park when it was resurrected by the state in 1964 as Confederate Memorial Park, a park that would be "a shrine to the honor of Alabama's Citizens of the Confederacy."

Before heading out I recommend you visit the visitor center and museum to get a feel for what you will be walking through, since most of the buildings were demolished over eighty years ago. While there is no park entrance fee, there is a small admission for the museum. Don't forget to pick up a brochure that has more details

Many of the Confederate veterans who once lived at the retirement home are buried in this cemetery that has a gorgeous view of the valley below.

about this hike. Many of the sites along the trail are numbered, and you'll appreciate the brochure for that extra information.

Once you've oriented yourself, begin the trip on the park's Nature Trail, directly across the road from the visitor center, for a nice walk in the woods. One impressive feature on the Nature Trail is the second-largest yellow poplar tree in Alabama. When last officially measured, the tree had a circumference of 174.5 inches and stood 105 feet tall. The canopy of the tree is 70 feet wide.

You'll quickly see that the trails are not marked but are easy to follow since most are wide fire lanes or dirt and gravel roads. There are several side roads you can wander down that will take you to other points of interest not described here. Again, all are easy to follow.

Some of the highlights of the hike include passing a spring that flows at a rate of 10 gallons per minute and was the source of water for the home. The trail will also take you past the remains of an old dam built in 1905 to harness that spring, the Old Marbury Methodist Church, and the site's reservoir and pumping station. The reservoir is an impressive large white structure that once held 85,000 gallons of water that was pumped to a tower and then into the home.

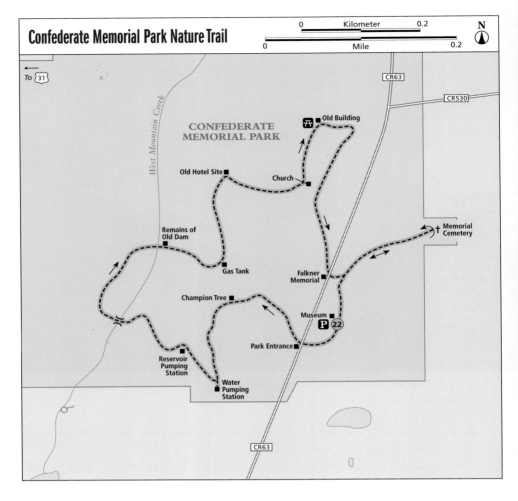

Confederate Memorial Park Nature Trail

CONFEDERATE
MEMORIAL PARK

West Mountain Creek

To {31}

CR63

CR530

Old Building

Old Hotel Site

Church

Remains of
Old Dam

Memorial
Cemetery

Gas Tank

Falkner
Memorial

Champion Tree

Museum

P 22

Reservoir
Pumping
Station

Park Entrance

Water
Pumping
Station

CR63

N

Kilometer

Mile

The hike culminates with a visit to Cemetery #2. This is a beautiful and peace-ful resting place high atop a hill overlooking the green valley below. Entering the cemetery you are immediately greeted with the grave of the man who started it all, Jefferson Manly Falkner.

Miles and Directions

0.0 Start at the parking lot in front of the museum. (***Note:*** Be sure to pick up a brochure at the museum that lists the historic sites along the route.) Cross the road to the west. There is a wooden fence here with a sign that reads Nature Trail. The trail is a wide dirt footpath.

0.1 Come to a sign that reads Nature Trail on the left and a trail leading in from the north. Turn left (west) here onto a gravel footpath. Many signs dot the trail through this area, identify-ing the plants you will see. In less than 0.1 mile, come to the second-largest poplar tree in the state on the right. It also happens to be the largest poplar in Lawrence County.

0.2 Come to a Y intersection in the trail. Take the left fork (south). In about 200 feet come to a T intersection. Turn left (south).

0.3 Arrive at the remains of a water-pumping station. The trail veers to the right (northwest). In less than 0.1 mile, come to the remnants of a reservoir pumping station that was used to supply water to the facility in the early 1900s. Follow the trail around the white building and cross a stream on a wooden bridge. A small trail comes in from the right. Continue straight (southwest).

0.5 Cross a wooden bridge over a spring. The trail parallels the stream to the right for a short distance. Come to another T intersection. Take a right and head north.

0.6 Pass the remains of an old dam and pond on the left.

0.7 The trail returns to the dirt path that you started on. Turn left (north) onto the dirt path and pass a cylindrical metal gas tank on the right that was used for cooking and lighting at the home.

0.8 Pass the site of the old hotel as the trail swings around to the north. A grassy field is on your left (north). The Old Marbury Methodist Church can be seen to your right.

0.9 Turn right (east) onto a short, narrow 4-foot-wide gravel path. In about 100 feet pass a picnic area and an old building that was used for gatherings on your left. Turn right (southwest) onto a dirt road and in a few yards pass the church. Continue straight (south) past the church on the dirt road to the paved park road (heading toward the museum).

1.1 Pass by the J. M. Falkner monument and a stand of memorial cedars on the right. Just before the museum turn left (northeast) onto a paved side road that heads up a hill.

1.3 Arrive at Cemetery #2. After exploring the cemetery and taking in the views, turn around and retrace your steps to the main park road. When you arrive, turn left (south) and return to the museum parking lot.

1.4 Arrive back at the parking lot.

23 Smith Mountain Loop

Smith Mountain stands high above the banks of Lake Martin. The Smith Mountain Trail winds its way up the craggy mountain, offering breathtaking panoramic views of the lake itself, and culminates at the summit at an old Alabama Forestry Commission fire tower that was manned from 1939 to 1980. The tower has since been completely restored and can be climbed for an even better view.

Start: At the Smith Mountain trailhead on the north side of the parking lot
Distance: 0.9-mile loop
Hiking time: About 1.5 hours
Difficulty: Moderate up rocky hillsides and bluff
Trail surface: Dirt and rock footpath
Best seasons: Sept to May
Other trail users: None
Canine compatibility: Leashed dogs permitted

Land status: Deeded Alabama Power property
Nearest town: Dadeville
Fees and permits: None
Schedule: Year-round
Maps: USGS Dadeville, AL; *DeLorme: Alabama Atlas & Gazetteer*, page 39, G7
Trail contact: Cherokee Ridge Alpine Trail Association, PO Box 240503, Eclectic 36024; cherokeeridgealpinetrail.org

Finding the trailhead: From the intersection of AL 49/South Broadnax Street and West Lafayette Street in Dadeville, take West Lafayette Street west 1.3 miles and turn left onto Young's Ferry Road. Travel 3.3 miles and turn left onto Smith Mountain Drive. The parking area and trailhead is ahead in 0.5 mile at the end of the road. GPS: N32 48.692' / W85 50.119'

The Hike

OK, quiz time. When you look at the state seal of Alabama, what do you see? Water. Lots of water. The state is a myriad of rivers and lakes. One of those lakes is Lake Martin, a beautiful 40,000-acre lake formed by the damming of the Tallapoosa River by Martin Dam. The lake is a popular bass fishing and boating destination, but thanks to the efforts of a group of trail builders called the Cherokee Ridge Alpine Trail Association (CRATA), Lake Martin is also becoming a hiking destination. One of the most popular, beautiful, and historical hikes CRATA has created is this 1-mile loop around the top of Lake Martin's Smith Mountain.

The mountain itself is unassuming, standing at only 780 feet above the lake, but as far as the state of Alabama was concerned, the large gneiss boulders and outcropping atop the mountain was the perfect location to establish a fire lookout station with an unobstructed, panoramic view of the rolling hillsides below.

The mountain is part of what is known as the Smith Mountain Historic District, with the center of activity being the mountaintop. The Alabama Power Company owned much of the forest in the area, which was harvested and used in the

Standing 90 feet above the summit of Smith Mountain, the fire tower provides a spectacular view of the surrounding mountains and Lake Martin.

construction of the dam, so as you can see that the power company was keen on protecting the forest from fire. In 1939 they built the Smith Mountain Fire Tower to do just that.

The tower opened to great fanfare. Many dignitaries attended the ceremony including state foresters, officials from Alabama Power, and county officials. The local Kiwanis Club sponsored a fish fry at the event.

The tower is 90 feet tall measured from the base of its legs to the bottom of the cabin. The cabin is 7 feet tall and the roof 2 feet taller, making it a total of 89 feet tall.

As the US Department of Interior described it, "[T]he tower had eleven landings and twelve flights of stairs. [It is] essentially an erector set composed of piers, legs, stairs, landings, and cab."

Just after its construction Alabama Forestry began manning the tower, and in 1941 the Civilian Conservation Corps (CCC) built a five-room district ranger station at the base of it. It was a stone foundation with wooden frame building, a cistern, grease and oil rack, map tables, a filling station shelter, pit latrine, and picnic grounds. A telephone was also installed. A set of stone stairs ran up a short distance from one level of the rock outcropping to the station.

The tower remained manned until 1980, when the Forestry Commission closed its doors and removed the lower landing and stairs so people wouldn't climb to the top. And that's the way the tower and Smith Mountain remained until 2011, when that group of volunteer trail builders from CRATA entered the story. With generous donations from construction companies and Alabama Power, the team set about building this amazing little trail and also restoring the fire tower to its original glory.

Today the tower has been completely rebuilt and can be accessed by hikers. Remember that the tower is only accessible from sunrise to sunset. It is the tallest structure in the area. If you hear thunder or see lightning, get out of the tower and below the mountaintop immediately.

The trail itself is a narrow dirt and rock footpath with beautiful wildflowers lining the way in the spring and early summer. You will be scampering over some boulders and walking beside the large gneiss outcroppings. Needless to say there are plenty of beautiful views of the lake from here.

Poor Ol' Kaw-Liga

One of Alabama's most famous singer-songwriters was the late Hank Williams. Over his career Williams penned hundreds of songs including hits like "Hey, Good Lookin'" and the tearjerker "Your Cheating Heart."

The story goes that Hank was spending a few days on Lake Martin in the town of Kaw-Liga, which was named after a legendary Indian from these parts. As he gazed out his cabin window, he saw a wooden cigar store Indian and came up with a love story about the statue, Kaw-Liga, who fell in love with a wooden Indian maiden that he could see across the way in an antiques store. But with a heart of knotty pine, Kaw-Liga never could express his love for her. The original wooden Indian was stolen years ago and has never been found.

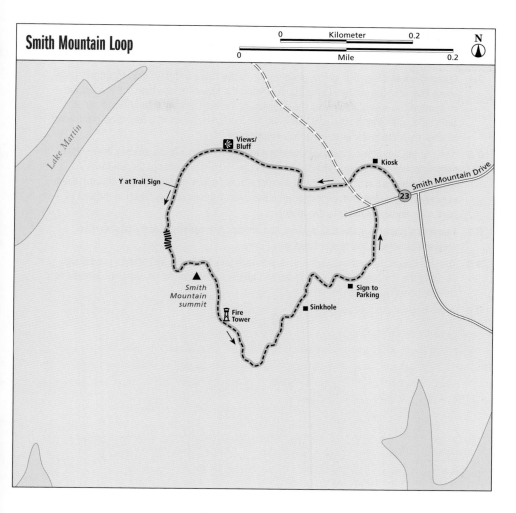

Smith Mountain Loop

0   Kilometer   0.2

0   Mile   0.2

N

Lake Martin

Views/ Bluff

Kiosk

Y at Trail Sign

Smith Mountain Drive

23

Smith Mountain summit

Fire Tower

Sign to Parking

Sinkhole

As you near the top, you will climb the stairs built by the CCC in 1941 and arrive at the foundation of the original ranger station. CRATA has plans to eventually rebuild the structure and make it into a mountaintop museum.

The path is well blazed with white paint markings. CRATA uses standard double blazes (dit-dots) to indicate turns in the trail.

Miles and Directions

0.0   Start at the trailhead on the north side of the parking lot. The entrance to the trail is clearly marked with a white and red sign reading To Tower. In 400 feet come to a kiosk that displays basic rules for hiking the trail. A large wooden sign reads To Tower/To Little Smith Mountain Trail.

0.1   Cross the dirt road to the south.

0.3 The trees begin to thin out and you start seeing views of the surrounding hills to the north along a nice rock bluff and outcropping. There is an Alabama Power No Trespassing sign here. The path is a 2-foot-wide rocky bed lined with mountain laurel.

0.4 Come to a Y at a sign that points the direction to the tower and the Smith Mountain/Lakeshore Trail. Take the left fork to the south (toward the tower). In less than 0.1 mile, come to another Y at a sign that points the direction to the boat landing/Island Hop Trail/Little Smith Mountain Trail (to the right). Take the left fork to the south. In a few yards climb a set of wooden stairs to the east, up a rock outcropping.

0.5 Arrive at the top of the mountain, passing a foundation with a brick chimney. There is a cement bench on the north side. Follow the ridge to the southwest to the fire tower. A kiosk here has a list of climbers and summit toppers and a register (please sign in). Great views are found here and, of course, atop the tower. After exploring, return to the trail (it continues under the tower to the south).

0.7 Come to a sinkhole in the trail. A short wooden bridge crosses it, but it's best to walk around the hole, as the bridge looks very rickety.

0.8 The trail leaves the outcroppings and ducks back into the forest. In 100 feet pass a sign showing the direction back to the tower and ahead to the parking lot. Continue straight to the northeast.

0.9 Arrive back at the trailhead.

24 Horseshoe Bend Loop

An easy walking trek, the Horseshoe Bend Nature Trail loops around the site of the Battle of Horseshoe Bend, a bloody and decisive battle that led to the end of the Creek Indian War but also shaped the course of history for the tribes of the region over the next few decades, culminating in their removal from the land over the "Trail of Tears." The hike leads you to key historic sites of the battle and along the banks of the Tallapoosa River.

Start: North side of Overlook parking lot
Distance: 2.5-mile loop
Hiking time: About 1.5 hours
Difficulty: Easy over rolling hills
Trail surface: Dirt footpath, small amount of asphalt trail
Best seasons: Year-round
Other trail users: None
Canine compatibility: Leashed dogs permitted
Land status: National military park
Nearest town: Alexander City

Fees and permits: None; donation requested
Schedule: Year-round, daily 8 a.m. to 5 p.m.; visitor center open daily 9 a.m. to 4:30 p.m.; closed Thanksgiving, Christmas, and New Year's Day
Maps: USGS Buttston, AL; *DeLorme: Alabama Atlas & Gazetteer*, page 39, D8; trail map and brochure available at the visitor center
Trail contact: Horseshoe Bend NMP, 11288 Horseshoe Bend Rd., Daviston 36256; (256) 234-7111; nps.gov/hobe/

Finding the trailhead: From Alexander City at the intersection of AL 22 and Madison Street, take AL 22 east 12.8 miles. Turn right onto Hamlet Mill Road (AL 49) and travel 4.7 miles. The park entrance is on your left. Turn left into the park and stop by the visitor center, then continue 0.1 mile to the Overlook parking area. The trail begins here on the north side of the parking lot. GPS: N32 58.832' / W85 44.093'

The Hike

Stepping out of your car at the Horseshoe Bend National Military Park, you will be immediately struck by the silence, the quiet serenity that surrounds you. Today only the occasional festival or reenactment disrupts the solitude, but just over one hundred years ago the scene was quite different when a bloody battle was waged here that helped seal the fate of Native Americans.

The park is located on the flat section of a U-shaped bend in the Tallapoosa River near Alexander City. The Creek Indians who lived here called it Cholocco Litabizee ("horse's flat foot"). Americans called it Horseshoe Bend.

The Creek Nation was actually a conglomeration of tribes that moved from the southwest United States to the southeast, to what is now Georgia, Alabama, Florida, and the Carolinas. Eventually these different tribes merged to form a politically aligned confederacy called the Muscogee Nation. Generally the tribes were divided by the Chattahoochee River. Because of this, when the British arrived on the scene,

A cannon used in the famous Battle of Horseshoe Bend stands silently guarding a monument to the battle.

they began calling them "Creek" Indians. The Creek and British enjoyed a strong trade relationship for many years.

Following the American Revolution the bond between the newly formed country and the Creek Nation was strengthened when a treaty was signed in New York in 1790. Immediately after the signing US Indian agent Benjamin Hawkins began implementing a series of programs designed to improve the Creek Nation's way of life, especially in agriculture.

By 1810, however, a split erupted between Creek tribes, separating them into two factions. One tribe, the Red Sticks, or Upper Creek, believed in Indian nationalism and feared the growing expansion of white settlements into the South. In 1813 a group of Red Sticks were told erroneously that war had broken out between the United States and the Creek Nation. Upon hearing this, the Red Sticks attacked and murdered several frontier families. A Creek tribal council captured, convicted, and executed those who were involved in the murders, but Red Stick chief Menawa vowed to eliminate everyone connected with the executions and remove white influences from the region once and for all.

With that the Creek Indian War began and lasted until 1814. Battles were fought throughout the region, with General Andrew Jackson in charge of US forces. Despite outnumbering the Creeks in every battle, Jackson could not bring a decisive end to the war. The situation worsened in July 1813 when a group of Creeks ambushed a Red Stick ammunition train. In retaliation the Red Sticks attacked and massacred 250 settlers in Fort Mims, located just outside present-day Bay Minette.

The decisive battle was waged here at Horseshoe Bend on March 17, 1814. Most of the battle was fought by 2,000 men from a Tennessee militia and 600 allied Cherokee and Creek Indians. By the end of the battle, 1,000 Red Sticks were dead, and soon after, this land was ceded to the United States. The battle forced an end to the

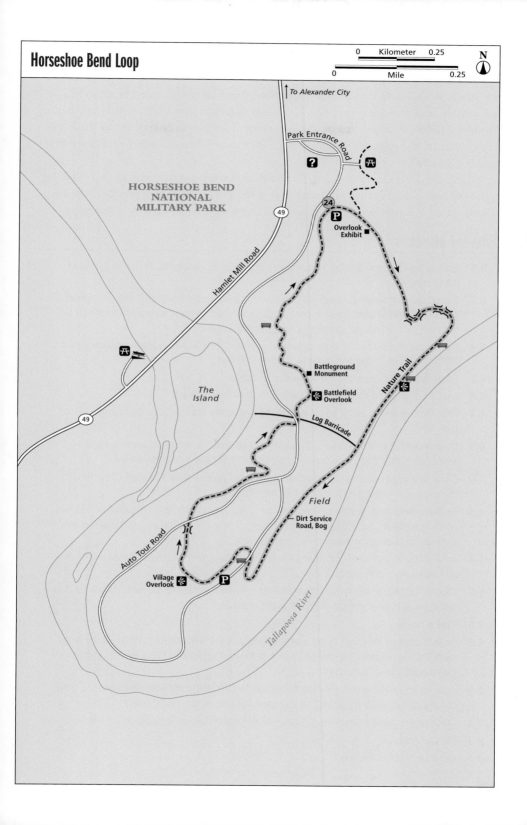

war and eventually led to the forced removal of the tribes from the region in what is known as the "Trail of Tears."

While the looping trail here at Horseshoe Bend takes you through some beautiful scenery and views of the wide Tallapoosa River, it also leads you to key battle locations. Before heading out, be sure to watch the 15-minute film about the battle, which will set the stage for what you are about to see. Admission is free, but a donation is requested.

Along the unmarked path you will pass many informational exhibits that describe what you are seeing, each with a roof over it for a little shade and benches. The hike is a very easy 2.5-mile loop over gravel and dirt footpaths about 3 to 4 feet wide.

Miles and Directions

0.0 Start at the Overlook parking area. The trail begins as a paved path on the north side of the parking lot.

0.1 A short, 50-foot walkway takes you to the overlook above the battlefield and an informational kiosk. When done viewing, head back to the main trail and turn right (southeast). Here the path is crushed gravel as it heads into the woods.

0.4 Walk alongside a nice seasonal stream on your right. In 100 feet cross the stream over a 20-foot wooden bridge and again in another 100 feet.

0.5 Cross the stream twice more over wooden bridges.

0.6 Pass a bench. Start seeing the Tallapoosa River to the left (east).

0.7 Pass another bench and a better view of the river to the left (east). Young bamboo plants grow here.

0.9 Cross an old dirt service road to the southwest (a brown post with a very small black arrow points the direction in front of you). In 200 feet pass a bog on your left.

1.0 Come to a large open field on your left (east) side. The trail skirts the edge of the field to the southwest before heading back into the woods.

1.3 Pass another bench just before crossing the paved tour road to the northwest. In 300 feet come to a parking lot and walk along the north side of the lot. The trail continues on the west and is once again paved for a short distance.

1.4 Arrive at the Village Overlook. After viewing and reading, turn left and continue on the dirt and gravel path to the north.

1.6 Cross a footbridge over a ditch, then cross the paved tour road to the north. Listen for the rushing waters of a long set of shoals in the distance.

1.8 Pass a bench.

1.9 Cross the paved tour road to the southeast. Here in the field across the road, white poles mark The Barricade. Follow the south side of the parking lot and rejoin the trail (now a paved path again) to the north.

2.0 Arrive at an exhibit overlooking the battlefield. In 100 feet to the northeast, view the grave of Lemuel Purnell Montgomery. The trail turns left here at the exhibit (north).

2.1 Come to the battle monument. Continue on the dirt and gravel footpath to the northwest.

2.3 Pass a bench.

2.5 Arrive back at the trailhead.

SOUTH REGION

They say the Black Belt (South) Region of Alabama has culture and history as rich as its land; this trek through the area will prove that statement is not just a slogan.

The region, which is known for its deep, rich, black topsoil that can grow just about anything, especially cotton, is where the state of Alabama was born. Here, from just above the Gulf Coast to just north of Montgomery, you will walk the long since deserted streets of Old Cahawba and Old St. Stephens. Now active archaeological parks, both towns were the cradle of early Alabama. Old St. Stephens was the first territorial capital of the state, while Old Cahawba was the first official state capital before it moved to Montgomery. Both might be ghost towns now, but walking the long-forgotten streets will bring their spirits back to life.

Another walk will take you in the footsteps of one of the most famous explorers to hit American soil, botanist to the king of England, William Bartram, who "discovered" and cataloged much of the flora and fauna of the region in the mid-1700s as well as documented the everyday lives of the Native Americans and early European settlers who lived here.

And, of course, the journey would not be complete without a walk down the streets of Selma. The town's motto is "from Civil War to Civil Rights." Selma was once a booming munitions-building town during the Civil War; bookending that one hundred years later, the city became the epicenter of the civil rights movement when protestors who were attempting to march to the state capital in Montgomery were thwarted on their first attempt and suffered tragic consequences at the hands of armed police officers blocking their way on the Edmund Pettus Bridge. This will be your opportunity to walk the bridge yourself and learn of the events of that day and the subsequent triumphant signing of the Civil Rights Act, which came about because of these brave men and women.

25 Bartram Trail

Follow in the footsteps of famed botanist to King George III, William Bartram, along the Bartram Trail at the Tuskegee National Forest. Bartram walked this region in the mid-1700s and documented the plants, wildlife, landscapes, inhabitants, and his many adventures in his popular book *Travels with William Bartram.* You can explore the same forest, streams, creeks, and bogs on this winding, 6.4-mile out-and-back hike.

Start: From the eastern trailhead on US 29
Distance: 6.7-mile shuttle (see hike description and "Miles and Directions" for other options)
Hiking time: 2.5 to 3 hours
Difficulty: Easy to moderate due to distance
Trail surface: Dirt footpath, wooden bridges and boardwalks
Best seasons: Year-round
Other trail users: Cyclists, hunters (see "Special considerations")
Canine compatibility: Leashed dogs permitted
Land status: National forest

Nearest town: Tuskegee
Fees and permits: None
Schedule: Year-round, daily sunrise to sunset
Maps: USGS Little Texas, AL; *DeLorme: Alabama Atlas & Gazetteer*, page 46, C4/C5
Trail contact: Tuskegee National Forest, 125 National Forest Rd. 949, Tuskegee 36083; (334) 727-2652; www.fs.usda.gov/main/alabama/home
Special considerations: Hunting is allowed in fall and winter; visit www.fs.usda.gov/main/alabama/home/ for seasons.

Finding the trailhead: From the intersection of AL 15 and US 29/US 80 in Tuskegee, take US 29/US 80 east 7.3 miles. US 80 and US 29 split at this point. Continue straight on US 29 North 1.1 miles. The well-marked trailhead is on your left directly across the street from the Little Texas Volunteer Fire Department, with enough room for about 15 cars. GPS: N32 28.727' / W85 33.834. **Directions for optional shuttle:** From the trailhead described above, turn right onto US 29 and head southwest. Travel 0.9 mile and turn right onto AL 186 West. Travel 2.1 miles and turn right onto FR 949 (the turn is clearly marked with a Tuskegee National Forest sign). In 0.2 mile the ranger station and parking is on your left. Shuttle GPS: N32 28.730' / W85 36.540'

The Hike

Alabama has had its share of famous explorers come through in its early history: Alonso de Pineda, Pierre Le Moyne d'Iberville, Hernando DeSoto, and the first native-born American naturalist and artist, William Bartram.

The son of an unassuming Quaker farmer and renowned naturalist in his own right, John Bartram, William was a failure as a farmer. His real calling was observing and documenting the natural world around him. Bartram was what you might call a Renaissance man today; he was an artist, writer, and botanist.

Born in Philadelphia, Bartram was appointed botanist to King George III of England. Between the years 1775 and 1778, he traveled over 2,400 miles through what is

Walking along a leaf-covered boardwalk through a seasonal bog on the Bartram Trail

now the states of Alabama, Florida, Georgia, Mississippi, Louisiana, Tennessee, and the Carolinas, documenting his experiences along the way. His adventures in Alabama took him to areas that are now the present-day cities of Mobile, Montgomery, and Auburn, plus the Mobile-Tensaw River Delta, to name only a few. He made his way through this section of Alabama (Macon County and the Tuskegee National Forest) in 1778.

While Bartram earned acclaim for his research back in the 1700s, his biggest claim to fame came from the book he wrote that documented his travels. The book was aptly titled *Travels with William Bartram*, but it was written in a style unheard of at the time. Instead of being a dull, stodgy science book, his writing was a mix of flowery prose interspersed with observations and illustrations of plants, wildlife, and landscapes. Oh, and a few rollicking tales of battles with alligators, crossing wide and foreboding rivers, and weathering tremendous storms.

Bartram relished meeting new cultures, and his writings paint a vivid picture of these encounters and what life was like for the local Native American tribes and early European settlers to the region.

Avid hikers have probably walked a number of trails named the "Bartram Trail" or some derivative of that name, like the Bartram Trail in Georgia or the Bartram Canoe Trail near Mobile. Could all these trails be identified as areas where William Bartram might have walked? The answer is yes! His journals were so detailed that finding his route was fairly simple. Some of the trails might not be exactly where Bartram's feet trod, but they are very close, so you will be walking virtually in his footsteps. I recommend visiting the Bartram Trail Conference website (bartramtrailconference. wildapricot.org) to view an excellent map of his travels through the Southeast.

The Bartram Trail at Tuskegee National Forest was the first trail in the state designated as a National Recreational Trail and features beautiful wildflowers, flowering dogwoods and magnolias, and assorted wildlife like wild turkeys and white-tailed deer. You will be experiencing virtually what Bartram did hundreds of years ago.

As I re-walked the trail for this book, I at first thought it had been relocated. It looked very different. But no, it was the same trail, but a prescribed burn had taken place not long ago, and much of the foliage was still trying to return. The trail is fairly easy to follow, especially with the intermittent white, metal diamond blazes. You will cross many creeks and bogs over some old bridges on the eastern side, and boardwalks on the western after passing near the ranger station. Remember, water features are seasonal and may not be there when you visit.

You have a couple different options when hiking the trail. Of course there is the out-and-back route described here. You could do a daylong hike and walk the entire 8.5 miles from end to end (not shown on map). You can do a shorter 4.2-mile hike from the east trailhead to the ranger station or a 4.5-mile jaunt to the Pleasant Hill parking area and trailhead. All of these options require a shuttle vehicle. If you're ambitious and want an overnight backpacking trip, try doing the entire trail as a 17-mile out and back, using one of the campsites located along side trails.

A sad side note is that the prescribed burn mentioned earlier took out some wonderful wooden benches on the eastern side. These benches had passages from Bartram's book engraved in them. You will see one or two, but mostly they are burned-out frames. The western side, however, still has the benches. Read the passages and feel what William Bartram felt walking these woods.

Miles and Directions

0.0 Start from the western side of the parking area. The trail for the most part is a good 2- to 3-foot-wide dirt footpath throughout. The path begins covered in a thick layer of pine duff, then slowly changes to a leaf-covered trail as the environment changes. A little ravine can be seen to the right. The trail parallels US 29 for a bit, so you will hear highway noise for a short section at the beginning. One of the old benches carved with the sayings of William Bartram can be seen just after you head out, on a small hill to your left (south).

0.2 Come to an old logging road. Turn right (north) and in 50 feet pick up the trail again into the woods on the left (west). In less than 0.1 mile, pass a sign indicating a wildlife food plot on the left. Notice the very young bamboo plants growing thickly alongside the trail.

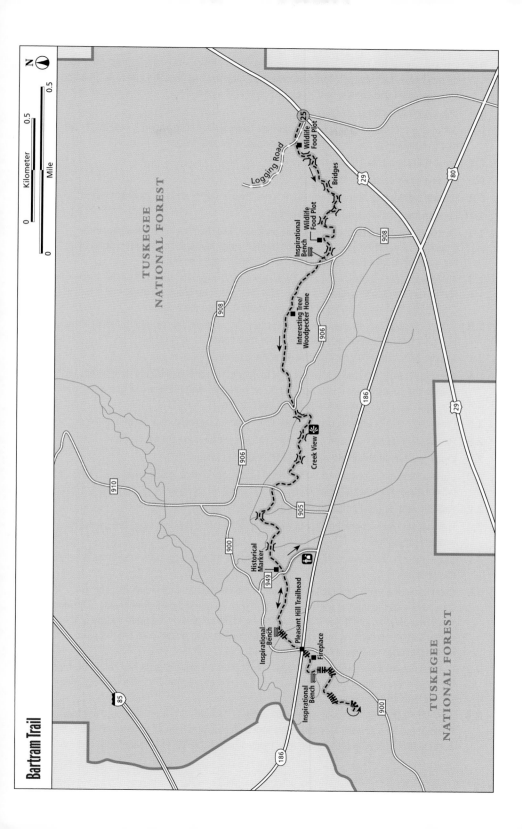

Bartram Trail

N

Kilometer
0   0.5   0.5

0   Mile   0.5

TUSKEGEE NATIONAL FOREST

Logging Road

Wildlife Food Plot

Bridges

Wildlife Food Plot

Inspirational Bench

Interesting Tree/ Woodpecker Home

Creek View

Historical Marker

Inspirational Bench

Pleasant Hill Trailhead

Fireplace

Inspirational Bench

TUSKEGEE NATIONAL FOREST

85

186

900

949

900

905

906

908

910

906

908

186

29

29

80

25

0.3 Cross an aging, 30-foot wooden bridge over a creek. At the time of this writing, the wood on this bridge had rotted in spots, so cross carefully. You may lose the trail for a bit after crossing; just head straight to the south to pick it up again.

0.4 Cross a 10-foot bridge over a creek.

0.6 Come to a Y intersection and take either fork. They rejoin in less than 0.1 mile at the bottom of a hill where you cross another creek over a wooden bridge.

0.7 Cross a creek over a 10-foot bridge.

0.8 Cross a creek over a 10-foot bridge.

0.9 Cross a small creek over a short bridge. A small pine savannah is to your right (north).

1.1 Pass another wildlife food plot on the right.

1.3 Cross another creek over a short 4-foot bridge. In less than 0.1 mile, pass one of the inspirational benches on the left. It was burned pretty badly during the prescribed burn but survived, barely. The saying reads, "erect stems, arise from its roots."

1.4 Arrive at the dirt FR 908. A flat fiberglass sign as you approach the road points to the right (northwest). Turn right onto the road. In 100 feet look for a diamond marker on a tree to the left (west). Turn right here and back onto the trail into the woods.

1.8 Pass an interestingly shaped tree and next to it, in a unique, burned-out, 5-foot-tall stump of a pine tree, a "duplex" woodpecker home (two holes).

2.1 Top out on a small hill and walk the ridgeline for a bit.

2.4 Arrive at FR 906. The trail comes out at a hairpin turn in the road. Go straight across the road to the southwest and pick up the trail on the other side (it's marked with a flat, brown fiberglass sign letting you know who can use the trail).

2.5 Cross a 10-foot boardwalk over a creek. As of this writing some boards were missing.

2.6 Topping a hill get a nice view of the creek you just crossed to your right (north).

2.7 Cross a seasonal creek and bog over a 60-foot-long bridge.

2.8 Cross a seasonal creek over a 20-foot-long bridge. Soon after look up and see a lone bigleaf magnolia among the pines.

3.2 Walk straight across FR 905 to the north.

3.4 The trail parallels a creek on the left with deep banks. In a few feet cross the creek over a wooden footbridge.

3.7 Cross another creek over a 25-foot-long boardwalk. Start seeing more magnolias through this section.

3.9 Come to FR 949 at a historical marker and National Recreational Trail (NRT) sign. Go straight across the road to the southwest and pick up the trail on the other side. (*Option:* You can make this into a 4.2-mile point-to-point hike by parking a shuttle vehicle at the ranger station and ending the hike here by turning left (southeast) onto the road. The ranger station is on your right in 0.3 mile.)

4.3 Pass an inspirational bench on the right. In less than 0.1 mile, cross a bog over a 50-foot boardwalk. Soon after cross another bog over a 70-foot boardwalk, then a few feet later a shorter 20-foot boardwalk.

4.5 Arrive at FR 900. Turn left and *cautiously* cross AL 186/US 80 (it's a very busy highway). Arrive at the Pleasant Hill Mountain Bike Trail trailhead. Turn right to continue on the Bartram Trail. Just after making the turn, cross a bog over a 100-foot boardwalk. There is a distinct change in the ecosystem here as you make your way into a bog, wetland, and bottomland area. (**Option:** You can park a shuttle vehicle at the Pleasant Hill trailhead to make this a 4.5-mile point-to-point hike.)

4.6 Pass an old stone fireplace just off the trail on the left.

4.7 Pass an inspirational bench on the right.

4.8 Cross a seasonal creek and bog over a 100-foot boardwalk. In less than 0.1 mile, cross another bog over a 500-foot-long boardwalk.

5.0 Cross another bog over a boardwalk. The blazes disappear for a time at this point. Keep heading to the southwest.

5.2 Come to a long 200-foot-long boardwalk. This is your turnaround for the hike described here. Turn around here and follow the trail back to the ranger station and your shuttle vehicle. (**Note:** As of this writing I could not make it to Choccolocco Creek due to a bridge being out. If you can go farther, it is worth your while to add an additional 0.5 mile to your trek to see the wide creek.)

6.4 Arrive back at the historical marker. Turn right onto the paved road to head to the ranger station and your shuttle vehicle.

6.7 Arrive at the ranger station.

26 Fort Toulouse-Fort Jackson Loop

The Fort Toulouse-Fort Jackson Loop is another great hike with several thousand years of history rolled into one. You will be retracing the steps of nomadic hunters who roamed this land thousands of years ago, as well as those of botanist to King George III, William Bartram, and visiting the site of the forts that at one time or another were controlled by the Spanish, French, British, and Americans.

Start: Parking lot in front of visitor center
Distance: 2.0-mile multi-loop
Hiking time: About 1.5 hours
Difficulty: Easy over rolling hills
Trail surface: Dirt and crushed gravel footpath, boardwalks
Best seasons: Sept to May
Other trail users: Cyclists on dirt roads
Canine compatibility: Leashed dogs permitted
Land status: National historic park
Nearest town: Wetumpka

Fees and permits: Day-use fee
Schedule: Year-round, daily sunrise to sunset; visitor center daily 8 a.m. to 5 p.m.; closed Thanksgiving, Christmas, and New Year's Day
Maps: USGS Wetumpka, AL; *DeLorme: Alabama Atlas & Gazetteer*, page 45, C8
Trail contact: Fort Toulouse-Fort Jackson National Historic Park, 2521 W. Fort Toulouse Rd., Wetumpka 36093; (344) 567-3002; forttoulouse.com

Finding the trailhead: From the intersection of AL 112 (West Bridge Street) and AL 111 in Wetumpka, take AL 111 south 0.2 mile and turn right onto South Main Street. Travel 0.8 mile and turn right onto AL 9 South. Travel 0.3 mile and turn left onto Old Montgomery Highway. In 0.8 mile turn right onto Fort Toulouse Road. In 3.4 miles you will arrive at the park entrance. Pay your day-use fee at the entrance kiosk or to the guard on duty and continue straight another 0.2 mile. The visitor center parking and trailhead is on the left. GPS: N32 30.335' / W86 15.170'

The Hike

Fort Toulouse-Fort Jackson National Historic Park is more than just the site of a historic nineteenth-century fort. Its history goes far beyond that, reaching back to 5,000 BC when the first Native Americans roamed this land. Since that time this location on the banks of the Coosa River has seen almost nonstop human occupation and plenty of history that helped build this country.

Archaeologists discovered that nomadic hunters roamed this region around 5,000 BC. They finally "settled down" and began building and cultivating their culture and civilization here during what is called the Mississippian period (AD 1100–1400). These tribes were known as mound builders, and throughout the south—along its myriad of deltas and rivers—they built tall dirt and stick mounds, by hand, to be used for ceremonies, as temples, and as housing for tribal leaders. You will have a chance to see one of the remaining mounds at the park along this hike.

A view of the moat and one of the last remaining visible points of an early incarnation of the fort that once stood here at Fort Toulouse–Fort Jackson

Famed explorer Hernando DeSoto was one of the first Europeans to explore this river-laden region in 1540. By the 1700s France and Britain were fighting for control of this land, with what is now the southeast United States divided into separate French and British territories.

In an attempt to halt the advance of Britain into the Louisiana Colony, the French, by invitation of their Creek Indian trading partners, constructed a fort on the territory's eastern side here at the confluence of three rivers—the Tallapoosa, Coosa, and Alabama. It was named Fort Toulouse after the son of King Louis XIV.

By the mid-1700s the French and Indian War was raging, and when it was over in 1763 the French were on the losing end and were forced to turn over much of their territory to Britain, including the fort. The Brits, however, were never able to man the fort and were forced to abandon it thanks in part to local Creek Indians who were loyal to their French trading partners.

Eventually the fort fell into disrepair and was reclaimed by nature until it was rediscovered in 1776 by the botanist to King George III, William Bartram, who found the ruins of the old fort during his explorations in the area. Bartram took note of the rich and fertile land around the fort and noted in his journals that this area was the "most eligible situation in the world for a city."

Years later, following the Battle of Horseshoe Bend in 1814, General Andrew Jackson made his way to this same location and established a new earthen fort that was named Fort Jackson. From here he began a military campaign against both Britain and Spain that culminated in the Battle of New Orleans in 1815.

> In early American history the North and South were as different as night and day, and it all came to a head during the Civil War. But there was one more thing they didn't agree on—Christmas. Northerners thought celebrating Christ's birth as a holiday was a sin while the South saw it as a social event. In 1836 Alabama became the first state to recognize Christmas as a holiday.

Before heading out I recommend hitting the visitor center to see the exhibits and pick up a book or two to orient yourself.

You will begin the hike on the south side of the visitor center on a wide, crushed-gravel footpath simply called the Nature Trail. The path soon turns into a 2- to 3-foot-wide dirt footpath. For almost a mile you will be wandering through a beautiful floodplain forest of southern red, water, and laurel oaks, flowering dogwoods, yaupon holly, sweet gum, and Atlantic white cedar with colorful black-eyed Susan lining the path. Remember that a floodplain is just that, and the trails can be deep in mud and water after a good rain. Of course this leaves boggy areas, so be prepared with insect spray in the summer months.

Eventually the loop opens up atop a bluff for a beautiful river view. As you head back toward the trailhead, you will visit the site of the forts. You can quite clearly make out the diamond-shaped corners and earthworks of Fort Jackson and in the center pay a visit to a rustic cabin of the period.

Miles and Directions

0.0 Start at the trailhead on the south side of the parking lot. In 50 feet pass a monument to Jean-Louis Fonteneau, a sergeant in the French Colonial Marines who died at the fort in 1755.

0.1 A short side trail to the left (east) takes you to two tombstones. Continue straight ahead to the south and cross a creek over a wooden footbridge. Come to a Y intersection and take the left fork to the southeast.

0.2 Come to a wide deck with informational signs and benches. In less than 0.1 mile, cross a seasonal creek over a 60-foot wood bridge with steel railings. In 200 feet come to a T intersection; turn left (west).

0.3 Come to another deck with informational signs and benches. Head down a flight of stairs to the south. You leave the crushed-gravel path at the bottom as the trail becomes a dirt footpath. It's very green and lush through here in late spring and early summer. In less than 0.1 mile, come to another T intersection. Turn left (south). In 100 feet cross another seasonal stream over a footbridge.

0.4 Come to a Y. A boat launch is to the left (east). Take the right fork to the south (a sign here points the way to the waterfront).

Fort Toulouse–Fort Jackson Loop

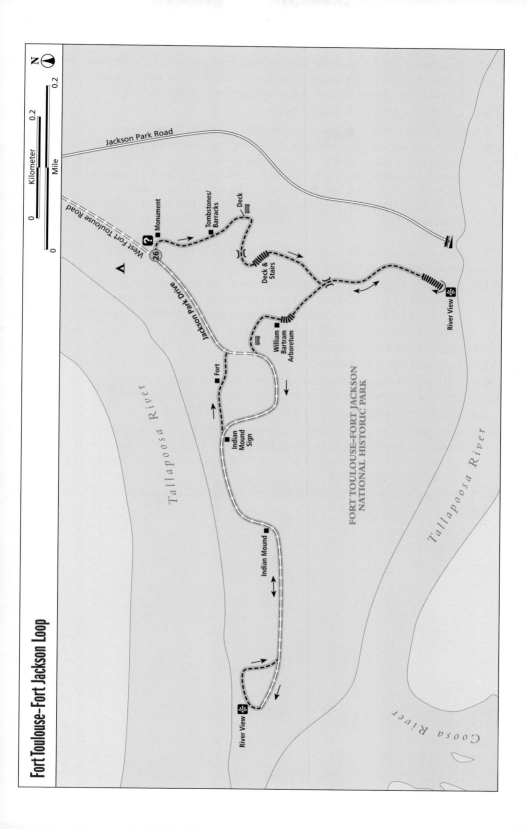

Jackson Park Road

West Fort Toulouse Road

Monument

Tombstones/Barracks

Deck

Deck & Stairs

26

Jackson Park Drive

Fort

Indian Mound Sign

Indian Mound

River View

William Bartram Arboretum

River View

Tallapoosa River

FORT TOULOUSE–FORT JACKSON NATIONAL HISTORIC PARK

Tallapoosa River

Coosa River

N

Kilometer

0   0.2

Mile

0   0.2

0.5 Head down a series of railroad tie stairs and cross a boggy area (could be fairly deep after a good rain). Continue straight to the southwest. In 100 feet arrive at your first look at the Tallapoosa River. When ready turn around and head back to mile 0.4.

0.6 Arrive back at the Y at mile 0.4. Take the left fork.

0.7 Take a series of wooden stairs up to a large deck.

0.8 Arrive at the top of the stairs at a large deck with signage describing the William Bartram Arboretum. Turn left (north) onto a short, crushed-gravel path. In 175 feet the trail ends at a gravel area with benches. You can see the fort to the right (northwest). Head west until you come to a dirt road. In 100 feet turn left (southwest) onto the dirt road and follow it around to the north. There are excellent views of the fort and the diamond shape of the structure along the route to your right. Beautiful Spanish moss–laden trees line the route on your left.

1.0 The road bends to the left (west). A large sign points the direction to the Indian mounds. Follow the dirt road to the west.

1.1 Come to an Indian mound on the right marked by a large sign reading Mississippian Phase Mound Circa 1100–1400 AD. You can move off-trail and explore the area, then continue on the dirt road. The road turns into mostly grass as you follow the edge of a large field.

1.2 The path ducks back into the thick forest.

1.3 Cross a dirt road to the northwest.

1.4 Come out on an open bluff overlooking the river. There is a bench here. Turn right (northeast) and follow the grassy path around, making a small loop back to mile 1.3.

1.5 Return to the dirt road and turn left (east) to head back to the fort.

1.8 At the Indian mound sign you passed at mile 1.0, get off the road and head straight (northeast) toward the fort on an unmarked grassy path. In just over 200 feet, arrive at the log cabin that was once part of the fort. After exploring, head straight from the fort to the east to return to the dirt road.

1.9 Arrive at the dirt road. Turn left (northeast) onto the road and head back to the trailhead.

2.0 Arrive back at the trailhead.

27 Selma Historic Walk

Nothing sums up the history you will experience in the town of Selma more than their motto, "From Civil War to Civil Rights." On this 1.8-mile city walk you'll see fascinating architecture in the buildings and churches, elegant hotels from the past, and of course, the site of "Bloody Sunday" in 1965, the Edmund Pettus Bridge.

Start: At the corner of Selma Avenue and Broad Street in front of the Selma-Dallas County Library
Distance: 1.8-mile loop with out and back
Hiking time: About 1 hour (add time for visiting sites and reading historical markers)
Difficulty: Easy
Trail surface: Cement sidewalk
Best seasons: Year-round
Other trail users: Vehicles at street crossings
Canine compatibility: Leashed dogs permitted

Land status: City owned
Nearest town: Selma
Fees and permits: None
Schedule: Year-round, daily, no set hours
Maps: USGS Selma, AL; *DeLorme: Alabama Atlas & Gazetteer*, page 43, D10
Trail contact: Selma and Dallas County Tourism and Convention Bureau, 912 Selma Ave., Selma 36701; (800) 457-3562; selma alabama.com

Finding the trailhead: From the intersection of US 80 and US 80 Business Route (BR)/Broad Street, take US 80 BR north 2.9 miles. The starting point is located on the right at the corner of Selma Avenue and Broad Street at the library. The best place to park is 1 block to the east behind the library on Washington Street. GPS: N32 24.549' / W87 01.228'

The Hike

In *Hiking through History Alabama* I've shied away from city walks and rail-trails as much as possible. After all, while the book is about history, it is also about hiking, and city walks just don't fit well in that mix—with a couple of notable exceptions: the city of Mobile with over 300 years of history, the Vulcan Trail with its mining history, and the town of Selma.

Before you head out, be sure to stop by the Selma–Dallas County Tourism Department, on the corner of Water Avenue and US 80 (just past the Edmund Pettus Bridge), and pick up a copy of the *Walking Tour of Selma* brochure. It will give you additional details about points of interest on this walk.

Selma is a quiet, quaint, unassuming city on the banks of the Alabama River. One of the state's more recent tourism marketing promotions used the slogan, "From Civil War to Civil Rights." In that one short phrase, the history of Selma is summed up nicely. But there is more to the city's story than the Civil War and the tragic events of March 7, 1965, a date now remembered as "Bloody Sunday." Selma's history began in 1820 and eventually led to a promise that men and women of all races and

An iconic location for the civil rights movement in the 1960s, the Edmund Pettus Bridge was the site where, after walking only 6 blocks on their march from Selma to Montgomery, demonstrators were brutally attacked in what has become known as "Bloody Sunday."

nationalities can live together and prosper. This city walk, the Selma Historic Walk, retraces a bit of that history.

When you drive into Selma, you first get the feeling that you're in a typical Southern town with buildings dating back to the late 1800s to 1920s, but step out of the car and you can feel the history. Looking around, you will notice some buildings boarded up and for sale, but don't let that fool you. The city is revitalizing in a big way, and more and more people are experiencing what it has to offer.

The area in which the city lies was first documented by the French in 1732. It was named for the French provincial governor of the area at the time, Jean Baptiste Le Moyne. When Europeans began frequenting the area, they called it the "High Soap Stone Bluff." In 1815 the name changed again when a Tennessee settler, Thomas Moore, built a cabin on the bluff and it became known as "Moore's Bluff."

Finally a US senator and eventually the vice president of the United States under President Franklin Pierce, William King, came to the area, and much like early Europeans before him along other stretches of Alabama's thousands of miles of rivers, King saw that the high bluff at this bend in the river would make the settlement a prominent river port and commercial center. The city of Selma was officially incorporated in 1820, its name coming from a poem written by a thirteenth-century poet, Ossian, titled "The Song of Selma."

It wasn't long before King's vision became reality, and the city became a thriving river port shipping cotton and later a major manufacturer of war materials for the Confederate army and navy during the Civil War. The Confederate ironclad CSS *Tennessee*, which fought in the Battle of Mobile Bay, was built and launched here. A cannon, the Brooke Rifle, the only surviving one from the battle, can be seen on this walk.

Bloody Sunday

The quiet town of Selma, Alabama, would find its place in history beginning March 7, 1965. Over the next three weeks an event occurred that historians call the political and emotional peak of the civil rights movement in the 1960s—the Selma to Montgomery March.

Selma, like many small Southern towns at the time, was resistant to Black voting. In January and February 1965, Martin Luther King Jr. and the Southern Christian Leadership Conference (SLCC) led a series of peaceful marches for voting rights to the Dallas County courthouse. One of those demonstrating, Jimmy Lee Jackson, was fatally shot by a state trooper during the march.

Angered, the demonstrators planned another march, this time to the state capital in Montgomery. On March 7, 600 demonstrators lined up and began the 80-mile trek, but no sooner had they cleared the eastern end of the Edmund Pettus Bridge, they were greeted by state troopers and local police. When the demonstrators refused to turn around, the police opened fire with tear gas and billy clubs. More than fifty people were hospitalized.

The one difference of this march from others like it was that this one was televised, not only in the United States but also around the world. King was put in a difficult situation. The federal government asked him to put a hold on another march until a court ruling about the protest was handed down, guaranteeing the marchers federal protection. Supporters demanded immediate action.

King relented to his followers and put out a call for demonstrators to flock to Selma to restart the march, which they did, but on March 9 the protestors were again turned back.

Finally, on March 21, with federal protection, the marchers made it to Montgomery, and in four months the federal Voting Rights Act was signed into law.

A view of the famous Edmund Pettus Bridge from a bluff above the Alabama River. It was here that the brutality against those fighting for civil rights during the 1960s was seen around the world thanks to television.

It was here in Selma that the Civil War's Battle of Selma occurred, which turned out to be the last engagement led by Confederate general Nathan Bedford Forest.

Along the first section of this walk, you will pass some beautiful churches over one hundred years old. Step inside and take a look at the architecture. There is the First Baptist Church that was organized in 1842 but located to this spot in 1900. Nearby is the First Presbyterian Church, which dates back to 1893. During the Civil War the church's pastor, Reverend Richard Small, was killed. Legend has it that the Lady Banksia rosebush outside the church lost all its petals when the reverend's body was returned here.

Making your way down Selma Avenue, you will pass the Selma Walton Theater. Originally a theater for movies and vaudeville, this 1914 building became the home of the Selma Performing Arts Center and, according to the tile inlay in front of the building on the sidewalk, is now once again the Selma Walton Theater.

Soon you will be at the iconic location that everyone knows the city for, the arched steel bridge called the Edmund Pettus Bridge. In 1965 there was nothing special about the bridge, but that all changed with terrifying swiftness in an event that brought Selma and race relations in the country to the forefront. On March 7, 1965, marchers organized in downtown Selma and planned to march to the state's capital in Montgomery. As they crossed the bridge, they were met by state troopers and local law enforcement armed with billy clubs and tear gas, driving the marchers back across the river. The entire event was televised around the country and outraged the nation. Eventually their efforts would lead to the signing of the Civil Rights Act, which outlawed discrimination of any kind and guaranteed equal rights in voting, employment, and education.

As you wrap up the walk, you will see the Bridge Tender's House, where the families who used to run the Selma turn bridge (before the Pettus Bridge) lived and worked, and the St. James Hotel, the only remaining riverfront antebellum hotel in the Southeast. The hotel was built by Dr. James Dee. When Dee had to leave for the Civil War, he placed his former slave, Benjamin Sterling Turner, in charge of operations.

And that's only a small bit of the historic buildings and locations you will pass in this 1.8-mile loop. Now let's go take a walk.

Miles and Directions

0.0 Start at the corner of Selma Avenue and Broad Street (US 80) in front of the Selma-Dallas County Public Library. Head north on Broad Street on the brick sidewalk. In less than 0.1 mile, pass the Brooke Rifle on the right.

0.1 Just pass the Brook Rifle, on the corner of Broad and Dallas Avenue to your right, is the William Rufus DeVane King home, which is now city hall. Turn left (southwest) onto Dallas Avenue. Across the street to your right is the First Presbyterian Church, which was built in 1893. Head straight to the southwest on Dallas Avenue.

0.2 At the corner of Dallas and Lauderdale Street on the left is First Baptist Church, which was built in 1900. Cross Lauderdale and continue straight on Dallas Avenue. In less than 0.1 mile, at the corner of Church Street and Dallas Avenue, the Church Street United Methodist Church is on your left. Turn left (southeast) onto Church Street.

0.3 Turn left (northeast) onto Selma Avenue.

0.4 Cross Lauderdale Street and arrive at St. Paul's Episcopal Church. Turn right and cross Selma Avenue to the southeast, and on the opposite side arrive at the Selma Walton Theater. Continue straight to the southeast on Lauderdale.

0.5 Turn right onto Alabama Avenue. As you walk the street, the Dallas County courthouse is on the right, the federal building on the left.

0.6 Cross Church Street and on the other side turn left and follow Church Street to the southeast. Just before the road makes a sharp bend and turns into Water Avenue you arrive at the Arsenal Place Pillars. Continuing only a few yards on Church Street, you arrive at the old Carneal Auto Building, which is now the home of performing arts in the city. From here walk around the bend. Church Street now becomes Water Avenue. There are several views of the Alabama River to your right along this stretch.

0.7 Pass the monument to Bienville.

0.8 As you near Broad Street/US 80, pass the Harmony Club on the left and the home of the *Selma Times-Journal* on the right. In just a few yards arrive at Broad Street/US 80. Turn right (southeast) and follow Broad Street/US 80, crossing the Edmund Pettus Bridge on the sidewalk.

1.1 Arrive at the National Voting Rights Museum and Institute on the right. After visiting the museum, there is a memorial park across the highway you may want to visit, but this is a dangerous and busy road to cross. I don't recommend crossing here. I'll talk more about this in a moment, but right now turn around and head back to Water Avenue.

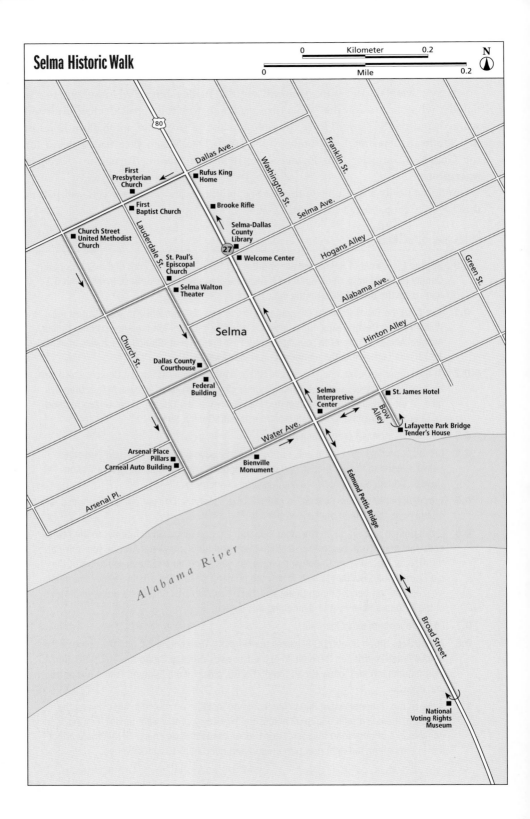

Selma Historic Walk

0 — Kilometer — 0.2

0 — Mile — 0.2

N

First Presbyterian Church

Dallas Ave.

Rufus King Home

Washington St.

Franklin St.

Selma Ave.

First Baptist Church

Brooke Rifle

Church Street United Methodist Church

Lauderdale St.

Selma-Dallas County Library

27

Hogans Alley

Green St.

St. Paul's Episcopal Church

Welcome Center

Selma Walton Theater

Alabama Ave.

Selma

Hinton Alley

Church St.

Dallas County Courthouse

Federal Building

Selma Interpretive Center

St. James Hotel

Bow Alley

Lafayette Park Bridge Tender's House

Water Ave.

Arsenal Place Pillars

Carneal Auto Building

Bienville Monument

Edmund Pettis Bridge

Arsenal Pl.

Alabama River

Broad Street

National Voting Rights Museum

1.4 Back at Water Avenue turn right and cross Broad Street/US 80. On the other side arrive at the Songs of Selma Park. Walk down to the viewing area on a high bluff above the Alabama River for an excellent view, then turn around and head back to Water Avenue. (***Option:*** If you want to view the memorial park on the opposite side of the river, turn right here and cross the Edmund Pettus Bridge once again, this time on the opposite (east) side. Once over the bridge the park is on your left. This adds an additional 0.6 mile to the walk.)

1.5 Back on Water Avenue turn right and head northeast on the road. In less than 0.1 mile, turn right down Bow Alley to view the Lafayette Park Bridge Tender's House where the people who manned the old Selma turn bridge used to live and work. You'll have another view of the river and bridge. Return to Water Avenue.

1.6 Back on Water Avenue you are now at the St. James Hotel, the only existing riverfront antebellum hotel remaining in the Southeast. After visiting the hotel, cross Water Avenue to the north, then turn left and head down the opposite side of the street to the southwest.

1.7 Arrive at the Selma Interpretive Center on the corner of Broad Street/US 80 and Water Avenue. When done visiting, turn right onto Broad Street/US 80 and head northwest.

1.8 The Selma Welcome Center, complete with souvenirs, is on your right at the corner of Broad Street and Selma Avenue. Cross Selma Avenue and arrive back at the beginning of the walk.

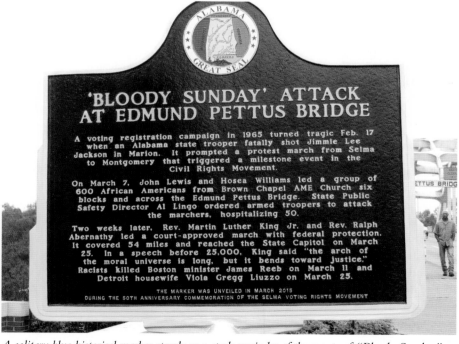

A solitary blue historical marker stands as a stark reminder of the events of "Bloody Sunday," when marchers heading to Montgomery to protest for their civil rights were met with the full force of local and state police.

28 Old Cahawba Archaeological Park

Walk the long since abandoned streets of the once-thriving antebellum town of Cahawba at Old Cahawba Archaeological Park. Stroll down the dusty dirt roads of the first Alabama state capital and visit remains of the Crocheron plantation, the New Cemetery and Negro Burial Grounds, the Civil War prison known as Castle Morgan, and the old one-room schoolhouse and Methodist Church.

Start: From the park's visitor center
Distance: 4.9-mile multi-loop
Hiking time: 2.5 to 3 hours
Difficulty: Moderate due to length
Trail surface: Clay and gravel road, a little asphalt
Best seasons: Year-round
Other trail users: Cyclists, motorists, equestrians
Canine compatibility: Leashed dogs permitted
Land status: Alabama Historic Commission property

Nearest town: Selma
Fees and permits: Day-use fee
Schedule: Year-round, daily 9 a.m. to 5 p.m.; visitor center daily noon to 5 p.m.; closed Thanksgiving, Christmas, and New Year's Day
Maps: USGS Blackwell Bend, AL; *DeLorme: Alabama Atlas & Gazetteer*, page 43, E9
Trail contact: Old Cahawba Archaeological Park, 9518 Cahaba Rd., Orville 36767; (334) 872-8058; www.preserveala.org/oldcahawba.aspx

Finding the trailhead: From the intersection of US 80 and AL 22 in Selma, take AL 22 west 1.5 miles and turn right to continue on AL 22. Travel 8.5 miles and turn left onto CR 9. Travel 3.4 miles and turn left onto Cahaba Road. The visitor center is on the right. GPS: N32 19.180' / W87 06.274'

The Hike

A major cotton distribution center, a Confederate prison camp for Union soldiers, and the first capital of Alabama—Old Cahawba has seen it all, and this ramble along the dusty dirt roads of the Old Cahawba Archaeological Park will give you a sense of what life was like here in the early 1800s.

Six years after the Creek Indian War of 1813, Alabama became a state and, of course, they needed a state capital. As the newly formed state legislature met in Huntsville, the "permanent" location for the new capital at the confluence of two of the state's largest rivers, the Alabama and the Cahaba, was being surveyed and constructed.

The location seemed like a good idea. The two rivers were thriving steamboat routes hauling cotton from the Black Belt of Alabama to the Gulf of Mexico down to Mobile for exporting. The problem was that the rivers were prone to dangerous and damaging flooding, not to mention it had a serious mosquito problem, and by 1826, after outbreaks of yellow fever, it was decided to move the capital to Tuscaloosa and then eventually to Montgomery.

The old one-room schoolhouse still stands along one of the backstreets of Old Cahawba.

It's easy to be confused between Old Cahawba and Old St. Stephens. At first glance it looks like both are claiming to be the first capital of Alabama, but there is quite a big distinction. Old St. Stephens was the first territorial capital of Alabama, long before the region became a state (hence their motto, "Where Alabama Began"). Old Cahawba was the first *state* capital.

Despite the relocation of the capital, the area remained the county seat and continued as a vibrant shipping town high atop the river's bluff, with cotton being king. With the addition of a railroad line, the population increased to 3,000 by 1859.

The economic boom in the tiny city was cut off, literally, during the Civil War when the Union navy blockaded the ports along the Gulf of Mexico, effectively stopping any overseas cotton trade. In fact, in 1863 a major cotton warehouse was converted to a POW camp to hold Union soldiers.

Called the Cahaba Military Prison, the camp was designed to house 660 men, but by 1865 there were 3,000. As you can imagine, conditions were deplorable, with polluted water and only one fireplace to warm the men during frosty winters. That fireplace still stands today, and you will see it along this hike.

The prison became known as "Castle Morgan" by locals who renamed it in honor of Confederate general John Morgan. The camp had a tragic ending when in 1865, with an estimated 2,300 passengers aboard, 1,700 of those Union veterans just released from the camp died aboard the paddle wheeler *Sultana*. The boat was carrying six times the number of passengers that it could safely handle. The ship's boilers exploded from the load and the swift river currents.

By the end of 1865, after a massive flood, the city finally died, the population moved on, and it was reclaimed by nature—that is, until 1973 when the site was purchased and opened as an active archaeological park by the Alabama Historic Commission.

Today a stroll through the park takes you to the glorious but short past of what is now known as the South's most famous ghost town. Some of the highlights include a visit to two cemeteries, the New Cemetery and the Negro Burial Grounds. The latter was started around 1819 as a slave cemetery but was used until the final burial in 1959. Contrasting this unassuming cemetery is the New Cemetery, which features ornate tombstones of the day.

You will also pass the remains of the Crocheron Mansion. In 1865 following the Battle of Selma, Confederate general Forrest and Union general Wilson met here for a few hours to discuss exchanging prisoners. The two shared cigars, drinks, and conversation before heading back to war. The circular brick columns are all that remains of the mansion. Bricks from the rest of the mansion were pilfered by locals. The only reason the columns still stand is because of their unique design, which made the bricks useless to scavengers.

There is way too much history to include here. Be sure to stop by the visitor center, where the extremely friendly staff will tell you more about the history and give you *many* brochures so you can learn more.

While you can easily drive the dirt roads of Old Cahawba, I prefer to walk them, and that's why I included it in *Hiking through History Alabama*. You get a sense of what life might have been like back in 1819 as you walk a side road and visit the old one-room schoolhouse and the old Methodist Church.

Miles and Directions

0.0 Start at the visitor center parking lot. Head southeast on Capitol Street. The route is a paved road.

0.3 Turn right (south) onto the dirt Oak Street. A sign here points the way to the New Cemetery.

0.9 Arrive at the New Cemetery. Take your time to explore the tombstones and pay your respects to those buried here from back in the early to late 1800s. When done exploring, turn around and retrace your steps up Oak Street to the north.

1.3 Turn right onto the dirt Sixth Street South.

1.5 Arrive at the Perine Mansion Well, constructed in 1857. Turn around and retrace your steps to Oak Street.

1.7 Turn right and head north on Oak Street.

2.1 Turn right onto the dirt Second Street South. The road loops around and in less than 0.1 mile, arrive at the remains of the one-room schoolhouse and the foundation of the old Methodist Church. Follow the road north and back to Oak Street.

2.3 Turn right (north) onto Oak Street.

2.4 Turn right (southeast) onto the paved Capitol Street.

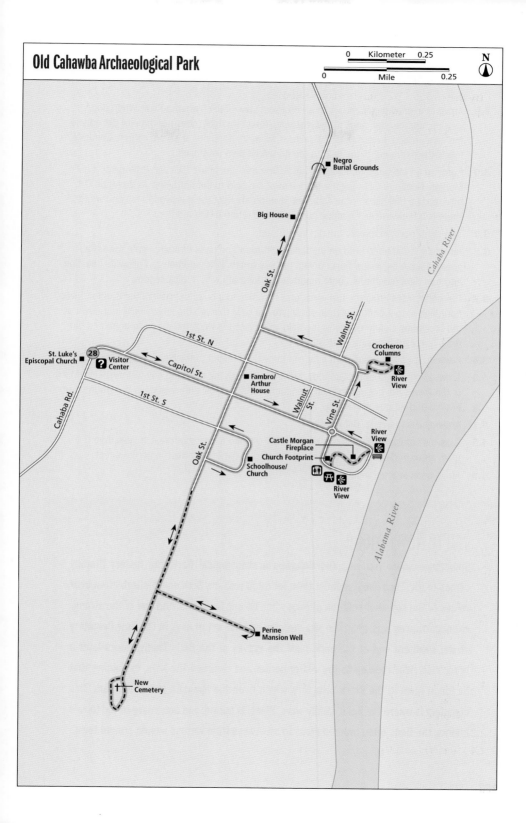

Old Cahawba Archaeological Park

0 Kilometer 0.25
0 Mile 0.25

N

Negro
Burial Grounds

Big House

Oak St.

Walnut St.

Crocheron
Columns

River
View

St. Luke's
Episcopal Church

Visitor
Center

1st St. N

Capitol St.

28

Cahaba Rd.

1st St. S

Fambro/
Arthur
House

Walnut
St.

Vine St.

River
View

Castle Morgan
Fireplace

Church Footprint

Schoolhouse/
Church

Oak St.

River
View

Perine
Mansion Well

New
Cemetery

Cahaba River

Alabama River

2.7   A dirt road veers off to the right (south). Follow the dirt road to the south and east and arrive at a restroom. The former site of the Civil War prison camp, Castle Morgan, is on the left.

2.8   Arrive at a small picnic area with an excellent view of the Alabama River. When done viewing, retrace your steps to the restroom, then turn right (north) and follow the edge of the field around. In less than 0.1 mile, arrive at the footprint of an old church. Continue to follow the perimeter of the field to the northeast then southeast.

3.0   Come to an old brick fireplace. This is all that remains of the Civil War POW camp Castle Morgan. Continue following the perimeter of the field to the northeast. In less than 0.1 mile, pass a nice view of the Alabama River on the right (best viewed in fall and winter). There is a bench here. Continue northwest and return to the road.

3.1   Turn right (northeast) onto the dirt Vine Street.

3.2   Turn right (southeast) onto an unmarked dirt road and pass through a gate toward a grassy field. A big yellow finger points the way to the right (southeast). Follow its direction and turn right (southeast) onto a narrow dirt footpath with a thick canopy.

3.3   The path circles around a few yards until it comes to a beautiful view of the Cahaba River from high atop a bluff. Continue circling to the west through the grassy field and arrive at the Crocheron Columns. Follow the field straight to the west and return to unnamed dirt road. Turn right here onto Vine Street.

3.6   Come to a T intersection. Turn right (northeast) and head to the Negro Burial Grounds.

4.0   Arrive at the Negro Burial Grounds. Meander through the field and pay your respects. Many of the graves are not marked but are identified by shallow depressions in the ground. Turn around and retrace your steps.

4.1   Arrive at the majestic "Big House."

4.5   Pass the Fambro/Arthur house on the left. Continue to the southwest. In less than 0.1 mile, arrive back at the paved Capitol Street. Turn right (northwest) onto the street.

4.9   Arrive back at the trailhead.

You're Never Alone

Sometimes when you visit Old Cahawba Archaeological Park, the history literally comes to life. They call it a ghost town for more reasons than one. Visitors often hear voices or the sound of children playing when no one is around. And one of the strangest occurrences was when the site director lost her set of keys in the New Cemetery at the southern end of the park, near the graves of the Bells family. Hours later a horseback rider rode up to the visitor center and returned the keys, explaining that he found them in the Black cemetery, which is on the opposite end of the park. This cemetery is where the Bells' family slave, Pleas, is buried, and according to the town's history, the Bells often ordered Pleas to steal keys from various people around town.

29 Nancy's Mountain

It is a story as old as time itself. The story of lost love never found. That is the story of Nancy, but does her ghost still walk this trail heading to the banks of the Alabama River, waiting for her son and husband to return from the war? Walk the Nancy's Mountain Trail early in the morning with a light fog and mist and see what you think. Wait! Over there—is that Nancy?

Start: From the trailhead at the south end of the parking lot
Distance: 2.0 miles out and back with loop
Hiking time: 1 to 1.5 hours
Difficulty: Easy to moderate
Trail surface: Dirt footpath
Best seasons: Fall–spring
Other trail users: None
Canine compatibility: Leashed dogs permitted
Land status: US Army Corps of Engineers
Nearest town: Franklin
Fees and permits: None
Schedule: Year-round, daily sunrise to sunset

Maps: USGS Franklin, AL; *DeLorme: Alabama Atlas & Gazetteer,* page 50, E1
Trail contact: US Army Corps of Engineers Mobile District, PO Box 2288, Mobile 36628; (251) 690-2505; www.sam.usace.army.mil/Missions/CivilWorks/Recreation/AlabamaRiverLakes.aspx
Special considerations: Hunting is allowed in fall and winter. Visit www.sam.usace.army.mil/Missions/CivilWorks/Recreation/AlabamaRiverLakes/Hunting/WildlifeUseBrochure.aspx for seasons.

Finding the trailhead: From the intersection of US 43 and US 84 in Grove Hill, take US 84 east 20 miles. Turn left onto Lena Landegger Highway. Travel 8.4 miles and turn left onto AL 41 North. Drive 9.3 miles and turn left onto CR 17. Travel 2.9 miles and turn right onto an unnamed dirt road (a brown USACE sign shows you where to turn). Follow the road 1.5 miles to the parking lot near the Davis Ferry and the Alabama River. The trailhead is on the south side of the parking lot. GPS: N31 43.475' / W87 28.167'

The Hike

You may have heard this story before. Every town, city, and village across the country has something similar. It's a story as old as history itself, the story of lost love and a never-ending search.

This hike at the US Army Corps of Engineers' Haines Island Park is, on its own, a beautiful walk in the woods. The path is lined with Christmas ferns and American beech, water oak, and yellow poplar trees. Snowy white dogwoods flower here in the spring. In the fall the hardwoods flame brightly with orange, red, and yellow color.

But there is a story here on this mountain. It's a story that's part history and part legend. It's the story of Nancy.

You may not believe in ghosts, but walking the Nancy's Mountain Trail on a foggy early morning may make you change your mind.

From all accounts Nancy was a strikingly beautiful woman. She was known to have dressed in white gowns of the antebellum period. Nancy, her husband, and son lived on the top of this double-humped mountain on a bend in the Alabama River.

It was sometime during the Civil War that Nancy's son decided to enlist in the Confederate army to fight for the Southern cause. As was the case in many families both North and South, it wasn't long before word came that her boy had died in battle but a body was never found.

In shock and disbelief Nancy walked day after day down the mountain to the river where there was a steamboat landing. She carried a pail of fresh water for her son to drink in case he would someday return on one of the boats.

Overwhelmed by his wife's grief, as well as his own, Nancy's husband took matters into his own hands and made it his mission to locate his son either dead or alive.

No one knows how long her husband was gone, but eventually word arrived at Nancy's doorstep that her husband had been found dead, frozen to death near the grave of an unknown soldier near Lookout Mountain, Tennessee.

Soon after, Nancy disappeared from the mountain and was never seen again. No one knows where she went. Her house fell into ruin and was reclaimed by nature. But not long after her disappearance, locals began reporting seeing a woman walking the mountain in the dark. Her beauty was indescribable, her dress a white antebellum gown of the period. In her hand she carried a lantern as she glided silently to the riverbank where the old steamboat landing was, and where the current Davis Ferry paddles back and forth.

To this day many people say they have seen this ghostly figure, and all agree it must be Nancy awaiting the return of her husband and son. Rangers with the Corps of Engineers will tell you stories about people camping on the mountain only to be found running down the hillside, white as ghosts, claiming to have seen her.

Arrive early in the morning just as the sun is rising, a light mist rolling in off the river, and see what you think. Walking the trail, as I did in these conditions, will make you wonder. You might find yourself looking around; goosebumps might rise on your arms. Is it because you have just heard the story, or is Nancy really there? I will tell you this: My black Labrador Archer usually leads the way on my hikes. This is the only time he followed behind me and I had to make him walk the trail. Spooky!

Whoa, shake it off, and let me tell you just a little bit about the trail itself. The path you will be taking up the mountain is actually two trails, the Big Leaf Magnolia and the Ironwood Trail. The trail starts with a short walk up the Big Leaf Magnolia Trail before branching off to the Ironwood. It's a little odd, but when you get to the opposite end of the Ironwood, you will see a sign along a dirt road that reads Nancy Mountain, but when you started it was the Ironwood.

The trail is intermittently blazed with stainless steel diamond markers and is a fairly well-maintained dirt footpath. After reaching the opposite and of the Ironwood, retrace your steps and finish walking the Big Leaf Magnolia Trail. This is also a narrow dirt footpath but a little more overgrown than the Ironwood, and many of the interpretive signs are no longer visible. There are his-and-her composting toilets near the intersection of the two trails and one at the trailhead.

The Cable Ferries of Alabama

The Alabama River is dotted with many small towns. Bridges crossing the river in these parts are few and far between, but at Haines Island, where Nancy Mountain is located, there is a unique mode of transportation across the river—a cable ferry.

The ferry began operations in the 1970s and rides across the river attached to a cable suspended high above. A six-cylinder Chevrolet motor powers a paddle wheel that moves the one-vehicle boat across. Small cars up to even large dump trucks use this ferry daily, and you can see it at the landing on the north side of the Nancy's Mountain Trail parking lot.

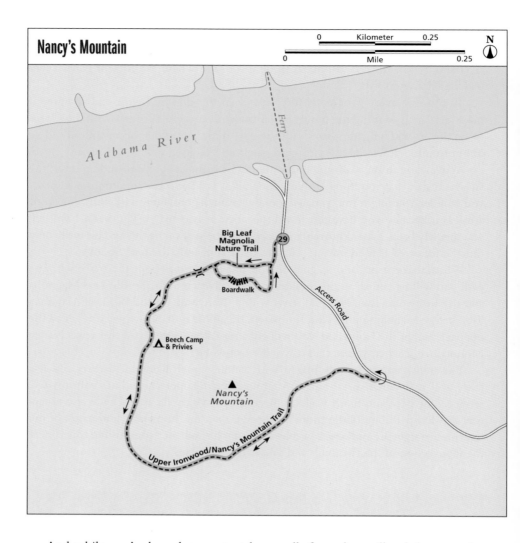

And while you're here, be sure to take a walk from the trailhead down to the riverbank to watch the old Davis Ferry in action as it shuttles vehicles, one at a time, back and forth across the Alabama River. As you watch the ferry, you may want to look behind you. You never know who might be there—maybe Nancy!

Miles and Directions

0.0 Start from the trailhead at the south end of the parking lot. A short 10-foot-long footbridge crosses a ditch here; on the other side look for a sign pointing to the right for the Lower Ironwood Trail and to the left for the Magnolia Trail and Upper Ironwood Trail. Turn left. The trail is a wide, root-strewn dirt footpath with a thick canopy. (**Note:** There is a nice elevated privy here to the right of the footbridge.) In less than 0.1 mile, pass a working hand water pump on the left and a large Big Leaf Magnolia Nature Trail sign on the right with a map of the short loop trail etched into it. In less than 0.1 mile, come to a Y intersection. A wooden 4x4 post with a painted green leaf is in the middle of the fork. Take the right fork to the west and continue on the Big Leaf Magnolia Trail. The trail narrows to a 2- to 4-foot-wide path and is littered with magnolia leaves.

0.1 Come to a Y. A sign in the fork points to the left and the Big Leaf Magnolia Trail and to the right to the Upper Ironwood Trail and Beech Camp. Take the right fork to the southwest onto the Upper Ironwood Trail. The trail is intermittently blazed with stainless steel diamond-shaped markers nailed to trees.

0.2 Cross a short 10-foot bridge over a runoff.

0.3 The trail narrows to about a foot wide in places as it winds around the side of the hill. In less than 0.1 mile, pass a set of men's and women's privies on the left. There is a Y in the trail here. The right fork takes you to a primitive camping area. Take the left fork to the south. The path widens out to a good 10 feet and is more of a grassy old service road.

0.8 The trail narrows again and is lined with young bamboo.

0.9 Come to a dirt road and a sign that reads Nancy's Mountain Trail. This is your turnaround. Did you see Nancy? Retrace your steps to mile 0.1.

1.7 Back at the Y at mile 0.1, take the right fork to the south to continue on the Big Leaf Magnolia Trail. Just after the Y cross a 20-foot-long bridge over a runoff. The path is less maintained, so you will probably have to navigate blowdowns. The sides of the trail are shored up with railroad ties to prevent erosion.

1.9 Cross a 60-foot-long boardwalk that, as of this writing, was a bit rickety, so mind your step.

2.0 Arrive back at the trailhead.

30 Old St. Stephens Loop

Journey back in time to the first territorial capital of Alabama along the Old St. Stephens Loop. The trail winds through an active archaeological site where students and professors from state universities continue to uncover the past of this once-thriving river city. Along the route you will visit old town wells, walk the rediscovered streets, and visit the Globe Hotel dig where archaeologists are working to bring the past back to life.

Start: Trailhead adjacent to the parking lot
Distance: 1.9-mile multi-loop
Hiking time: About 2 hours
Difficulty: Easy to moderate due to some hills
Trail surface: Dirt footpath and road
Best seasons: Late Feb to May and Sept to Nov
Other trail users: Equestrians
Canine compatibility: Leashed dogs permitted

Land status: City historic park
Nearest town: St. Stephens
Fees and permits: Day-use fee
Schedule: Year-round, daily 7 a.m. to 3 p.m.
Maps: USGS Saint Stephens, AL; *DeLorme: Alabama Atlas & Gazetteer*, page 48, H5
Trail contact: Old St. Stephens Historical Commission, PO Box 78, St. Stephens 36569; (251) 246-6790

Finding the trailhead: From Jackson and the intersection of AL 69 and US 43, take US 43 south 8.4 miles. Turn right onto Mobile Cutoff Road and travel 1.9 miles. Turn right onto Gib Bailey Road/Cement Plant Road. Travel 0.8 mile and come to a fork in the road. Take the right fork onto an unnamed street (Cement Plant Road continues on the left fork). The park entrance gate is ahead on the right in 0.2 mile. After paying the attendant, continue another 1 mile to the parking lot and trailhead. The trail begins at the information shelter, which has details about the park and its history. GPS: N31 33.315' / W88 02.220'

The Hike

You will notice that many of the historical hiking trails of Alabama lead down paths through forests where something of significance happened, but there is nothing tangible that you can see to get a true feeling of what occurred there. That's not the case at Old St. Stephens Historical Park, a vibrant and active archaeological site where scholars and universities come each year to uncover the history of the first territorial capital of Alabama.

As with most settlements the history of Old St. Stephens revolves around a river, in this case the Tombigbee River. In 1789 the Spanish governor of Mobile, Juan Vincente Folk, realized that the sharp bend at this location would be a perfect spot for commerce along the river. Immediately after the bend is a set of shallows that larger ships couldn't navigate. Folk built a fort high atop the limestone bluffs that overlook the river, and as he predicted, ships would sail up from Mobile to this bend and dock, and passengers and cargo would disembark to ride by stagecoach or wagon to other parts of the developing region.

Archaeologists work to bring the history of the once bustling Globe Hotel to life.

In 1799 Spain and the United States signed the Treaty of San Lorenzo, which transferred this land to the fledgling nation; it became part of the Mississippi Territory, and the town began growing exponentially, with the population increasing from 190 to 7,000.

In 1804 the superior court judge for the Mississippi Territory, Ephraim Kirby, wrote a letter to President Thomas Jefferson describing the people of St. Stephens as "illiterate, wild and savage, of depraved morals, unworthy of public confidence or private esteems, litigious, disunited, and knowing each other, universally distrustful of each other."

Despite that blistering review St. Stephens was a bustling town, and at the height of its success it sported high-class boardinghouses, hotels, theaters, and the state's first chartered school, Washington Academy. When the Alabama Territory was established in 1817, St. Stephens became the first territorial capital, thus giving the park its motto, "Where Alabama began."

Success was short lived, however, for soon the territory became a state and the state capital was established in Cahawba, and with that move so went the population, which relocated a few miles away to New St. Stephens.

The town gradually fell into ruin and was reclaimed by nature—that is, until the Alabama Historic Commission and archaeology departments from state universities rediscovered this grand old Alabama city. Today you can walk the actual streets of this long-forgotten town to get a glimpse of its historic past.

The beautiful placid waters of the old limestone quarry at Old St. Stephens

The trail begins by weaving its way through dogwood and redbud trees along the ancient streets. Signs along the way tell the story of what life was like in the town during its heyday. Each city block is marked off, showing you the layout of the town with the actual street names at corners, such as High Street and Chambers Street. Many individual properties are marked with their original house numbers.

One of the highlights of this hike is the site where archaeologists are unearthing the grand Globe Hotel. The Globe was once the main stopping point and lodging for travelers and businessmen throughout the region. Built in 1816 the hotel was a large stone structure with a detached kitchen, stables, its own well, and slave quarters. Today when you visit the site, you can see the ongoing archaeological work. And if you visit the Archaeological Institute of America's website, www.archaeological.org, do a search on Old St. Stephens to find out when the next digs will be taking place. It's fascinating to talk with the researchers about the town's history.

The trail itself isn't marked with the exception of the street signs on corners. It's basically a ramble, and while I have given you a general route to follow, feel free to explore the many dirt roads that wind through the park. By the way, camping is available here above and below the quarry, and swimming is allowed in the quarry at the designated swimming area.

Miles and Directions

0.0 Start at the trailhead a few yards to the southeast of the parking lot. The trail begins to the right of a small building that houses informative panels describing the town's history and the site's archaeology. In a few short yards, come to a Y intersection. The right fork is the return route; take the left fork (east) and a few yards later cross a short bridge over a creek. Another short walk takes you to a sign that reads "You are now crossing Chambers Street" and describes where you are, but the rest of the sign is hard to read. Follow the path up the hill to a dirt road and turn right (east) onto the road. To the left is the archaeological building.

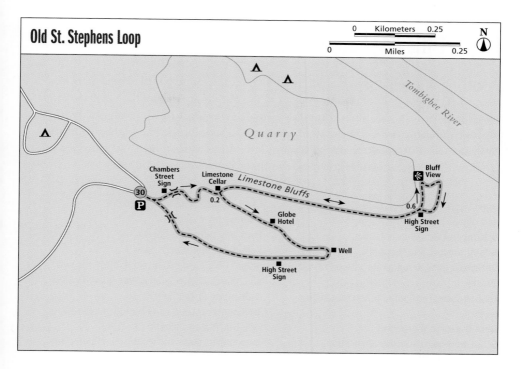

0.2 Pass the remnants of a limestone cellar labeled 142 High Street and a marble marker. Just past this the trail comes to a Y (a sign reading High Street is in the center of the Y). Take the left fork (northeast). Along this wide dirt road section, you are walking atop the limestone bluffs of a quarry with beautiful blue water. (**Note:** You can walk out to the bluff's edge on several short side trails, but be warned, they are high and dangerous!)

0.6 Come to a Y. Take the left fork (north). The trail narrows and has a nice enclosed feel.

0.7 Just after passing a wide path to the right, continue straight (north) a few yards to get a look at the beautiful limestone bluffs behind you. Turn around and head back to the wide path you just passed, turn left (east), and follow the dirt road. In less than 0.1 mile, the trail comes to a Y. Take the left fork down into a gully and back up the other side to the dirt road at the top of the hill. Turn right (south) onto the dirt road.

0.8 Return to the Y from mile 0.2 (the High Street Y). Take the left fork and head west on the wide dirt road. To your right along this section, 4x4 white posts mark the property lines of houses that once stood here; some have signs marking the address. There are also signs with articles from newspapers of the day (late 1800s).

1.3 Come to the archaeological dig of the Globe Hotel.

1.4 Pass a well house on the right. Circle around the well to the south and pick up the dirt road on the other side. Turn right here onto the dirt road to the southeast.

1.6 Come to a sign that reads 132 High Street and a narrow 2- to 3-foot-wide dirt footpath coming in from the left. Turn left (west) onto the footpath.

1.7 A trail comes in from the left. Keep heading straight (west).

1.8 Come to a creek crossing. There are two bridges here; use the smaller one on the left.

1.9 Arrive back at the trailhead.

31 Little River State Forest

A little out-of-the-way gem that locals flock to in the summer, Little River Forest is a lasting reminder of the amazing work that the young men of the Civilian Conservation Corps (CCC) did during the Great Depression to help create the world's greatest infrastructure and beautiful outdoor recreation areas. The highlights of this hike include walking along the glistening Little River Lake, which was dammed by hand by the CCC, and an original gazebo that still stands atop a hillside.

Start: From the parking lot at the bathhouse and office
Distance: 4.8-mile double loop
Hiking time: 2.5 to 3 hours
Difficulty: Easy to moderate with one good incline
Trail surface: Dirt footpath and road, some asphalt
Best seasons: Year-round
Other trail users: Cyclists, equestrians
Canine compatibility: Leashed dogs permitted

Land status: State forest property
Nearest town: Atmore
Fees and permits: Day-use fee
Schedule: Year-round, daily 9 a.m. to 5 p.m.
Maps: USGS Uriah East, Uriah West, Huxford, and McCullough, AL; *DeLorme: Alabama Atlas & Gazetteer*, page 57, D6
Trail contact: Little River State Forest, 580 H. Kyle Rd., Atmore 36502; (251) 862-2511; www.forestry.state.al.us/little_river_state_ forest.aspx?bv=6&s=2

Finding the trailhead: From the intersection of I-65 at exit 57 and AL 21, take AL 21 north 11 miles. Turn right onto H. Kyle Road and travel 0.4 mile to the pay station. Travel 0.2 mile to the park office; park here at the office. This is the start of the trail. GPS: N31 15.436' / W87 29.129'

The Hike

Hidden away just north of the town of Atmore on AL 21 is this little gem, Little River State Forest. Like many of the state parks and forests in the state, Little River was a creation of the Civilian Conservation Corps during the Great Depression. This double loop will take you to two highlights of their work here, Little River Lake and an original, and impressive, gazebo.

The country was in the grips of the Great Depression. Millions of people, approximately 25 percent of the country, were broke, homeless, and desperate. In 1932 newly elected President Franklin Roosevelt proposed a plan to help the masses get back on their feet with good, honest work and in turn get the economy moving again. It was known as the New Deal. Out of the myriad New Deal initiatives he proposed came the CCC, a program designed to help preserve and protect our natural resources while at the same time provide meaningful work for men ages 18 to 23 (later 17 to 28). On March 31, 1933, the bill was passed into law, and in less than forty days the first enrollee was employed.

Still standing after all these years, the gazebo built by the CCC in 1935 continues its vigil atop a hillside.

When people visit a park that was built by the CCC, they expect to see massive stone fire towers or dining halls. Here at Little River State Forest it is the small but equally impressive work that stands out.

The south loop of this double-loop hike is along the Bell/CCC Trail, which is actually two trails. The Bell Trail was named for a former park ranger, Paul Bell, who built the trail. The CCC Trail is the actual road the workers used to move men and materials into the forest to build the park.

The centerpiece of the park is the 2,100-acre Little River Lake (also known as Blacksher Lake), a creation of the CCC. As you leave the trailhead on the Bell/CCC Trail, you will immediately cross a spillway that looks virtually the same as it did in 1935 when the park was first opened. From here you will cross the hand-built earthen dam that created the lake. This was a monumental, backbreaking task, as each layer of dirt was shoveled in by hand. You can see a film of the workers actually building the dam and cabins in a film called *Down Mobile Way 1935*, which can be viewed online at www.youtube.com/watch?v=N23Vpy6VTmw. (The segment about this forest comes at about the 10-minute mark.)

The Bell Trail follows the banks of the shimmering lake, which is a joy to swim in during the hot summer months and a great place to wet a line for a little fishing. The trail eventually moves away from the lake and after a moderately steep climb reaches its connection with the CCC Trail. Be sure to turn around here to get a view of the surrounding hillsides. It's a beautiful and unexpected sight.

As you walk down the wide dirt and gravel CCC Trail, keep a lookout for CCC-built stone culverts that run beneath the road to divert rainwater underneath.

The second loop of this trip is the Gazebo Trail, which takes you to the trail's namesake. This trail is my personal favorite in the park, especially in the spring when white flowering dogwoods are blooming. The path was originally built by the CCC when the park opened. I am also a bit partial to this trail because I worked on it too. In 2004 and 2005 a series of devastating hurricanes hit the Gulf Coast. The park's infrastructure was in ruins and the trails were all but obliterated. I joined volunteers with the Alabama Hiking Trail Society, and we completely rebuilt the trail on its original track.

The trail is named for a wooden gazebo that stands proudly atop a hillside on the trail's eastern end. Step inside the gazebo and look up to see the tightly connected hand-cut framework of the roof. This structure is a testament to the skill of the CCC workers, having withstood many major hurricanes and south Alabama's fierce summer storms.

The trail crosses a nice but seasonal stream over a wooden footbridge at mile 0.6. The bridge was being rebuilt as of this writing but will hopefully be back in operation by the time you read this. If not, you will have to do a little rock-hopping to get across.

Both of the trails are blazed with yellow paint blazes. The blazes use the dit-dot method of marking. What this means is that whenever the trail makes a sharp turn there will be two paint blazes one on top of the other. The top blaze is offset to the direction of the turn.

Miles and Directions

0.0 Start at the park office and bathhouse to hike the 2-mile Bell/CCC Trail first. Both trails are blazed with the yellow markings of the Alabama Trail. Head southwest along the banks of the lake toward the park's pay station and entrance.

0.1 The trail comes to a 50-foot-long footbridge that spans the lake's spillway. Cross the bridge heading to the south, then turn to the east and head back toward the lake. At the lake turn right and follow the dirt road atop the earthen dam.

0.3 Pass a T fishing pier that extends out into the lake on the left (east).

0.4 Come to a T intersection. To the right is the dirt road CCC Trail, which is your return route. Turn left (southeast) into the woods. The trail is now a dirt footpath.

0.5 Cross a short, 20-foot metal grate bridge over a small stream.

0.6 Come to a Y. Take the right fork to the southwest. (**Note:** The left fork is a side trail that takes you to a nice walk along the banks of the lake. It eventually meets back up with the main trail at mile 0.7.)

0.7 The side trail to the lake rejoins the main trail from the northeast. Continue about another 20 feet and come to a Y. Take the right fork to the southeast. (**Note:** The left fork is the forest's property line, which is marked with yellow-and-white rings around the trees and has

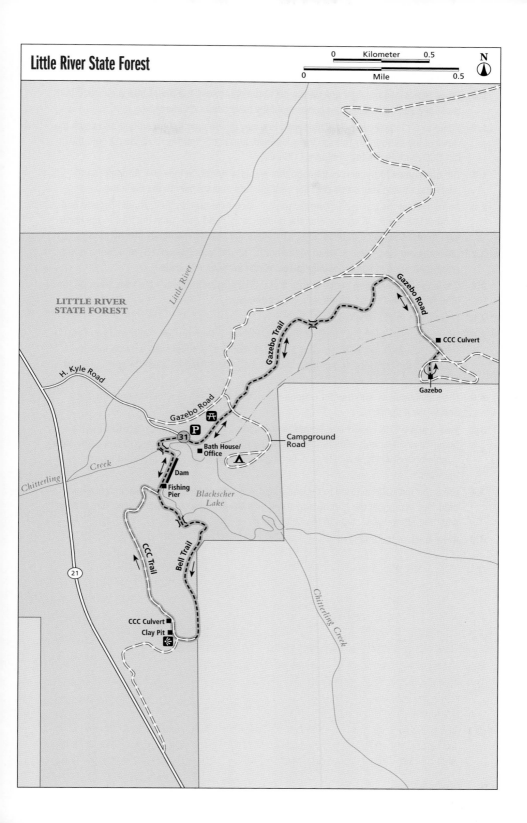

Little River State Forest

0   Kilometer   0.5

0   Mile   0.5

N

LITTLE RIVER
STATE FOREST

Little River

Gazebo Road

Gazebo Trail

CCC Culvert

Gazebo

H. Kyle Road

Gazebo Road

Campground
Road

Bath House/
Office

Chitterling   Creek

Dam

Fishing
Pier

Blackscher
Lake

Chitterling Creek

CCC Trail

Bell Trail

21

CCC Culvert

Clay Pit

a grass-covered service road along the perimeter.) Soon the trail begins a pretty decent climb up the hill to the intersection with the CCC Trail.

1.0 Come to a Y. Take the right fork up the hill to the southwest. The trail is now a dirt road that is usually well maintained but can sometimes have deep ruts after heavy rain.

1.1 Come to a T intersection. Straight ahead is a clay pit. Be sure to turn around and catch the views of the surrounding hills to the southeast. Turn right (northwest) at the pit onto the dirt CCC road. This is the unblazed CCC Trail.

1.7 The trail comes to the end of the loop that you first started at mile 0.4. Turn left (northeast) and retrace your steps over the earthen dam and spillway to the trailhead.

2.0 Arrive back at the trailhead. (*Option:* You can stop here and do the 2.8-mile Gazebo Trail another later time.) To continue on the double loop, head away from the lake to the northeast toward the picnic pavilion and picnic area. The trail here is neatly mowed grass.

2.2 Cross the dirt Campground Road to the north. The trail now follows a 3- to 4-foot dirt and grass path through some beautiful pines. Watch for deer in this area.

2.6 Come to a 78-foot-long bridge across a seasonal stream that feeds the lake. Once on the other side of the bridge, turn to the left (northeast).

2.8 Cross a dirt road to the east.

2.9 The trail merges with a dirt logging road that comes in from the left. Keep going straight (north), following the blazes. In about 100 feet come to a double yellow blaze indicating a turn. Turn left (north) and leave the dirt road, continuing on a narrow grass and dirt footpath.

3.0 The trail intersects with the dirt Gazebo Road. Turn right here (southeast) onto the road and follow it uphill.

3.3 Pass a stone CCC culvert that funnels water from a stream under the road. This area is beautiful in the spring, with hundreds of white blooming dogwoods. In 200 feet come to a double blaze indicating a right turn. Turn right (southwest) onto a narrow dirt footpath into the woods.

3.4 Cross the dirt Gazebo Road to the southeast and scramble up a short hill. In a few hundred feet, you reach the gazebo and some nice views of the surrounding hills. Turn around here and retrace your steps to the trailhead.

4.8 Arrive back at the trailhead.

GULF REGION

Along the golden beaches, barrier islands, and dark delta waters of Alabama's Gulf Coast is an amazing record of human history dating back over 1,000 years.

You will journey deep into the second-largest river delta in the country, the Mobile-Tensaw River Delta, where a true wilderness adventure awaits when you visit the towering man-made mounds of the Mississippian period Indian. These Native Americans formed one of the earliest civilizations and communal systems in the United States.

European history along the coast dates back over 300 years to when the city of Mobile and the surrounding area had an identity crisis—first being controlled by Spain, then France, then Britain, then the United States, and for a time the Confederacy. You will experience much of that history while walking the city streets of Mobile, paying visits to historic buildings, landmarks, and the waterfront that made Mobile an important port city. You can also pay your respects to Mobile luminaries on a walk through Magnolia Cemetery, the second-oldest cemetery in the city.

And then there is Civil War history. Walk in the steps of those who fought the famous Battle of Mobile Bay at Fort Morgan and Fort Gaines. It was here in 1865, after one of his ironclads was sunk by a Confederate mine, that Union admiral David Farragut uttered those immortal words, "Damn the torpedoes! Full speed ahead!" and went on to win a decisive victory. That victory led to the last major battle of the war at the former town of Blakeley. You will visit the battlefield that was taken by Union troops and led to the taking of the last Confederate port city.

32 Mound Island

Venture into the dark wilderness of the second-largest river delta in the country on the Mound Island hike. Alligators and wild boars lurk about on the island and along the nearby waterline as you hike the rain forest–like trail to ancient Indian mounds over a thousand years old.

Start: From the creek banks on the south side of the island
Distance: 1.1 miles out and back
Hiking time: About 1 hour
Difficulty: Easy
Trail surface: Dirt footpath
Best seasons: Sept to early May
Other trail users: Hunters (See "Special considerations")
Canine compatibility: Leashed dogs permitted
Land status: State conservation property
Nearest town: Stockton
Fees and permits: None to hike the island; fee to take a guided boat or kayak tour, free if you have your own canoe/kayak

Schedule: Year-round, daily sunrise to sunset
Maps: USGS The Basin/Stiggins Lake, AL; *DeLorme: Alabama Atlas & Gazetteer*, page 56, G1
Trail contact: Mound Island/Bartram Canoe Trail Info: Alabama Department of Conservation and Natural Resources, 64 N. Union St., Ste. 468, Montgomery 36130; (334) 242-3484; lands.dcnr.alabama.gov/Bartram. Canoe/Tour Guide Info: Delta Safaris, 4891 Battleship Pkwy., Spanish Fort 36527; (251) 259-8531; www.5rds.com.
Special considerations: Hunting is permitted in the Delta and on Mound Island. Visit outdooralabama.com/hunting/ for dates.

Finding the trailhead: The following route is to the trailhead used by the Delta Safaris tour boat. *Before* heading out contact them for tour dates and times (see "Trail contact") to be sure they are running a tour and to reserve a seat. For paddling information contact ADCNR or Delta Safaris (see "Trail contact"). To Lower Bryant's Landing from the intersection of I-65 at exit 31 and AL 225 in Bay Minette, take AL 225 north 2.2 miles. Turn left onto Lower Bryant's Landing Road. Travel 1.3 miles and park near the dock. GPS: N30 58.231' / W87 53.075'; Island GPS: N31 00.534' / W87 56.039'

The Hike

Take a walk on an island deep in the wilderness known as the Mobile-Tensaw River Delta to a site that was inhabited by humans over a thousand years ago—Mound Island.

The Mobile-Tensaw River Delta is the second largest in the country right behind the Mississippi Delta, with over 250,000 acres of bottomland forest, brackish tidal marshes, cypress–gum swamps, and floodplain, making this one of the largest intact wetlands in the country. The wildlife is amazing with alligators, blue herons, and wild boars, to name only a few. But tucked away in this almost rain forest–like environment only minutes from downtown Mobile is an island that was inhabited by humans

This sign is the only indication that you are walking through a truly unique, historic area in the middle of the wilderness known as the Mobile-Tensaw River Delta.

thousands of years ago. It's called Mound Island and is where we are heading for this 1.1-mile out-and-back hike.

The Native American inhabitants on Mound Island lived in what is known as the Mississippian period, which generally began around AD 1000. During this time tribes were settling along the Mississippi River and moving out into other areas of the Southeast, including here on the Gulf Coast. Early explorers called them "Mobilians."

What made Mississippians unique is their mound-building abilities. Here on Mound Island, eighteen of these mounds, made of dirt and sticks, were built—all by hand. The dirt was dug out of the ground with shell hoes, then carried by hand one cane basket at a time to its location. It took hundreds of years to complete all the mounds.

The taller mounds were about 45 feet tall. The tallest here, Mound "A," was reserved for the chief. The next tallest, Mound "B," was for the religious leader. This mound is actually about as long as a football field. Midsize mounds were for the "upper middle class," and the workers lived at ground level.

Farther north near present-day Tuscaloosa, another Mississippian period community, Moundville, appears to have been a thriving economic and political community, but Mound Island looks like it might have been more of the spiritual capital. It is believed that the island was "where the Gods are," and tribes would come here to offer sacrifices.

We'll talk about how to get to the island in a minute, but first a little about the trail. As I said, you will be walking through a landscape that resembles a rain forest. The trail isn't blazed, but it is well used, so you should be able to follow it pretty well.

Tall, deep rows of palmetto line the trail on both sides. Because of this thick growth, you will only be able to see two of the eighteen mounds. You will first arrive at Mound "A" and can climb to the top. Watch for holes dug by opportunists looking for artifacts to sell. Next you'll visit a large borrow pit. It is believed that this is where at least some of the dirt used to build the mounds came from. Finally you'll arrive at the base of Mound "B." This is normally very overgrown so that's about all you can see of it.

Now some important safety notes: First, remember that this is a delta and is prone to flooding—*dangerous* flooding. If the flood stage is over 19 feet, do not attempt to go to the island. There also are some notable wild animals to keep your eyes peeled for. In the summer the mosquitoes are brutal. Wait until late fall through late winter to visit. Don't be surprised if you see alligators sliding off the banks as you pull up. Gators are normally afraid of humans, but don't tempt fate and keep a wide berth. You also need to watch for wild hogs, which can be ferocious fighters. If you see any, be prepared to shimmy up the nearest tree pronto.

There are a couple of ways to get to the island and this trail. If you have your own canoe or kayak, you can paddle to it on the Bartram Canoe Trail (see "The Bartram Canoe Trail" sidebar for more information and safety tips), or you can go on one of the many guided paddling trips where you can rent a kayak.

Since I had done the paddle before, I opted this time to take a guided tour boat to Mound Island. I sailed in with a group of excited tourists on a cruise set up by Delta Safaris. It was an excellent tour, and the guide and captain were very knowledgeable about the history of the island and the ecosystem of the delta. I highly recommend it (see "Trail contact" above for details.)

The Bartram Canoe Trail

The most adventurous way to visit Mound Island in the heart of the Mobile-Tensaw River Delta is by paddling the Bartram Canoe Trail. The trail is a series of marked waterways down narrow bayous and channels. Sloughs like Bottle Creek are scenes ripped right off a picture postcard of the South, with massive oak and cedar trees adorned with long, flowing strands of Spanish moss. Alligators will be literally sliding off the banks as you round bends or lurking just beneath the surface near your boat.

The trail takes you deep into the cypress-tupelo swamps and marshes where over fifty rare and endangered species of plants and wildlife can be seen. And to make it even more exciting, you can camp right in the middle of all this on one of a number of floating campsites.

The delta is not for neophyte paddlers, however. Even though the trail is marked, the myriad inlets still make it easy to get lost. Unless you're an experienced paddler with navigational skills, it's best to venture out with an experienced guide.

Learn more about the trail and obtain maps online at lands.dcnr.alabama.gov/Bartram/.

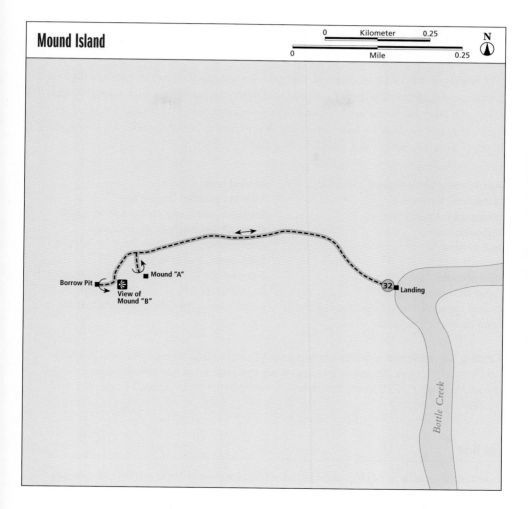

Miles and Directions

0.0 Start at the landing on Mound Island on the banks of Bottle Creek (see "Trail contact" and the hike description for travel options to the island). Climb up the steep bank and head west on the well-worn trail. The path is thickly lined with palmetto.

0.4 Arrive at the base of Mound "A." A side trail on your left steeply climbs 300 feet up the slope to the top. When you're done exploring, climb back down to the trail.

0.5 Turn left (west) onto the trail.

0.6 Arrive at the borrow pit. After a good rain this could be knee deep in water with snakes. Turn around and start the walk back.

0.7 Come to a Y. Take the right fork and in a few yards arrive at the base of Mound "B." Walk back to the Y, turn right (east) and head back to the trailhead.

1.1 Arrive back at the trailhead.

33 Chickasabogue Park Loop

Thousands of miles of inlets, bayous, and back bays along the Gulf of Mexico allowed pirates, and some outlaw gangs, to hide out from the law. The Chickasabogue Park Loop will take you to the banks of one of those many rivers, Chickasaw Creek, where legend has it there may be buried treasure. Who knows? The trail also leads to the old Myers Cemetery, which was established in 1849.

Start: Parking lot trailhead at sports field
Distance: 3.9-mile loop
Hiking time: About 1.5 hours
Difficulty: Easy
Trail surface: Dirt footpath and road, some asphalt
Best seasons: Sept to May
Other trail users: Cyclists
Canine compatibility: Leashed dogs permitted
Land status: County park

Nearest town: Chickasaw
Fees and permits: Day-use fee
Schedule: Year-round, daily 7 a.m. to 5 p.m.
Maps: USGS Chickasaw, AL; *DeLorme: Alabama Atlas & Gazetteer*, page 62, B3; trail maps available at entrance gate
Trail contact: Chickasabogue Park, 60 Aldock Rd., Eight Mile 36613; (251) 574-2267; mobilecountyal.gov/living/parks_chickasabogue .html

Finding the trailhead: From the intersection of I-65 and Whistler Street in Prichard, take Whistler Street west 2 miles. Turn right onto Aldock Road and travel 1 mile. The park entrance is straight ahead. After paying the attendant, the trailhead is ahead on the right in about 0.1 mile. GPS: N30 46.868' / W88 06.288'

The Hike

Located just north of Mobile in Saraland is Chickasabogue Park, a 1,100-acre family-friendly park with plenty to do including disc golf, bike riding, camping, and hiking. In all, the park has 17 miles of hiking and biking trails that wind their way through a pine and mixed hardwood forest.

Archaeologists have determined through the discovery of ancient campsites that Native Americans of the Woodland period lived here around 1500 BC. In 1711 the governor of the French city of Mobile, Jean Baptiste Le Moyne, relocated members of the Apalachee tribe here to the banks of Chickasaw Creek, where they stayed until 1732 when they moved across the Mobile–Tensaw River Delta to what later became the town of Blakeley.

As far as historians know, Europeans first settled in what is now Chickasabogue Park in 1787 when Spanish Grandee (nobleman) Don Diego Alvarez was awarded a grant of land here. In his request for the grant, Alvarez noted that he had already lived here for five years.

Several other families settled along the banks of the creek over the next few years. One of note was Frederick Daniel Myers. Born in Orangeburg, South Carolina, Myers and his sons David, Daniel, and John built a sawmill on the creek. Myers also established a small village here with a public school, gristmill, and brick kiln. Myers died in 1866 and is buried in the cemetery that bears his name, which you will visit on this hike.

In the mid-1800s the outlaw Cooper Gang set up shop near the banks of Chickasaw Creek. The gang was famously known for robbing stagecoaches and businesses, but their side business was in the slave trade. It was a unique operation—the gang would promise to help runaway slaves escape to the North only to sell them to other plantations throughout the South.

The area in which the park lies saw a sharp increase in its population when, during the closing months of the Civil War, 700 residents from the nearby town of Whistler flocked here seeking refuge as the Union army attacked and took over their town.

Three different trails are used to complete this loop: the Indian, Beach, and Cemetery Trails. The Indian Loop leads to the banks of Chickasaw Creek where the Cooper Gang once hid out and pirates like Jean Lafitte plied the waters burying their illegal bounty. Along the Cemetery Trail we will pay our respects to Frederick Myers and his family at the family cemetery.

All the trails are well maintained with one notable exception as you're trying to locate Myers Cemetery, but otherwise they are nice 2- to 3-foot-wide dirt footpaths with a few dirt road walks. The forest is thick with pine, a hardwood mix, and bigleaf magnolia trees giving you an excellent canopy even in the hot, humid days of summer.

But having said that, you still may want to skip the summer hiking here. Being in close proximity to the creek and traveling through many bogs, you will encounter mosquitoes. The only other drawback is on the far eastern side of the Cemetery Trail where you are within shouting distance of I-65. Early morning hikes are OK, but later in the day the traffic noise is disturbing.

Remember, the trails are shared with mountain bikers, so keep your eyes peeled. Trails marked with yellow blazes are for hikers, red for bikers, but they are easily confused at intersections. Just keep your head up and an eye out for them.

Before leaving be sure to visit the museum at the park's entrance, which is housed in the former Eight Mile A.M.E. United Methodist Church that was built in 1879 and moved here for this purpose. The museum features artifacts tracing the region's history all the way back to the early native inhabitants.

Miles and Directions

0.0 Start from the northwest end of the sports field parking lot off Aldock Road just past the park's entrance. Cross the road to the northwest using the crosswalk. A sign here reads Yellow—Hikers, Red—Bikers. The trail is a 4-foot-wide sand and dirt path, root strewn and very enclosed with a tight tree canopy. On this side of the loop there are mainly yellow paint blazes on trees with wooden signs at intersections. In less than 0.1 mile, come to a T intersection. A picnic pavilion is on the left; turn to the right (northwest) to continue on the trail.

0.1 Come to a Y intersection. To the right is the Cemetery Loop Trail. Take the left fork to the west to begin the Indian Loop Trail.

0.3 Cross a 15-foot boardwalk. All boardwalks have farm fence on them to provide secure footing in wet weather. After the boardwalk come to a depression that can be very wet after a good rain and a Y. Take the left fork to the northwest. Look for a sign that reads Indian Trail just after the Y. Bright green moss lines parts of this section.

0.5 Come to an intersection. To the left are some houses and straight ahead is a little extension of the Indian Loop Trail (a little finger in the trail). Turn here to the right (north) onto a wide gravel road.

0.7 Pass an old water pump on the right that still works so you can grab a drink. In less than 0.1 mile, come to a Y. A red-blazed trail continues straight. Take the left fork to the north to continue on the Indian Loop Trail. The path is dirt once again. To your left (west) you'll see a nice pond down at the bottom of a bluff. You will start seeing the creek through the trees.

0.9 Pass a side trail on the left that takes you to a backcountry campsite next to the creek. In a few yards come to a T intersection with a dirt service road. Turn to the left (west). Immediately come to a Y and take the left fork to the northwest to head to the creek. In less than 0.1 mile, pass the backcountry campsite on the left. The path becomes thick sand as it approaches the creek, with little canopy.

1.0 Arrive at the banks of the creek. Feel free to explore, then turn around and head back to the Y at mile 0.9. Another backcountry campsite is back here, so don't be surprised if you walk up on someone's tent. In less than 0.1 mile, arrive back at the Y at mile 0.9. Turn left (north) onto the wide dirt path.

1.1 Get another view of the creek, then turn around and retrace your steps to the Y at mile 0.9.

1.2 This return trail runs parallel to the inbound trail you just walked to the creek (you will see the water pump at mile 0.7 on the other side). Come to a Y and take the left fork onto the wide, yellow-blazed dirt path.

1.3 Cross a 50-foot boardwalk over a seasonal bog.

1.4 Come to a Y. Take the right fork to the east. The trail narrows to maybe 2 feet wide and is very enclosed. In less than 0.1 mile, take the left fork to the east at a Y. In a few yards cross a 5-foot puncheon bridge.

1.5 Cross another 5-foot puncheon bridge.

1.6 Pass an intersection with a red bike trail (Hidden Trail) and cross a 100-foot boardwalk over a seasonal wetland. The trail widens out to 4 feet.

1.7 Take the right fork to the northeast at a Y. Continue following the yellow blazes. In less than 0.1 mile, cross a gravel road next to the nature center (a series of displays in kiosks) on the left. A sign on the other side says Beach Loop Trail. Pick up the yellow-blazed trail there. From here on out, the trail has not only yellow paint blazes but also the red blazes of the biking trails. Wooden arrows show the way. Unfortunately you are getting close to I-65 and will start hearing it. It's not too disturbing in the morning, but as midday nears the traffic sound worsens.

1.9 Come to a T intersection. Turn right (south) to continue on the Beach Loop Trail.

2.0 Cross a road to the northeast and pick up the trail on the other side.

2.1 Come to a series of several signs that looks like a hodgepodge of directional cues. Turn right (southwest) onto an unmarked dirt foot trail that is thick with pine duff. In less than

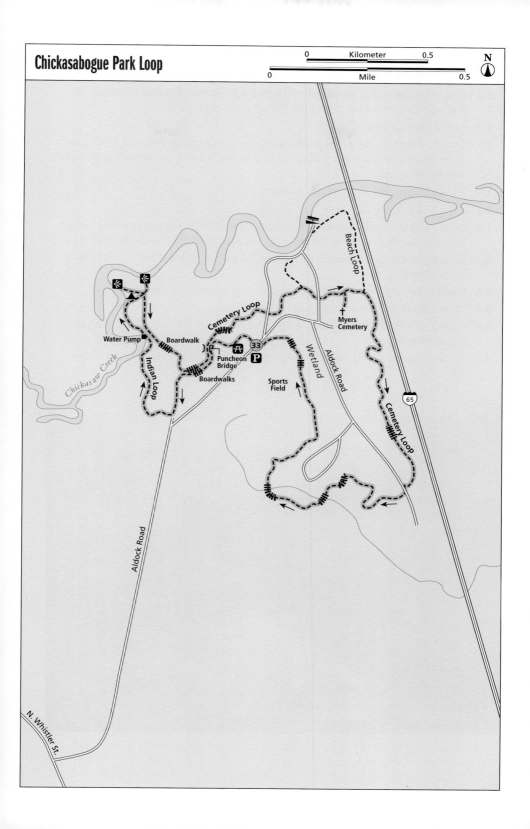

Chickasabogue Park Loop

Kilometer
0   0.5
Mile
0   0.5

N

Beach Loop

Cemetery Loop

Myers
Cemetery

Water Pump

Boardwalk

Chickasaw Creek

Indian Loop

33

Puncheon
Bridge

P

Boardwalks

Sports
Field

Wetland

Aldock Road

65

Cemetery Loop

Aldock Road

N. Whistler St.

0.1 mile, arrive at Myers Cemetery, which is surrounded by a chain-link fence. Pay your respects, then turn around and head back to the main trail.

2.2 Back at the intersection at mile 2.1, turn right and follow the yellow-blazed trail. You are now paralleling I-65, a few dozen yards through the trees on the left.

2.7 Cross a boardwalk over a bog.

2.8 Come to a road. Down the road to the right (north) is a bathhouse. Pick up the trail again across the road ahead to your left (south). Look for the Cemetery Trail sign where the path reenters the woods.

2.9 Come to a Y. Take the left fork to the northwest.

3.1 Cross a 15-foot-long boardwalk.

3.2 Cross a 100-foot-long boardwalk over a seasonal bog. The trail begins moving away from the interstate. You will pass several disc golf course tees and holes from here to your vehicle.

3.3 Cross a 100-foot-long boardwalk. In less than 0.1 mile, come to a Y. Take the right fork to the northeast.

3.6 Start paralleling the edge of the sports field (through the trees on your left.)

3.7 Cross a gravel service road to the east.

3.8 Cross a 50-foot-long boardwalk. In less than 0.1 mile, cross a 40-foot then a 100-foot-long boardwalk.

3.9 Come to a gravel parking area. The sports field parking area and your vehicle are on the left.

The beautiful placid waters of Chickasaw Creek, where pirates once hid away in the narrow coves and sloughs, is a highlight of this loop trail.

34 Confederate Breastworks Trail

The Confederate Breastworks Trail at Historic Blakeley State Park follows some of the best-preserved Civil War breastworks in the South and takes you to the site of the Battle of Blakeley, which is recognized as being the last major battle of the war. The trail winds its way to the battlefield where you will see gunner positions, the "Zig-Zag" that Union troops used to sneak up on the Confederate side, and two well-preserved redoubts.

Start: From the parking area on Old Blakeley Road

Distance: 3.0 miles out and back

Hiking time: About 2 hours

Difficulty: Easy

Trail surface: Dirt and grass footpath, gravel road

Best seasons: Sept to early May

Other trail users: Cyclists, equestrians, cars on dirt roads

Canine compatibility: Leashed dogs permitted

Land status: Alabama state historic park

Nearest town: Spanish Fort

Fees and permits: Day-use fee

Schedule: Year-round, daily 9 a.m. to sunset

Maps: USGS Bridgehead, AL; *DeLorme: Alabama Atlas & Gazetteer*, page 62, C5

Trail contact: Historic Blakeley State Park, 34745 State Hwy. 225, Spanish Fort 36577; (251) 626-0798; blakeleypark.com

Finding the trailhead: From the intersection of US 90 and AL 225 in Spanish Fort, take AL 225 north 4.4 miles. Turn left onto Upper Shay Branch Road. This is the park entrance and is well marked. In 400 feet come to the pay station where you can pick up maps and brochures. After paying the entrance fee, continue straight 0.3 mile and turn right (north) to continue on Upper Shay Branch Road. In 0.8 mile the pavement ends and becomes a gravel road and is now called Old Blakeley Road. Continue straight another 0.5 mile. An old, small shack is on the left side of the road with parking. Begin the hike here. GPS: N30 44.498' / W87 54.986'

The Hike

The Battle of Blakeley is recognized as the last major battle of the Civil War and one that guaranteed the taking of the last major Southern city in the Confederacy, Mobile. The recently reopened Confederate Breastworks Trail gives you the opportunity to experience the battlefield firsthand and see some of the best-preserved Civil War redoubts in the region.

I say reopened because over the past few years the trail was being relocated. It used to lie directly on top of the Confederate breastworks, which were in danger of being destroyed by hikers (if you see the maps in the early editions of *Hiking Alabama*, you'll see what I mean.) Now the trail meanders alongside the earthen breastworks, protecting them for future generations.

Before you hit the trail, you'll need a little perspective about the battle and why this fight was the final blow to the Confederacy. The city of Mobile along the

The view looking out over the Blakeley battlefield from Redoubt #5

Alabama Gulf Coast was the last major Confederate city standing during the war, and for good reason. The Port City was heavily fortified with two massive stone forts protecting the entrance to Mobile Bay at the Gulf, several earthen forts in the Mobile-Tensaw River Delta, plus heavily armed forts at Spanish Fort and Blakeley on the eastern shore of the bay. The bay also had a contingent of ironclads positioned offshore. In addition the bay itself was strewn with obstacles and mines designed to sink any advancing Union ships.

The first breach in the city's security came on August 23, 1864, when the Union navy won a major battle off Fort Morgan in the Battle of Mobile Bay, giving them easy access to the northern forts.

Seven months later Union troops were reinforced and began to sail and march up the bay's eastern shore. One detachment broke off and headed north toward the town of Spanish Fort, where it took thirteen days for the Union to defeat the Confederates. The second detachment headed east toward Pensacola, Florida, in a move designed to fool the Confederate generals into thinking they were heading to Montgomery. When the latter detachment reached the town of Pollard, Alabama, they turned and headed west, making a beeline to Blakeley.

On April 2, 1865, 16,000 Union soldiers took on the nearly 4,000 Confederate soldiers in the Battle of Blakely. Seven days later, on April 9, General Robert E. Lee surrendered to Ulysses S. Grant at Appomattox Courthouse in Virginia, effectively ending the Civil War. Six hours later, the Battle of Blakeley was over, making it the last major battle of the war.

When the smoke had cleared, 3,400 Confederate soldiers were captured, 250 died, and 200 escaped. It wasn't long until the city of Mobile was declared an open city and the Union army moved in.

The Confederate Breastworks Trail is a combination of dirt footpath, dirt and gravel road, and grassy walk through the battlefield. As you start the hike, you will be walking directly next to the earthen breastworks that Confederate soldiers hid behind waiting for the Union army. The breastworks will be on your right.

Red buckeye brightens the trail.

Next you come out to the main park road, which will take you past a beautiful little wetland and stream called Baptizing Branch and then to the main attraction, the battlefield itself.

Your first stop is Redoubt #5. This is one of the best-preserved redoubts in the region. Of course it has been shorn up to help keep it intact, but you can see how the Confederate army was positioned and the ports where their cannons peered out over the battlefield.

You will see ample signs and ropes blocking off the redoubt, telling you not to walk on it. Please heed the signs and help preserve this history.

As you cross the grassy battlefield, you will pass many trenches hand dug by forward-positioned gunners and then come to the Union side with its redoubt and an interesting trench called the "Zig-Zag," an approach trench that took the Union soldiers right up to the Confederates' doorstep near the redoubts.

As you enter the park, be sure to ask for a map and a brochure. Many of the features you will pass are numbered, and the brochure will give you more detailed information about the battle.

Miles and Directions

0.0 Start on Washington Avenue where Old Blakeley Road ends at the parking area next to an old shack. Cross the dirt road then turn left (west) onto the road. In 200 feet you pass the grave of a former ranger's dog, Biscuit, on your right; just after turn right (northeast) at the sign marking the Confederate Breastworks Trail. Notice the black cherry and magnolia trees along this section, and to your right (east) a large, linear mound of dirt that runs the length of the trail. This is the Confederate breastworks. The trail, a wide grass and dirt path with a thick canopy, follows alongside the breastworks.

0.2 Cross an old service road to the north. To your right (east) are the cannon, monuments, and entrance road to the park. In a few hundred feet pass a wide side trail, probably a service road, to the left (west). Continue straight to the northeast. The trail dips down between two hills here and can be boggy after a good rain.

0.3 In less than 0.1 mile, come to an intersection with a wide dirt and grass service road. On some maps this is called Old Blakeley Road. This road leads to a restroom and equestrian trailer parking area on the left, the entrance road to the park to the right. Continue straight on the main trail to the northeast. The trail narrows here to a 3- to 4-foot-wide dirt path. (***Note:*** There is another trail just off to the right of the main trail—the old Breastworks Trail, which is now barricaded and closed.)

0.7 The trail comes out to the gravel Battlefield Road. Turn to the right (northeast) onto the road.

0.8 The road travels between two very pretty wetlands formed by Baptizing Branch.

1.0 A sign to your right reads No Horses on Trail. Turn right (south) onto a narrow dirt footpath to walk directly behind Redoubt #5. Heed the sign! Do *not* climb on the earthworks! This is a historic site. Continue to the south.

1.1 The trail swings to the east then northeast as it comes around to the front of the redoubt. Come to a Y intersection here. The right fork is the old Breastworks Trail that is now closed. Take the left fork to the northeast and walk in front of the redoubt on a dirt road. In less than 0.1 mile, come to marker #16. Turn right (southeast) here and head across the battlefield.

A Little Town on the Delta

Historic Blakeley State Park is known not only for its famous Civil War battle but also for the rich history it had prior to 1865. Paleo-Indians lived on this land some 4,000 years ago. Beginning in the 1500s, as Europeans moved in, the land changed hands several times and fell under the rule of Spain in the late 1500s, France in the early 1700s, followed by Britain, then the United States in 1813. Soon after becoming a US territory, Josiah Blakeley bought this land and established the town of Blakeley.

Blakeley was chartered in 1814 and became a bustling port city that rose to rival neighboring Mobile. By 1828, however, a series of yellow fever epidemics coupled with the greed of land speculators forced the city of 4,000 to spiral into decay, and by the mid-1800s it was abandoned.

Today all that remains of the old port town are the 400-year-old live oaks that once lined the bustling city streets and a recently unearthed foundation—the original brick and wood base of the town's courthouse.

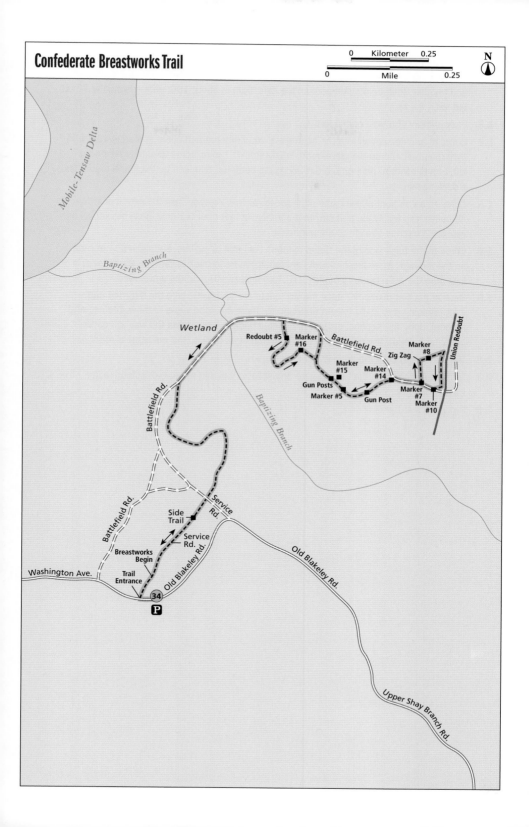

Confederate Breastworks Trail

Kilometer 0 0.25

Mile 0 0.25

N

Mobile-Tensaw Delta

Baptizing Branch

Wetland

Redoubt #5

Marker #16

Battlefield Rd.

Marker #15

Gun Posts

Marker #5

Marker #14

Gun Post

Zig Zag

Marker #8

Union Redoubt

Marker #7

Marker #10

Battlefield Rd.

Baptizing Branch

Battlefield Rd.

Service Rd.

Side Trail

Service Rd.

Old Blakeley Rd.

Breastworks Begin

Trail Entrance

Washington Ave.

Old Blakeley Rd.

34

P

Upper Shay Branch Rd.

1.2 Turn right (southeast) onto a dirt road. In less than 0.1 mile, pass a Confederate gun post on each side of the trail and marker #15 on your left. A few yards farther pass marker #5 and another Confederate gun post on the right, then in about 100 feet pass marker #6 on the left.

1.3 Pass another gun post on the left.

1.4 Come to an intersection with the main gravel road into the battlefield at marker #14. Turn right (southeast) onto the gravel road. In less than 0.1 mile, come to marker #7 on the left. Turn left (north) here onto a dirt and grass path. The path can be thick with mud after a soaking rain.

1.5 Come to a Y. In front of you is the ditch known as the "Zig-Zag." Take the right fork to the northeast and follow the trail next to the trench. In less than 0.1 mile, pass marker #8 on your left. Continue straight to the northeast.

1.6 Come to the back side of the Union redoubt. Feel free to explore, but again do not climb on the redoubt. When finished turn right (south) to head back toward the gravel road. In less than 0.1 mile, come to marker #10. Turn right (west) onto the gravel road.

1.9 Back at the Y at marker #7, take the left fork to the southwest onto the dirt road and start retracing your steps toward Redoubt #5. There are good views of the battlefield and redoubt along this section. Instead of heading back to the redoubt the way you came, continue to follow the dirt road to the north and head back to the main gravel road.

2.0 Turn left (west) onto the main gravel road.

2.3 Turn left (south) onto the Confederate Breastworks Trail and retrace your steps to the trailhead.

3.0 Arrive back at the trailhead.

35 Port City Historic Walk

Alabama's oldest city, Mobile, has over 300 years of history waiting for you to explore. From its historic riverside landing to almost 200-year-old churches and cemeteries to mid–1800 buildings that are experiencing a renaissance, there is a lot of ground to cover in this 3.5-mile loop around the Port City.

Start: From the Fort Conde parking lot on South Royal Street.
Distance: 3.5-mile loop
Hiking time: About 2.5 hours (varies depending on museums and stops)
Difficulty: Easy
Trail surface: Cement and brick sidewalk
Best seasons: Year-round
Other trail users: Joggers, cyclists
Canine compatibility: Leashed dogs permitted but not allowed in public buildings
Land status: City walk

Nearest town: Mobile
Fees and permits: None; small fees for museums
Schedule: Year-round, daily sunrise to sunset; contact those listed under "Trail contact" for museum hours
Maps: USGS Mobile, AL; *DeLorme: Alabama Atlas & Gazetteer*, page 62, D4
Trail contact: Mobile Bay Convention & Visitors Corporation, One S. Water St., Mobile 36602; (800) 566-2453; mobile.org

Finding the trailhead: From the intersection of I-10 at exit 26 and Water Street in Mobile, take Water Street 0.3 mile and turn left onto Monroe Street. In 300 feet turn right onto South Royal Street. In 300 feet the Fort Conde parking lot is on the right. Start the hike from here. GPS: N30 41.299' / W88 02.364'

The Hike

What would a book about historical hikes in Alabama be without a trek through the state's oldest city, Mobile? Mobile has a rich and eclectic history that dates back to the early 1500s, with the city proper finally established in 1702.

The earliest history records the region as inhabited by Native Americans until Spanish explorer Alonzo Alvarez Pineda landed here during his expedition to map the northern Gulf Coast in 1519. Twenty years later explorer Hernando DeSoto voyaged in looking for gold. His encounters with local natives were violent and bloody affairs. Finally, in 1559 Tristan de Luna established a settlement on the banks of what would later be called Mobile Bay, but a devastating hurricane soon put an end to that.

The city finally took hold in 1702 when French naval hero Pierre Le Moyne d'Iberville established a settlement on what would later be called the Mobile River at Twenty Seven Mile Bluff, twenty miles north of the location of present-day Mobile. D'Iberville's brother, Jean Baptiste Le Moyne de Bienville, urged his brother to move the settlement farther south on the river to a location near a local Indian tribe that the settlers had good relations with, the Mauvila. The new settlement was named Fort

Old meets new—a statue of famed explorer Pierre Le Moyne d'Iberville with the tallest building in the state, the RSA Tower, as a backdrop. D'Iberville would not recognize Fort St. Louis (later called Mobile), which he established here in 1702.

Louis de La Louisiana or Fort Louis de La Mobile (the anglicized version of Mauvila), the first French settlement on the Gulf Coast.

After that Mobile, like many later Gulf Coast cities, earned its nickname as a "City of Five Flags." The city was occupied and controlled by the French until 1763, the British until 1780, Spain until 1813, and the United States until 1862, when it was part of the Confederacy during the Civil War, then the United States again.

Just before the Civil War, Mobile was the third-largest seaport for exports in the country and the third-largest city on the Gulf Coast, but the war took its toll, and it wasn't until the advent of World Wars I and II that the city began to grow again, now as a major shipbuilding location.

That is only a brief history of the city. On this 3.5-mile loop you will be able to explore other interesting historic sites and buildings including the historic waterfront that made Mobile what it is today; the Battle House Hotel, which was built in 1851 and where Stephen Douglas stayed following his loss to Abraham Lincoln for president; the home of Confederate admiral and captain of the famous CSS *Alabama* during the Civil War, Raphael Semmes; and "Alabama's greatest showplace," the "most beautiful playhouse in all of Dixie," the Saenger Theater, which was built in 1927.

The walk heads down Government Street (US 90), so you will pass the domed Barton Academy, the first public school in Alabama. Built in 1835 Barton was named for William Barton, who authored the bill that created the public school system in the city.

Several churches grace this walk including the Government Street United Methodist Church, which was built in 1849 but remodeled to its present appearance in 1906. The congregation was said to "swarm" to the church, and it became known as the "Bee Hive."

Raisin' Cain

The phrase "Raisin' Cain" takes on new meaning in the port city of Mobile. It's a term that has been endeared to one of its favorite sons, Joe Cain.

Cain moved to Mobile from Philadelphia with his parents in 1832. He was quite intrigued with the mystic societies that paraded the streets of the city during early Mardi Gras celebrations.

During the Civil War the celebrations were curtailed, but immediately afterward the South and Mobile were ready to move forward. They just needed a party to get things started.

Cain and several members of a local mystic society decided to parade in the streets during the period just before Lent, and in 1867, manning a decorated charcoal wagon, Cain led a procession of partiers dressed as Indians down the streets of Mobile. The mystic society called themselves the "Lost Cause." Cain himself took on the persona of fictional Chickasaw Indian chief Slackabamarinico. The parade signified the end of the city's suffering from the war.

Today a special parade, the Joe Cain Parade, aka the "People's Parade," takes to the streets of Mobile the Sunday before Fat Tuesday to honor Chief Slac and Joe Cain.

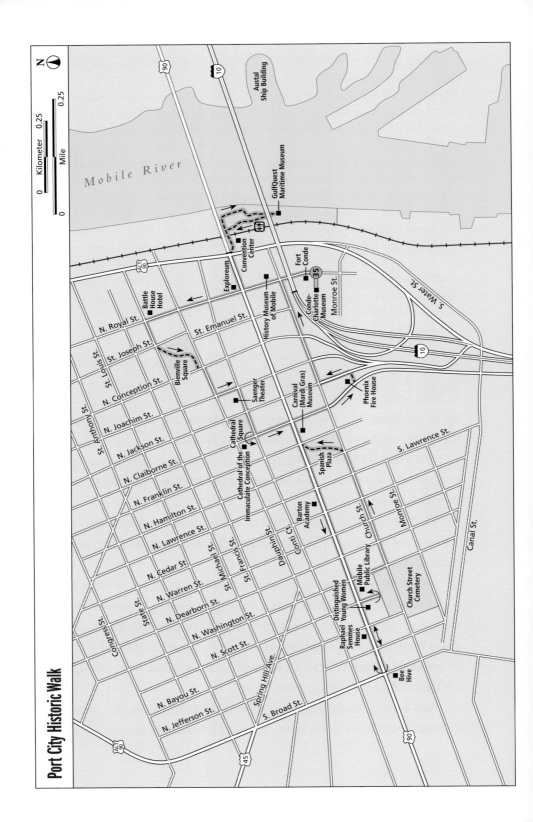

Port City Historic Walk

Mobile River

Austal Ship Building

GulfQuest Maritime Museum

Convention Center

Exploreum

Battle House Hotel

History Museum of Mobile

Fort Conde

Conde-Charlotte Museum

Monroe St.

Saenger Theater

Bienville Square

Carnival (Mardi Gras) Museum

Phoenix Fire House

Cathedral of the Immaculate Conception

Cathedral Square

Spanish Plaza

S. Lawrence St.

Barton Academy

Gonti Ct.

Dauphin St.

St. Francis St.

St. Michael St.

Mobile Public Library

Distinguished Young Women

Raphael Semmes House

Bee Hive

Monroe St.

Church Street Cemetery

Canal St.

S. Water St.

N. Royal St.

St. Louis St.

St. Joseph St.

St. Anthony St.

N. Conception St.

N. Joachim St.

N. Jackson St.

N. Claiborne St.

N. Franklin St.

N. Hamilton St.

N. Lawrence St.

N. Cedar St.

N. Warren St.

N. Dearborn St.

N. Washington St.

N. Scott St.

N. Bayou St.

N. Jefferson St.

Congress St.

State St.

Spring Hill Ave.

S. Broad St.

St. Emanuel St.

Church St.

N

Kilometer 0   0.25

0   0.25

Mile

90

10

ALT 90

35

10

ALT 90

45

90

Another church, and one you will want to walk inside to visit, is the Cathedral Basilica of the Immaculate Conception. The first bishop of Mobile, Michael Portier, commissioned the building of the church. Construction began in 1835 and was completed in 1850. The interior is beautifully adorned, the high rounded ceiling breathtaking, the sanctuary inspiring. When you visit, please be sure to make a donation to the Poor Box located inside next to the entrance to help the needy of the area.

And finally, there is the Church Street Cemetery, the city's oldest cemetery, established in 1819. Wander about the grounds and pay your respects to those who were laid to rest here, including Mobile's favorite son, Joe Cain, who brought Mardi Gras back home after it was halted during the Civil War.

I've listed this hike as taking 2.5 hours to complete, but you will pass many museums along the route that you may want to visit and linger in. They include the History Museum of Mobile (housed in the original Mobile city hall and market place), the GulfQuest Maritime Museum, the Exploreum Science Museum, the Phoenix Fire House, and the Mobile Carnival (Mardi Gras) Museum. See "Trail contact" to find information on schedules and admission fees.

Miles and Directions

0.0 Start from the Fort Conde parking lot. Head north on South Royal Street.

0.1 Pass the History Museum of Mobile on the right. The building was the former city hall and market place. Continue north on South Royal Street.

0.2 Come to the Exploreum Science Museum. Cross US 90 and on the other side turn right onto US 90.

0.3 Carefully cross South Water Street and head toward the waterfront. Once across continue straight to the east. *Carefully* cross the railroad tracks and head to the water.

0.4 Along the banks of the Mobile River, turn right (south) and walk through Cooper's Riverside Park to take in the view and the passing ships. Directly across the river is Austal Ship Building, which is continuing the city's maritime heritage.

0.5 Arrive at the new GulfQuest Maritime Museum, which traces the history of ships and all related subjects along the Gulf Coast. Turn around here and retrace your steps to mile 0.3.

0.6 Pass a public restroom on your left. In the winter an outdoor skating rink (honestly) is set up here on the right.

0.8 Back at South Royal Street turn right (north).

1.0 Come to the historic Battle House Hotel. Turn left (west) onto St. Francis Street.

1.1 Cross St. Joseph Street and arrive at Bienville Square. Cut across the square to the southwest and head to Dauphin Street.

1.2 Turn right onto Dauphin Street. This is the city's night spot, with many clubs and restaurants now using the historic buildings.

1.3 Turn left (south) onto South Joachim Street. In less than 0.1 mile, come to the historic Saenger Theater. Turn right (west) here onto Conti Street.

1.4 At the corner of Conti and South Jackson Street, cross the street. This is Cathedral Square. Cross through the grassy square to the west and in less than 0.1 mile, arrive at the Cathedral of the Immaculate Conception. Feel free to walk inside to see the beautiful architecture and shrine, but please be respectful. Also please make a donation to the Poor Box just inside the door to help the needy. When done step back outside, turn right, and head south on South Claiborne Street.

1.5 Turn right (west) onto US 90/Government Street.

1.7 Pass Barton Academy on the right.

2.0 Pass the home of Captain Raphael Semmes on the right.

2.1 Turn left (south) and cross US 90. On the opposite corner is the Government Street United Methodist Church, aka the "Bee Hive." On the other side turn left (northeast) and follow US 90 on the opposite side.

2.2 Pass the home of the Distinguished Young Women's competition (formerly America's Junior Miss). In less than 0.1 mile, turn right onto South Scott Street.

2.3 Arrive at the Church Street Cemetery, then retrace your steps to US 90.

2.4 Back at US 90 turn right (northeast).

2.5 Turn right onto South Washington Street. In less than 0.1 mile, turn left onto Church Street. The street is lined with houses dating back to the mid-1800s.

2.8 Cross South Hamilton Street and in a few feet come to Spanish Plaza, a tribute to the city's Spanish heritage. Cut straight through the park, passing the water fountain and a statue that is a tribute to Queen Isabella of Spain.

2.9 Back at US 90 turn right (northeast). In less than 0.1 mile, come to the Mobile Carnival (Mardi Gras) Museum on the right. Just past the museum turn right (south) onto South Claiborne Street.

3.1 Arrive at the Phoenix Fire Museum. Turn right (south) and walk around the building to the east, coming to Jackson Street. Turn left (north) onto Jackson Street.

3.2 Turn right (northeast) onto Church Street.

3.4 Turn right (south) onto South Royal Street.

3.5 Arrive at the Fort Conde Welcome Center. Admission is free. Continue south on South Royal Street less than 0.1 mile and turn right onto Theater Street. In a few yards pay a visit to the Conde-Charlotte Museum. When done exit the building and turn left onto Theater Street. In less than 0.1 mile, arrive back at your vehicle.

36 Magnolia Cemetery

Mobile's second-oldest cemetery, Magnolia, is a fascinating journey through 140 years of the Port City's 300-plus-year history. Elegant hand-carved tombstones and eloquently written epitaphs from the Victorian period surround you, and many of the city's luminaries have found peace here, including one of the founders of Mardi Gras in the United States, Michael Kraft; the son of Apache Indian chief Geronimo, Chappo; and the founder of Mobile's spectacular Bellingrath Gardens, Walter Bellingrath, to name only a few.

Start: Behind the office at the northeast corner of the National Cemetery
Distance: 1.9-mile loop
Hiking time: About 2 hours
Difficulty: Easy
Trail surface: Cement, gravel, and asphalt road, grass path
Best seasons: Year-round
Other trail users: Cars
Canine compatibility: Leashed dogs permitted

Land status: City cemetery
Nearest town: Mobile
Fees and permits: None
Schedule: Year-round, daily 7 a.m. to 5:30 p.m.; office open 8 a.m. to 5 p.m.
Maps: USGS Mobile, AL; *DeLorme: Alabama Atlas & Gazetteer*, page 62, D4
Trail contact: Magnolia Cemetery, 1202 Virginia St., Mobile 36660; (251) 432-8672; magnoliacemetery.com

Finding the trailhead: From the intersection of Broad Street and US 90 in Mobile, take US 90 West 0.8 mile. Turn left (south) onto South Ann Street. Travel 0.6 mile and turn left (east) onto Virginia Street. Travel 0.2 mile. The entrance to the cemetery is on the left. The driveway is a short single-lane one-way road that curves behind the administration building. Follow the road 100 yards and come to the intersection with the cement exit road. Turn left and in 100 feet turn left again. Park here off to the side of the road next to the National Cemetery. GPS: N30 40.446' / W88 03.791'

The Hike

The port city of Mobile is Alabama's oldest city, established over 300 years ago in 1702 by the French. The city's first cemetery was an old Spanish burial ground called the Campo Santo, which was open from 1780 to 1813. City officials thought the old cemetery was too close to the rapidly growing city and began looking for a new plot of land for this purpose. In 1819 they purchased a piece of property from William and Joshua Kennedy on Mobile's Church Street, but before the ink was dry on the paperwork, a yellow fever epidemic spread like wildfire through the city, killing almost 20 percent of the population, which filled the new cemetery rapidly.

It wasn't long before the city needed a new cemetery, and in 1836 they purchased 37 acres along what is now Virginia Street and opened the New City Cemetery, which was renamed the Magnolia Cemetery in 1867. Since that time the cemetery

Two impish cherubs watch over the LeBlanc grave at Mobile's Magnolia Cemetery.

has increased to over 100 acres in size. The cemetery is laid out in a grid pattern with early sections marked alphabetically and later sections marked numerically 1 through 34.

A walk through Magnolia Cemetery is a trip back in time to the Victorian era when death was celebrated with glorious hand-carved stone funerary art, and where around every corner you can pay your respects to some of Mobile's notable luminaries.

The hike begins at the gatehouse near the cemetery's office. Parking here is *very* limited, so I recommend driving past the office, turning left at the first intersection, and parking on the side of the road here. Head to the east to begin your journey.

The first stop will be at the memorial to Confederate soldiers and sailors of the Civil War. In all 1,110 are buried here, who either died on the battlefield or from disease from wounds. A moving and special memorial is here for the crew of the first operational submarine, the *Hunley*, which was built in Mobile but sank during its first engagement off the Carolinas with its crew onboard, many of them from Mobile. In 2004 sediment from the recovered submarine was brought here and interred in the cemetery, bringing a bit of the fallen home.

Soon you will pass the grave of Jarvis Turner, an Englishman who came to the United States and became a renowned stone carver. Many of his works can be seen as you walk the cemetery. Look for his moniker, "J. Turner," on the stones.

One of the most easily identifiable graves is that of Michael Kraft. It's easy to recognize because the headstone is normally adorned with colorful Mardi Gras beads. Although a celebration similar to Mardi Gras was held in Mobile just after its founding, in 1703, it was Kraft who actually started what we now know as Mardi Gras in 1830. The festive celebration didn't migrate to New Orleans until several years later, making Mobile the "Mother of Mystics."

Another famous Mobilian is buried here, Dr. Josiah Clark Knott. Dr. Knott was the founder of the Mobile Medical Collage and one of the doctors on the front lines during the yellow fever epidemic of 1853. At the time no one knew for sure where yellow fever came from or how it was transmitted. His research was the first to show that the disease was borne and transmitted by mosquitoes. Sadly Dr. Knott lost four children to the disease in September 1853. All are buried here along with himself and his wife, Sarah.

And of course there is the funerary art of the day, which is on display on many of the tombstones and mausoleums, each having its own symbolic meaning. For example, a shroud represents sorrow, a butterfly rebirth, a broken column the end of life, and a cross salvation.

That is only a small taste of what you will see at Magnolia Cemetery. Be sure to stop by the office and pick up a guide to the cemetery's walking tour to learn more about the extensive, rich history of Alabama's oldest city.

The Mother of Mystics

So where did Mardi Gras begin in the United States? Right here in Mobile, Alabama, and the man credited with starting this festive time of year is Mobilian Michael Kraft.

Now, a celebration similar to Mardi Gras was held in Mobile one year after its founding, in 1703. But it wasn't until New Year's Day 1830 that things became organized when a group of drunken partygoers, including Kraft, were walking home in downtown Mobile. They passed a general store with a selection of rakes, hoes, and cowbells outside. Of course, being in an inebriated state, the group armed themselves with the implements and paraded the streets making a raucous sound.

As legend has it, the mayor at the time brought the men into his home and suggested that they organize and let everyone have some fun. And they did. The following year, led by Kraft, the group organized the Cowbellion de Rankin Society, the first Mardi Gras organization, and the festive celebration officially began in the United States.

Miles and Directions

0.0 Start just behind the administration building at the northeast corner of the National Cemetery where you parked. A cement road heads north and south, and a gravel road (the one you parked on) travels east and west. Take the gravel road to the east.

0.2 Turn left (northeast) onto a cement road at the intersection of section 29 and 35.

0.3 Arrive at the Confederate Cemetery on the left (west). Continue straight to the northeast and in a few feet pass the monument to the crew of the submarine *Hunley* and the Confederate dead. Continue northeast and in less than 0.1 mile, turn left (northwest) at the Alabama State Artillery monument onto a gravel road. On the right are the Williamson Family plots.

0.4 Turn left (southwest) onto another gravel road and circle behind the Confederate Cemetery. In less than 0.1 mile, pass the resting place of General Braxton Bragg on the left. Continue straight a few feet until you reach a cement road. Turn left (east) onto the cement road.

0.5 Turn left (northeast) back on the original cement road, completing a short loop of the Confederate Cemetery (you pass the *Hunley* monument one more time).

0.6 Take a short side trip off the road to the left (west) and visit the resting place of Jarvis Turner and the Slatter Mausoleum. Return to the road and turn left (north). In less than 0.1 mile, turn left (west) onto a gravel road.

0.7 Come to section 9 on your right and in a few feet pass the grave of Michael Kraft, which is easily identifiable by Mardi Gras beads adorning the tombstone. Continue straight to the west.

0.8 The road bends to the south just before a maintenance building. Take the time to view the interesting hand-carved funerary art. In less than 0.1 mile, turn left (southeast) onto an asphalt road at the end of section 7. In about 100 feet pass the grave of Colonel John Hinson on the left.

0.9 Pass the grave of Dr. Josiah Clark Knott on the left. In less than 0.1 mile, at the end of section 7, turn left onto a grassy path and view some truly beautiful hand-carved funeral art. Retrace your steps to the road and turn left (east).

1.0 Pass the twin cherubs and the grave of the D'Ornellas Infant on the right. Continue straight. In less than 0.1 mile, as you come to sections 15 and 14, turn right (south) onto a dirt and grass road. In a few yards turn right (west) onto a gravel and asphalt road.

1.1 Pass the Wilson Mausoleum, then take your time to explore and view the largest concentration of hand-carved statues in the cemetery just past the mausoleum. In less than 0.1 mile, pass the graves of General John Herbert Kelly, George Huggins, and Henry Hitchcock on the right.

1.2 Pass the grave of General Ledbetter on the right. In less than 0.1 mile, at the intersection of sections 17 and 18, cross over a gravel road to the west and in a few yards view the Iron Woman on your right. Turn around and head back to the intersection you just passed and turn right (south). In a few yards pass the Jewish Cemetery to your left (east). Continue straight to the south.

1.4 Arrive at the Owen Mausoleum with its interesting and intricate stonework. Retrace your steps to the last intersection and turn left (west) onto a cement road. In less than 0.1 mile, pass the grave of Lieutenant John Comstock, who died in the Battle of Mobile Bay in 1864, on the right.

Magnolia Cemetery

1.5 The Greek-inspired pillars of the Bellingrath/Morse family resting place are on your left. Continue straight to the west and view the Woodman of the World section. In less than 0.1 mile, at the intersection of sections 22, 23, 26, and 27, turn left (south) onto an asphalt road.

1.6 Turn left (east) onto another asphalt road.

1.7 The Leflore Family graves are on your right. In just a few feet pass the National Cemetery on your right (southeast). The asphalt and concrete road continues to the southeast; a gravel road heads off to the north. Turn left onto the gravel road and head north.

1.7 Turn left (west) onto a grass path. In less than 0.1 mile, come to the Working Man's Timber and Cotton Benevolent Association section. Turn around and retrace your steps to the gravel road and turn right (south). In less than 0.1 mile, turn left (southeast) onto the asphalt and cement road. Pass the National Cemetery on your right.

1.9 Arrive back at your vehicle.

37 Village Point Park Preserve Loop

The cemetery of the first family of Daphne, dating back to the early 1800s; a giant oak tree where it is believed Andrew Jackson rallied his troops during the War of 1812; and the legend of pirates like Jean Lafitte hiding out under the bluffs is just some of the history awaiting you on this family-friendly loop hike through Daphne's Village Point Park Preserve.

Start: Village Point Park Preserve trailhead at Bayfront Park
Distance: 1.8-mile lollipop
Hiking time: About 1.5 hours
Difficulty: Easy
Trail surface: Gravel and dirt roads, boardwalks
Best seasons: Late Feb to mid-May and mid-Sept to early Nov
Other trail users: Cyclists, joggers
Canine compatibility: Leashed dogs permitted

Land status: City nature preserve
Nearest town: Daphne
Fees and permits: None
Schedule: Year-round, daily sunrise to sunset
Maps: USGS Bridgehead, AL; *DeLorme: Alabama Atlas & Gazetteer*, page 63, D6; brochures available online (see "Trail contact")
Trail contact: City of Daphne Parks and Recreation, 2605 US 98, PO Box 400, Daphne 36526; (251) 621-3703; daphneal.com/residents/parks-recreation

Finding the trailhead: From the intersection of I-10 and US 98 north of Daphne, take US 98 south 1.7 miles. Turn right onto Main Street (a Publix shopping center is on the right at the turn). In 200 feet turn right onto Bayfront Park Drive. Travel 0.4 mile to the parking area. The trailhead is well marked on the west side of the parking lot next to Mobile Bay. GPS: N30 37.793' / W87 55.117'

The Hike

Situated on the eastern shore of Mobile Bay in the town of Daphne, just south of the second-largest river delta in the country, the Mobile-Tensaw River Delta, there is a plot of land that may be small in size but is packed with some amazing history. It's called Village Point Park Preserve. Along the park's wide gravel, dirt, and boardwalk paths, you will visit the cemetery of the town's earliest settlers, walk the beach where pirates once roamed, and have a good-natured disagreement with your historian friends at the Jackson Oak.

The history of this location began well before Europeans first arrived. The delta once was much larger than it is today and extended farther south, making this a fertile land for farming and one that was teeming with wildlife and fish, the perfect location for civilization to take root. Archaeologists have found evidence of meeting areas and primitive campsites by Native Americans including Choctaws, Tensaws, Creeks, and Seminoles dating back to AD 1500. Large council meetings or "neutral ground" meetings were held in this area.

Jackson Oak is lovingly protected by a composite boardwalk. Historians debate whether General Andrew Jackson rallied his troops from these branches before heading off to a battle during the War of 1812.

Spain was the first European country to visit the area around 1557. They called the land La Aleda, or "the Village," hence the name Village Point. The first settlers to move in from across the pond were the French. In 1670 families like D'Olive set up residence here. Nothing remains of the old homesteads, but this hike will take you to the D'Olive Cemetery. Look carefully at the centuries-old tombstones and see the hand-carved inscriptions written in French. A small kiosk here will play an audio history of the family at the push of a button.

During this time stories of pirates plying the waters of Mobile Bay were told, and one pirate in particular, Jean Lafitte, supposedly hid along the bluffs along the banks of the bay. This hike takes you to a nice, long sand island on the bay's eastern shore. Could pirates have landed here at one time? No one knows for sure, but we do know that this was a landing area for the Union navy during the Civil War following the Battle of Mobile Bay, where northern soldiers disembarked on their way to the Confederate fort at Blakeley.

The French eventually lost the territory to Great Britain during the French and Indian War in 1763. In 1781 Britain and Spain fought a skirmish here, and later the area became part of the United States after the US defeated Britain in the War of 1812.

As the trail meanders around the property, you will come to a sprawling oak tree, the Jackson Oak. The tree is lovingly protected—to the point of having a composite boardwalk built around it so you can walk up to it but not touch it.

The tree earned its name from history when in 1814 it was discovered that Britain was using the Spanish port of Pensacola, Florida, for shipping. Despite protests the activity continued, and General Andrew Jackson finally amassed his 3,000 troops here at the Village and prepared to attack. Legend has that Jackson climbed the branches of the tree to address his troops before marching in for the attack. Check the Village Point website for guided hikes of the trails. If you can catch one where historians are leading the way, you will be fascinated to hear the good-spirited banter debating if this really occurred here, and if Jackson was heading to Pensacola or New Orleans.

Pirates of Mobile Bay

Several well-known pirates plied the waters of the Gulf Coast from Florida to Texas. Mobile Bay had its own share of pirates ducking in looking for a safe haven. One of those was the pirate Gasparilla (Jose Gaspar), who for thirty-eight years beginning around 1783 reportedly plundered 400 ships. Legend has it that he buried several chests of looted treasure along the banks of Mobile Bay. Famed privateer and smuggler Jean Lafitte is said to have buried up to $10 million in pirated treasure in the bay, and even hid his ships along the bluffs near the present-day Village Point Park Preserve in Daphne.

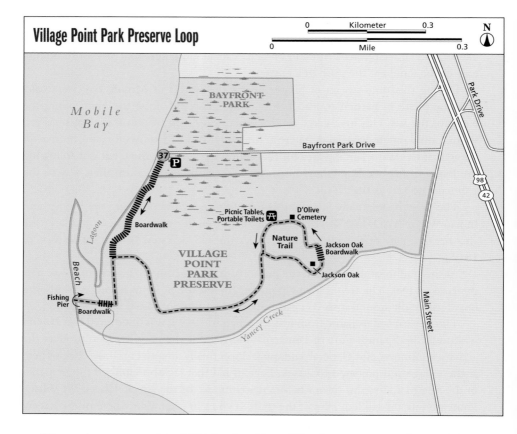

Village Point Park Preserve Loop

Mobile Bay

BAYFRONT PARK

Bayfront Park Drive

Park Drive

98

42

Picnic Tables, Portable Toilets

D'Olive Cemetery

Nature Trail

Jackson Oak Boardwalk

Jackson Oak

Boardwalk

Lagoon

Beach

VILLAGE POINT PARK PRESERVE

Fishing Pier

Boardwalk

Yancey Creek

Main Street

The park was created in 2004 by the City of Daphne to protect the area's history and the surrounding environment. The trail you will be walking was named a National Recreational Trail in 2011. It is not blazed or marked, but the wide gravel roads and boardwalks are very easy to follow.

Miles and Directions

0.0 Start from the Village Point Park Preserve trailhead located about 250 feet west of the parking lot on Mobile Bay. The trailhead is well marked. The hike begins on a boardwalk over a wetland.

0.2 Come to the end of the boardwalk. The trail becomes a wide dirt and gravel road and heads off in two directions, to the left (east) and straight ahead. For now, continue straight ahead to the south.

0.3 The trail turns to the right (west), crosses a boardwalk over a slough, and comes out on a small sand island. There is a fishing pier at the end of the bridge. When you're ready, turn around and retrace your steps to the end of the first boardwalk at mile 0.2.

0.5 Return to the south end of the boardwalk and turn right (east).

0.6 Come to a T intersection with another dirt road. Turn left here and head east. A right turn dead-ends at a locked fence and gate.

0.8 Pass a side trail with a bridge over Yancey Creek to your right (south). This is an access trail to the Harbor Place condominiums and is private property. Don't go there. Continue straight (east). In about 400 feet come to a fork in the trail. This is the southwest end of the trail's east loop. Take the right fork. In just a few feet, turn right (south) onto the D'Olive Plantation Nature Trail. There is a small sign indicating the trail entrance, but it can be hard to see when the area is overgrown. The trail is a narrow 2-foot-wide dirt footpath through a thick forest with a shady canopy.

1.0 Come to a boardwalk that encircles the massive Jackson Oak. The boardwalk is made of a composite material to alleviate problems with rotting. There is an audio kiosk here that tells the history of the oak tree, along with picnic tables off to the side. Continue on the dirt footpath to the north and in 200 feet cross a dirt service road. A sign points the way to D'Olive Cemetery.

1.1 Arrive at D'Olive Cemetery. Another audio kiosk tells the history of the D'Olive family and their plantation. After exploring the cemetery, continue west on the trail. In just a few hundred feet, there are Port-a-Johns and picnic tables. Shortly after arrive at the south end of the loop.

1.6 Return to the boardwalk. Turn right (north).

1.8 Arrive back at the trailhead.

38 Perdido River

The "Lost River," the Perdido borders Alabama and Florida and is the perfect location to lose yourself on the banks of a beautiful black-water river. You will be walking in the footsteps of early Spanish, French, and British settlers through cedar bogs and swamps and along white sand beaches.

Start: From the south trailhead
Distance: 2.8 miles out and back (optional longer trips; see hike description)
Hiking time: About 2 hours
Difficulty: Easy
Trail surface: Dirt, deep river sand, dirt and gravel road
Best seasons: Year-round; summer can be very buggy but the swimming is great.
Other trail users: Hunters (see "Special considerations")
Canine compatibility: Leashed dogs permitted
Land status: Alabama Forever Wild/Department of Conservation
Nearest town: Robertsdale
Fees and permits: None
Schedule: Year-round, daily sunrise to sunset

Maps: USGS Barrineau Park, FL; *DeLorme: Alabama Atlas & Gazetteer*, page 63, C10/D10
Trail contact: Alabama Hiking Trail Society, PO Box 235, Rockford 35136; hikealabama.org
Special considerations: Hunting is permitted on the Perdido River tract. Visit outdooralabama.com/hunting/ for dates. The Perdido is prone to flooding and the trails can be underwater. Do not hike when there are flash flood watches or warnings in effect. Check the water level through NOAA online at water.weather.gov/ahps2/hydrograph.php?wfo=mob&gage=BRPF1. Also, as of this writing the roads leading to the trailhead are deep sand. Improvements are being made, but until then I recommend traveling with two vehicles so one can get help if the other gets stuck.

Finding the trailhead: From the intersection of I-65 at exit 53 (Wilcox Road) and CR 64 in Robertsdale, take CR 64 north 7.1 miles. Turn right onto AL 112 (Old Pensacola Road). Travel 9.4 miles and turn left at Duck Place Road (Barrineau Park Road). Immediately after you turn onto the paved Duck Place Road, turn right onto the dirt River Road. Follow River Road for approximately 1.7 miles, then turn left onto Nims Fork Road. Travel 0.3 mile and turn right onto an unnamed road. Travel approximately 0.5 mile around a curve to the left, then turn right onto another unnamed road. Follow this road approximately 0.4 mile and cross railroad tracks, then take a right at the fork. Travel approximately 0.7 mile and turn left onto yet another unnamed road. Travel 1 mile. The road makes a sharp curve to the right. After the curve continue another 1.7 miles to a triangular clearing where you can park. The trail begins on the north side of this parking area. GPS: N30 39.477' / W87 24.244'

The Hike

The river that forms the current boundary between Florida and Alabama along the Gulf Coast was named Rio Perdido, meaning "Lost River," by early Spanish settlers to the region because the bay and river were difficult to locate from the Gulf. Over the years the name was anglicized to Perdido River. The Perdido, however, has been

The morning sun shines down on the placid waters of the Perdido River.

far from a lost river. Over the centuries humans have inhabited the banks of this meandering black-water river, living off its bountiful land and later fighting over it as a border between rival countries.

As with most areas of Alabama, Native Americans first called the river home somewhere between 1,000 to 1,200 years ago during a time known as the Woodland period, a period of time archaeologists use to designate pre-Columbian civilizations. Traces of pottery have been found all along the river.

Europeans first explored and settled the region in the 1500s, with both France and Spain laying claim to the territory. Between 1682 and 1763 the Perdido River formed the boundary between the Louisiana Colony of France and the Spanish colony of Florida, but following the French and Indian War in 1763, the British acquired both colonies. Twenty years later, in 1783, the United States and Britain signed the Treaty of Paris, effectively ending the American Revolution, which forced Britain to return its territory along the Gulf Coast to Spain.

In 1803 the United States purchased the territory just east of the Mississippi River from France in what was called the Louisiana Purchase. This meant that now the Perdido River was the border between the United States and Spain.

Complicated, isn't it? Well, this is where the back and forth ends; the Perdido River became part of the United States in 1819 when Spain ceded all of Florida to the United States. Today the only thing that the Perdido borders is the two states of Alabama and Florida.

After that time the river had a booming little turpentine industry in the middle of the long-leaf forest. The area was later purchased by timber companies, which owned the forest surrounding the river until the early 2000s when the Alabama Forever Wild program purchased the tract and has since opened it to hiking and canoeing.

You have a few options for walking the trail. The route described here is a simple 2.8-mile out and back to a large bend in the river and a huge white sandbar that's a great picnicking and swimming destination. The trail will lead you through a cedar bog and swamp with nice views of the river all along the route. The hike uses a combination of narrow dirt and sand footpaths and old logging roads. The trail is marked with yellow paint blazes and easy to follow.

Keep in mind that the Perdido is a conduit for rain runoff from many streams, rivers, and creeks as it flows to the Gulf of Mexico. The river is prone to flooding during times of heavy rain, not only from local rain but also from storms much farther north. Check the weather and avoid the trail if there are flood or flash flood warnings in effect. The trail will be underwater!

The trail is also in a wildlife management area, which means hunting is allowed. See "Special considerations" above.

The hike described here is only a subset of the much larger 9-mile-long trail. That gives you plenty more options for hiking the Perdido River, including doing a 9-mile point-to-point hike. This hike would require a shuttle vehicle at the opposite trailhead, which is located at Nelson's Branch, or you can make it into a really nice overnight 18-mile out-and-back backpacking trip. Camping is allowed on any of the sandbars along the river or in one of several new trail shelters built to accommodate hikers and paddlers on the newly opened Perdido Canoe Trail. Shelters are free to use, but reservations are required. Visit the Alabama Forever Wild website for information or to reserve a shelter at outdooralabama.com.

For more information on the trail and extended hikes with maps, visit the Alabama Hiking Trail Society website at hikealabama.org. Here you can also read about their efforts to extend the trail an additional 10 miles, making this a 20-mile-long trail and the first true backpacking path on the Alabama Gulf Coast.

Miles and Directions

0.0 Start from the parking area/trailhead. Head to the southwest on the dirt road that you drove in on. In less than 200 feet, turn right (northwest) onto a dirt road.

0.4 Come to a Y intersection in the road. Take the right fork (northeast).

0.7 A short 30-foot side trail to the right (east) leads to a bluff some 20 feet above the river with excellent views. Continue northwest on the dirt road. In less than 0.1 mile, the trail makes its way off the dirt road and into the woods on a dirt footpath. You cross several boggy areas through this section. After a few days of rain, this could be thick in mud or even rather deep puddles.

0.9 Cross a narrow 1- to 2-foot-wide stream (it's easy to hop across). The trail narrows to 2 feet wide, with thick foliage on either side.

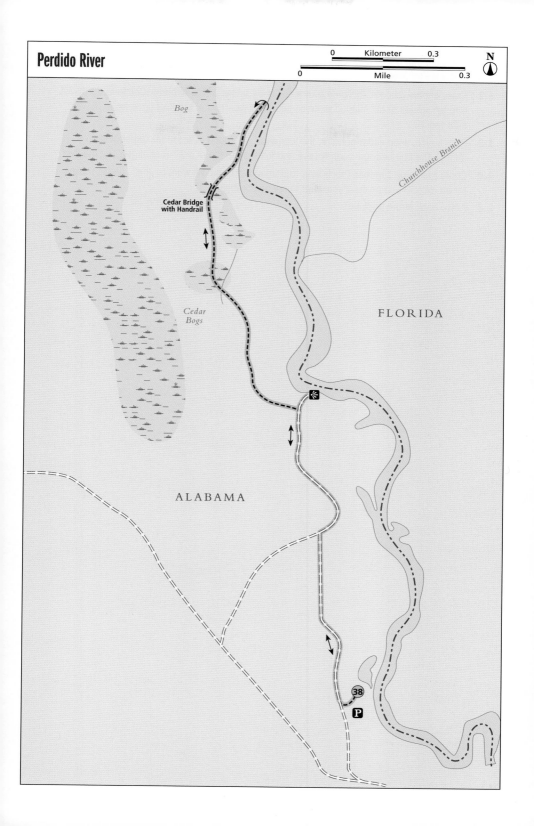

Perdido River

Bog

Churchhouse Branch

Cedar Bridge
with Handrail

Cedar
Bogs

FLORIDA

ALABAMA

38

P

0   Kilometer   0.3
0   Mile   0.3

N

1.0 Cross another boggy area. One part has a narrow 3-foot-wide stream that you cross on a cedar log footbridge.

1.2 Cross another stream, this time over a cedar log bridge with a handrail. Continue northeast through stands of tall Atlantic white cedars. Look for views of the river once again to your right (east).

1.3 Pass a nice, deep cedar pond on the left (west). The pond is seasonal, depending on rainfall. The trail bed turns sandy here and follows the top of a 20-foot bluff along the river.

1.4 Come to a large sandbar. This is your turnaround, but you will want to linger. It also makes for an excellent campsite if you want to spend the night.

2.8 Arrive back at the trailhead.

39 Fort Morgan Loop

From the ramparts of Fort Morgan, which overlook the symbolic divide between the Gulf of Mexico and Mobile Bay, you can almost hear the cannons roar, smell the sulfur of gunpowder, and feel the desperation of the Confederate soldiers as they clung to one of the last coastal fortresses in their possession during the Civil War. This is the site of the famous Battle of Mobile Bay where Admiral David Farragut, after watching the sinking of the ironclad *Tecumseh*, uttered these immortal words, "Damn the torpedoes! Full speed ahead!" over 150 years ago. But that battle is only a part of this massive stone fort's history, as you will discover on this coastal loop hike.

Start: Behind the museum at Fort Morgan Historic Site
Distance: 2.4-mile loop
Hiking time: About 2 hours
Difficulty: Easy to moderate
Trail surface: Brick or cement sidewalk, dirt, fine beach sand paths
Best seasons: Year-round
Other trail users: Cyclists, cars
Canine compatibility: Leashed dogs permitted
Land status: Alabama state historic park

Nearest town: Gulf Shores
Fees and permits: Day-use fee
Schedule: Year-round, daily 8 a.m. to 5 p.m.; museum open daily 9 a.m. to 4:30 p.m.; closed Thanksgiving, Christmas, and New Year's Day
Maps: USGS Fort Morgan, AL; *DeLorme: Alabama Atlas & Gazetteer*, page 64, B4
Trail contact: Fort Morgan State Historic Park, 110 State Highway 180, Gulf Shores 36542; (251) 540-7127; fort-morgan.org

Finding the trailhead: From the intersection of US 59 and AL 180 in Gulf Shores, take AL 180 west 20.4 miles and come to the site's pay station. After paying your admission fee, continue straight (west) 0.3 mile and arrive at the parking area. The museum is on the east side of the parking lot. Begin the hike behind the museum. GPS: N30 13.776' / W88 01.321'

The Hike

Two spits of land on the Alabama Gulf Coast jut out into the open waters of the Gulf of Mexico, acting as the symbolic demarcation line between the Gulf and Mobile Bay. To the west is the barrier island known as Dauphin Island, to the east the Fort Morgan peninsula. At the very western tip of this peninsula, you will find this hike, the Fort Morgan Loop.

Fort Morgan and its sister, Fort Gaines, across the bay, found themselves the centerpieces of one of the most famous naval battles of the Civil War and in US naval history—the Battle of Mobile Bay. But let's go back a few years before that, back before a single brick of Fort Morgan was laid, to the beginning of the peninsula's military history.

Most believe that the massive pentagonal stone structure here, Fort Morgan, was where the military history of this strip of land began. It actually began twenty-one

"For a short time the smoke [of the cannons] was so dense that the vessels could not be distinguished. Shot after shot was seen to strike and shells to explode on or about the vessels, but their sides being heavily protected by chain cables no vital blow could be inflicted."

—Confederate general Richard Page, commander of Fort Morgan, reporting on the shots fired at Union ships during the Battle of Mobile Bay

years earlier during the War of 1812. In 1813 the US Army built a small sand and stone fort here, Fort Bowyer, to guard against enemy attack.

In 1814 the British laid out a plan to take the city of Mobile and use it as a base of operations to take New Orleans. To do this they first had to take control of Mobile Bay, and the only thing that stood in their way was the tiny Fort Bowyer.

The fort was attacked twice by the British. The first attack came in September 1814 when four British warships and a contingent of marines and Creek Indians made their way to the fort from the Gulf. The British quickly found that they were outnumbered and outgunned. In the end the Americans sank one ship, the HMS *Hermes*, and forced the British to retreat.

In 1815 the British attacked again, but this time they overwhelmed the Americans with 3,000 troops compared to the fort's 300. The fight was in vain, however, because a month earlier a treaty had been signed ending the war, which dictated that all forts and territory be returned to US control.

Following the war President James Madison vowed that the country's coastline would always be ready to face enemy naval forces and ordered the building of what is known as "Third System Forts," forty-two almost impenetrable stone forts including Fort Morgan, which was completed in 1834.

Speed ahead to 1861 and the Civil War, when an Alabama militia took control of the fort and its sister across Mobile Bay, thus making Mobile one of the most highly fortified cities in the Confederacy. By August 1864, as the war was winding down, the city found itself the last sea port controlled by the Confederacy.

The Union navy under Admiral David Farragut took his fleet and began to move against the fort from the Gulf. His plan was to rush past the fort and take Mobile. As the first Union vessel, the USS *Tecumseh*, made its way past the fort, it hit one of the torpedoes and sank bow down beneath the waves. Ninety-two of its crew died including the captain. Several did survive with four swimming ashore only to be taken prisoner.

The Irony of It All

The next objective for Union troops following their victory at the Battle of Mobile Bay was to take the city of Mobile, one of the last port cities still controlled by the Confederates. The army began a march up the eastern shore of Mobile Bay, fighting several skirmishes with Confederate troops along the way until on April 8, 1865, Spanish Fort was taken and the following day the fort at Blakeley, just across the river from Mobile.

Three days later, fearing that the city would face the total destruction that other Southern cities had faced, the mayor of Mobile surrendered to the Union, saving it from destruction. The war was over for Mobile. The city had survived without a scratch. That would change in an ironic twist of fate on a summer afternoon one month later.

Just after noon residents began to see smoke rising from a warehouse on Beauregard Street. Over 200 tons of shells and powder were stored in the building. In a matter of minutes the ground began to shake, the stillness of the afternoon gave way to a rumble, and a massive explosion ripped through the sky. An account of the incident in the *Mobile Advertiser and Register* read, ". . . bursting shells, flying timbers, bales of cotton, horses, men, women, and children co-mingled and mangled into one immense mass."

When it was over, the explosion had created a hole 30 feet deep, killed 300 people, sank two ships in the Mobile River, and burned most of the northern part of the city to the ground.

Fort Morgan's cannons stand at the ready as they did more than 150 years ago.

Farragut became more resolute and, according to history, uttered those now immortal words, "Damn the torpedoes! Full speed ahead!" And the rest, as they say, is history; the Union army took the fort and later the Confederate fort at Blakeley and then the city of Mobile.

This nice 2.4-mile loop hike around the tip of the peninsula will take you to all of this rich history. You will pass the remnants of the original Fort Bowyer (later named Battery Bowyer when the military repurposed the huge dirt fort into a cement barricade during World War I) and the smaller Battery Dearborn. Both are massive cement structures that will tempt you to explore inside, but heed the warnings! Entry to these aging structures is dangerous.

In addition you will pass the foundation of the old barracks; the Federal Siege Line where the Union army attempted to take the fort by land; and Peace Magazine, an off-site powder house used by the military from 1902 to 1924—and of course the massive fort itself. As you walk through the fort's entrance tunnel, your hollow footsteps echoing off the brick walls, you can't help but feel the history seeping through the nearly 200-year-old brick and mortar.

After exploring inside the fort, you head north toward Mobile Bay where you will see a simple, small, orange and yellow buoy in the water. Near this marker is the resting place of the USS *Tecumseh* and its crew.

Visit the site's website (see "Trail contact") for dates of reenactments and candle-light tours where actors tell the story of the battle through the letters and memoirs of those who were there. And don't miss visiting the on-site Blue Star Museum, where you can learn more and view artifacts from the fort's past.

Miles and Directions

0.0 Start at the parking lot and head east to the museum. Be sure to visit the museum before heading out, then exit the building and walk around to the back of the structure. Begin by heading to the east across a grassy field; in a few yards pick up the red brick sidewalk. To your left (north) is Mobile Bay with its natural gas rigs, and to the right (south) the Gulf of Mexico.

0.1 The brick sidewalk bends to the north, giving you a chance to walk around and view the remains of an old barracks building. Some nice butterfly plants bloom here spring through summer. Continue heading east on the brick sidewalk. In less than 0.1 mile, the brick sidewalk turns to cement, with your best view of Mobile Bay to the left (north).

0.2 Pass the Union breastwork called Battery Lincoln to the right (south). Keep heading east; the cement sidewalk will turn into a brick path again. In less than 0.1 mile, come to an intersection. To your left (north) is Mobile Bay and the entrance road to the park. Straight ahead to the east is the administration building. Turn right onto the brick sidewalk and head south.

0.3 In less than 100 feet come to an intersection. To your right (west) is Battery Lincoln, which was used by Company C of the 20th Iowa Infantry. Turn left here and continue walking to the east on the brick path. To your right (south) across the field, you can see the massive Battery Bowyer, which you'll explore later in the hike. The brick sidewalk meanders into a small stand of pines that give you a bit of respite from the southern sun.

0.5 Pass a sign to your left about the varieties of raptors found here, including red-tailed hawks, Cooper's hawks and ospreys. In a few yards the sidewalk bends to the left (north) toward the entrance road. Don't follow it. Instead continue straight to the east on an abandoned old asphalt runway.

0.6 To your right (south) is an orange brick building, Peace Magazine. Turn here and cross the field to the south, and in less than 0.1 mile, arrive at the building. After exploring, turn left and continue down the dirt path to the east.

0.7 Arrive at Battery Dearborn. Feel free to explore but heed the warnings—explore the interior rooms at your own risk. Continue on the cement sidewalk in front of the building to the east.

0.8 At the east end of Battery Dearborn, the cement sidewalk ends. Continue straight a few feet and pick up a sandy footpath that loops around the end of the building on its east side. The path swings around the structure and heads back to the west on the opposite side of the building.

0.9 Now heading west and cresting a small hill, the back side of Battery Dearborn is on your right (north) side, the Gulf of Mexico and a cement seawall to your left (south). The trail is fine beach sand at this point.

1.0 Look for the Peace Magazine building through the trees to your right (north). There is a nice grove of palms here as well as huge mounds of wild rosemary. Off to the southwest you

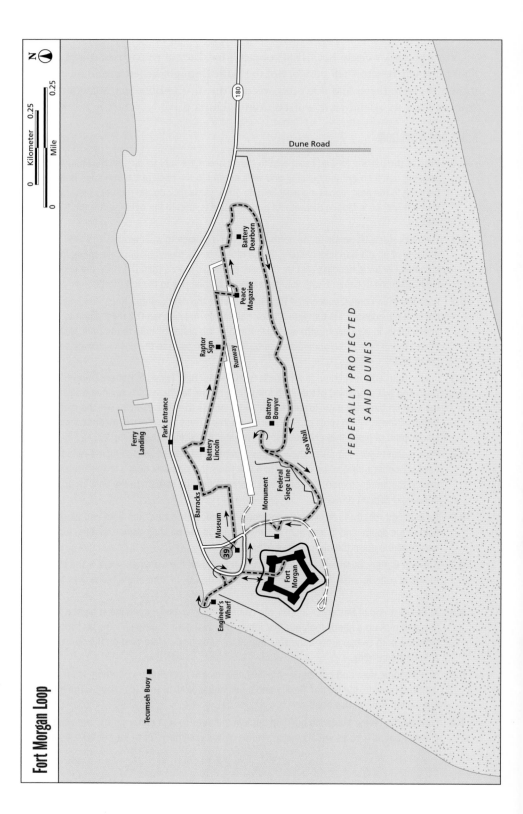

Fort Morgan Loop

N

Kilometer
0   0.25   0.25

Mile
0   0.25

Ferry Landing

Park Entrance

Barracks

Battery Lincoln

Raptor Sign

Museum

39

Engineer's Wharf

Runway

Peace Magazine

Battery Dearborn

Battery Bowyer

Sea Wall

Monument

Federal Siege Line

Fort Morgan

Dune Road

180

FEDERALLY PROTECTED SAND DUNES

Tecumseh Buoy

start getting wonderful panoramic views of the Gulf of Mexico with ships and barges making their way into Mobile Bay and the Sand Island Lighthouse on the horizon.

1.2 Climb a short hill behind Battery Bowyer. The back of the battery is a large hill with small trees and grass growing. Once at the top follow the base of Battery Bowyer to the west as the trail swings around to the front of the structure. You will see the breastworks of the Federal Siege Line on your left (west). We'll come back to that in a moment.

1.4 Arrive at the front of Battery Bowyer. Take a look around the exterior, but entry into this structure is prohibited. Turn around and head to the west once again, toward the Federal Siege Line. Once there follow the wooden breastwork to the left (south).

1.5 Several cannons peer through the Federal Siege Line, taking aim at the fort just as they would have been during the Battle of Mobile Bay.

1.6 Once at the southern end of the Federal Siege Line, turn right (west), walking almost directly on the old sea wall. In less than 0.1 mile, come to a dirt road. Turn right (north) onto the road and head back toward the fort entrance.

1.7 Pass a monument to those who fought here at the Battle of Mobile Bay and a marker for the first director of the historic site, Hatchett Chandler. Continue north on the dirt road.

1.8 Come to an intersection. A gravel road travels to the right (east) and heads back toward Battery Bowyer. An asphalt road heads straight to the north and left to the west. Turn left onto the asphalt road.

1.9 Arrive at the entrance to the fort itself. Turn left (south) and enter the fort. Take your time and explore the ramparts and ancient halls, then retrace your steps through the entrance.

2.1 When outside of the fort, turn left and head north on a cement sidewalk.

2.2 The cement turns briefly into a brick walkway then heads down a ramp known as the Engineer's Wharf toward Mobile Bay. In less than 0.1 mile, come to the end of the ramp for a magnificent view of the bay. Look for an orange and yellow buoy. This is the marker that approximately represents the final resting place of the USS *Tecumseh*. Turn around and head back to the parking lot.

2.4 Arrive back at the parking lot.

40 Fort Gaines Loop

Located on the eastern tip of Alabama's barrier island, Dauphin Island, this hike takes you not only through some magnificent wetlands and forest to do a little bird watching but also on a wonderful beach walk that culminates in a visit to historic Fort Gaines, a massive stone fortress that is the twin of Fort Morgan and, like its twin, played an important role in the Civil War's Battle of Mobile Bay.

Start: From the trailhead on the south side of the Audubon Bird Sanctuary parking lot
Distance: 3.4-mile scorpion loop
Hiking time: 2 to 2.5 hours
Difficulty: Easy
Trail surface: Dirt, grass, sand footpath, asphalt road
Best seasons: Year-round
Other trail users: Cars and bicycles on Bienville Boulevard, sunbathers on the beach
Canine compatibility: Leashed dogs permitted
Land status: City-managed historic site

Nearest town: Dauphin Island
Fees and permits: None
Schedule: Audubon Bird Sanctuary open year-round, daily sunrise to sunset; Fort Gaines open daily 9 a.m. to 5 p.m., closed Thanksgiving, Christmas Eve, and Christmas Day
Maps: USGS Fort Morgan and Little Dauphin Island, AL; *DeLorme: Alabama Atlas & Gazetteer*, page 64, B4
Trail contact: Fort Gaines Historic Site, 51 Bienville Blvd., Dauphin Island 36528; (251) 861-6992; dauphinisland.org/fort-gaines/

Finding the trailhead: From the intersection of I-10 at exit 17 and Rangeline Road/AL 193 in Theodore, take AL 193 south 6.8 miles. Turn left (east) to continue on AL 193 South. Travel 0.8 mile and turn right (south) to continue 17.9 miles on AL 193 South. Turn left (east) onto Bienville Boulevard. In 1.6 miles come to the Audubon Bird Sanctuary on the right. The trailhead is on the south side of the parking lot next to the large kiosk. GPS: N30 15.028'/ W88 05.238'

The Hike

During the Civil War the city of Mobile was described as being the most fortified city of the Confederacy. With several land forts surrounding it, two in the expansive delta and Mobile Bay, and two pre–Civil War masonry forts guarding the entrance to the bay at the Gulf of Mexico. One of those, on the eastern shore of the bay, is Fort Morgan. The other, on the eastern tip of Dauphin Island, is Fort Gaines.

Prior to 1817 only a few small earthen forts protected the wide opening between the Gulf and Mobile Bay. Following several attacks by the British on Fort Bowyer near the location of what would later become Fort Morgan, the federal government realized that these structures were no match for the rapidly modernizing weaponry of the day and began constructing what was called a Third System of Fortification. These would be large structures with tall, thick stone and brick walls that would be lined with heavy artillery.

A cannon stands high atop a battlement at Fort Gaines, keeping a silent vigil over Mobile Bay and the Gulf of Mexico.

Construction on Fort Gaines, which was named for a hero of the War of 1812, General Edmund Pendleton Gaines, began in 1818. The fort was to be the identical twin to its cross-bay relative, Fort Morgan. Plans called for a pentagonal-shaped structure with diamond-shaped bastions at the corners. Construction was halted in 1821 due to a lack of funding but was re-funded again in 1846. The work didn't resume until 1857.

On January 5, 1861, in anticipation of the state seceding from the Union, the then-uncompleted fort was seized by the Alabama state militia and eventually completed by the Confederates.

In 1862 Union admiral David Farragut successfully captured the city of New Orleans, but as his writings show, his eyes were on the city of Mobile but he was being held back by his commanders. In a letter to his son from February 1864, he wrote, "If

I had the permission I can tell you it would not be long before I would raise a row with the rebels in Mobile." He finally had his chance on August 5, 1864, when the Battle of Mobile began.

Farragut divided his flotilla into two columns. One consisted of four ironclads that would take out Fort Morgan. This column is the one that provided the famous Farragut quote, "Damn the torpedoes! Full speed ahead!" when the USS *Tecumseh* was sunk by a Confederate torpedo or mine.

The second column was a group of wooden ships that would take on the guns of Fort Gaines. The fleet bombarded the fort for three straight days while the battle raged across the bay. When the Union had secured Fort Morgan, the ironclads sailed across the channel and, at what is described as point-blank range, began shelling the fort. By August 8 the commander of Fort Gaines realized the cause was lost and surrendered. Nine months later, following the Battle of Blakeley, the city of Mobile fell into Union hands.

Today the guns of Fort Gaines are silent with only the occasional reenactment, but it is a fascinating site to visit. Often the fort's old blacksmith shop is open, holding demonstrations and encampments illustrating how life was back in 1862. The fort itself is recognized as one of the best preserved east of the Mississippi.

You can drive right up to the front gates of Fort Gaines, but why do that when you have this beautiful hike that can take you there along the trails of the Audubon Bird Sanctuary and the beaches of the Gulf of Mexico?

Pioneer II

Many know the story of the first operational submarine that ever saw combat, the Confederate submarine CSS *Hunley*. It is a heroic and tragic tale, with the crew losing their lives on its first mission. But there was another sub prior to the *Hunley*, *Pioneer II*.

As with the CSS *Hunley*, *Pioneer II* was built in Mobile by the same designer, Horace Lawson Hunley. It was 36 feet long, held a crew of five, and was powered by a hand crank that turned the propeller.

Pioneer II almost became the first operational submarine ever when it was towed down Mobile Bay to a point near Fort Morgan. The crew then took over and powered the sub. Apparently they went to Sand Island just outside of Mobile Bay in the Gulf of Mexico to get a bearing, but the seas were too much for the tiny craft and it was swamped, causing it to sink. The crew managed to escape without loss of life.

The sanctuary has been recognized as one of the most significant bird migration sites in the world. Starting at the sanctuary's parking lot, trails will take you past beautiful, placid ponds teeming with turtles and frogs and hundreds of species of birds like mockingbirds, cardinals, and ospreys. The path heads south to the Gulf of Mexico where you head east with a panoramic view of the Gulf—the Sand Island Lighthouse, which was built in 1838, on the horizon. Bottlenose dolphins may be seen playing in the Gulf surf.

Walk the beach to the very eastern tip of the island and round the bend on Bienville Boulevard to get your first glimpse of the massive stone walls of the fort, a dark gray cannon aiming ominously over the Gulf, waiting for foreign invaders.

Miles and Directions

0.0 Start from the trailhead on the south side of the parking lot. The trail begins to the right of the large Audubon Bird Sanctuary sign and heads out on a long boardwalk over a wetland.

0.2 Pass a section of the boardwalk that veers off to the right and ends at a dirt path. You'll come back to this in a moment; right now continue straight to the south. In about 50 feet come to an observation deck with a great view of Gaillard Lake. Turn around and retrace your steps to where the dirt path veers off from the boardwalk.

0.3 Turn left (west) onto the wide dirt and grass path called the Pond View Trail. (**Option:** Continue straight on the boardwalk for more views of the wetland and lake. The boardwalk leads to the Sand Dune Edge Trail, where you can turn to the left (west) and pick up the trail described here at mile 0.6.) Continuing on the main trail, in less than 0.1 mile, come to a Y intersection with a bench in the middle of the fork. Take the left fork to the west.

0.4 A short 50-foot side trail on the left (east) leads to a bench and a great view of Gaillard Lake. In less than 0.1 mile, pass a bench on the right and a sign about the birds of prey you may see along the trail. In less than 0.1 mile, a trail comes in from the right (west). Continue straight to the south.

0.5 Pass a short side trail on the left that leads to another bench and view of the lake. The path begins to turn a bit sandier.

0.6 Come to a Y. The left fork is the Swamp Dune Edge Trail. Take the right fork to the south, climbing a sand dune using a boardwalk. The path is lined with beautiful green, fragrant sand rosemary bushes. At the top of the hill is a small observation deck with a bench that overlooks the Gulf of Mexico and an osprey nesting pole. Continue straight to the south on the boardwalk until you arrive to the shores of the Gulf. In less than 0.1 mile, arrive at the beach. Look for the Sand Island Lighthouse on the horizon. Turn left (east) onto the beach.

1.0 Pass a small pavilion on the left (north), where you will turn on the way back from the fort. Right now continue straight to the east. Notice the foundations of houses that did not survive past hurricanes on your left.

1.3 Pass the Dauphin Island Sea Lab on the left. In less than 0.1 mile arrive at Bienville Boulevard. Turn right (east) onto the paved road. As you circle around the eastern tip of the island, you can see Fort Morgan on your right across the mouth of Mobile Bay; Fort Gaines is on your left.

1.7 Turn left (south) and head toward the fort's main entrance, passing the remains of a nineteenth-century ship on the way.

Fort Gaines Loop

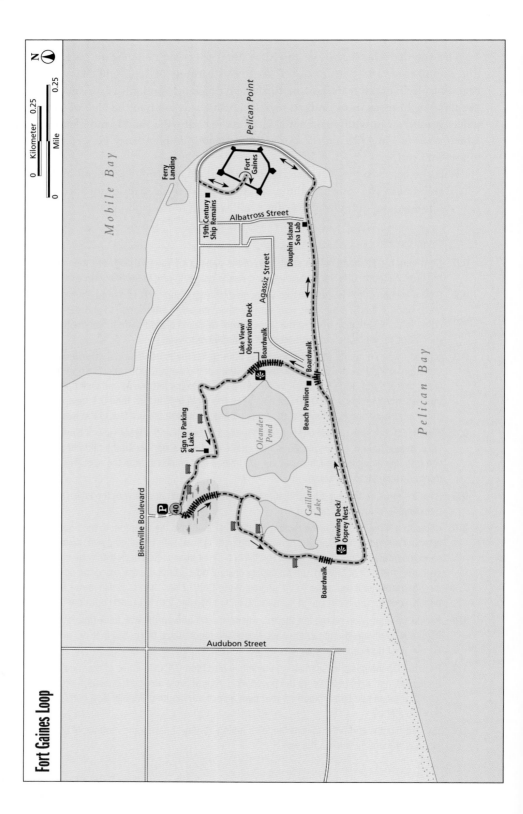

Mobile Bay

Pelican Point

Ferry Landing

19th Century Ship Remains

Fort Gaines

Albatross Street

Dauphin Island Sea Lab

Agassiz Street

Lake View/ Observation Deck

Boardwalk

Boardwalk

Beach Pavilion

Sign to Parking & Lake

Bienville Boulevard

Oleander Pond

Gaillard Lake

Viewing Deck/ Osprey Nest

Boardwalk

Pelican Bay

Audubon Street

N

Kilometer

0   0.25

0   0.25

Mile

1.8 Come to the entrance of the fort. Pay your entry fee and explore the fort, then retrace your steps to the pavilion on the beach at mile 1.0. (*Option:* If you want to shorten the trip, as you leave the fort, turn left onto Bienville Boulevard and follow it back to the trailhead, a walk of 0.7 mile.)

2.7 Arrive back at the pavilion you passed at mile 1.0. Turn right (north) onto a boardwalk. Please stay off the sand dunes! Immediately after the turn there is a bench. The trail is lined with saw palmetto and scrub pine. Look up and see how past hurricanes snapped many of the pine trees like twigs.

2.8 Come to an exit point off the boardwalk in front of you. Turn left (northwest) to continue on the boardwalk; in a few feet the boardwalk ends and becomes a sandy path with little to no canopy.

2.9 Cross a short boardwalk over a wetland. In less than 0.1 mile, come to a nice platform that overlooks Oleander Pond.

3.0 The trail is a wide dirt and grass path once again. Come to a Y. The campground is to the right. Take the left fork to the northwest. In less than 0.1 mile, pass a small trail coming in from the right. Continue straight to the northwest. Once again there is a good canopy for shade.

3.1 Come to an intersection with a 10-foot-wide grass path. A sign here points the way to the Swamp Dune Edge Trail (the way you came), campground to the right, parking straight ahead. Turn left (west) onto the path. In less than 0.1 mile, pass a bench on the right.

3.2 A side trail comes in from the right (north) with a sign that has an arrow pointing to the left and reads Lake and Parking, and another sign that points to the right and reads Parking. Turn right (north) onto the narrow dirt- and pine-straw-covered trail.

3.3 Pass a bench on the right and some large magnolia trees. In less than 0.1 mile, pass a bench on the left and, in just a few more feet, come to an intersection with another dirt trail. If you turn left (southwest), you would return to Gaillard Lake. Turn right (northwest) onto the dirt trail.

3.4 Arrive back at the trailhead.

Appendix A: Clubs and Trail Groups

Alabama Forever Wild: Alabama Department of Conservation and Natural Resources, 64 N. Union St., Montgomery 36130; (334) 242-3484; alabamaforever wild.com.

Forever Wild is an arm of the Alabama Department of Conservation and Natural Resources whose mission is to purchase and protect lands of historical and environmental significance and provide recreational opportunities.

Alabama Hiking Trail Society: PO Box 231164, Montgomery 36123; hike alabama.org.

AHTS is a statewide nonprofit organization with a mission to design, build, and maintain safe hiking trails across the state.

Alabama Historic Commission: 468 S. Perry St., Montgomery 36104; (334) 242-3184; preserveala.org

Alabama Trail of Tears Association: PO Box 71085, Tuscaloosa 35407; national tota.org/alabama-chapter/

Appendix B: Additional Resources

Appalachian Highlands 1937. National Park Service, 1937. Video: https://www.you tube.com/watch?v=jUJTSm1IUgY

Bartram, William. *Travels of William Bartram*. New York: Dover Publications. Print.

Down Mobile Way 1935. National Park Service, 1935. Video: www.youtube.com/ watch?v=N23Vpy6VTmw

Pasquill, Robert G. *The Civilian Conservation Corps in Alabama 1933–1942: A Great and Lasting Good*. Tuscaloosa: University of Alabama Press. Print.

About the Author

Joe Cuhaj grew up in Mahwah, New Jersey, near Harriman-Bear Mountain State Parks. It was here, near where the first sections of the Appalachian Trail were built, that his love of hiking and the outdoors began. After high school Joe enlisted in the US Navy, where he met his wife, Maggie. The two moved to her hometown, Mobile, Alabama, and now live on the Eastern Shore of Mobile Bay in Daphne.

Joe spent many years in radio broadcasting before changing careers, becoming a software programmer for a local company, where he still works by day. By night Joe is an author and freelance writer, having penned five books: *Hiking Alabama* (FalconGuides), *Paddling Alabama* (FalconGuides), *Baseball in Mobile*, *Best Tent Camping: Alabama*, and an e-book of short stories titled *Living in a Banana Dream*. He has also written many articles for magazines and online publications on a wide variety of topics ranging from the environment to political issues to the media. Find out more about Joe online at www.joe-cuhaj.com.

American Hiking
Society

Because you
hike.
We're with you
every step of the way

As a national voice for hikers, **American Hiking Society** works every day:

- Building and maintaining hiking trails
- Educating and supporting hikers by providing information and resources
- Supporting hiking and trail organizations nationwide
- Speaking for hikers in the halls of Congress and with federal land managers

Whether you're a casual hiker or a seasoned backpacker, become a member of American Hiking Society and join the national hiking community! You'll enjoy great member benefits and help preserve the nation's hiking trails, so tomorrow's hike is even better than today's. We invite you to join us now!

American
Hiking
Society